ROUTLEDGE LIBRARY EDITIONS: RELIGION IN AMERICA

Volume 3

THE POLITICS OF ETHNIC PRESSURE

THE POLITICS OF ETHNIC PRESSURE

The American Jewish Committee Fight Against Immigration Restriction, 1906–1917

JUDITH S. GOLDSTEIN

LONDON AND NEW YORK

First published in 1990 by Garland Publishing, Inc.

This edition first published in 2021
by Routledge
2 Park Square, Milton Park, Abingdon, Oxon OX14 4RN

and by Routledge
52 Vanderbilt Avenue, New York, NY 10017

Routledge is an imprint of the Taylor & Francis Group, an informa business

© 1990 Judith S. Goldstein

All rights reserved. No part of this book may be reprinted or reproduced or utilised in any form or by any electronic, mechanical, or other means, now known or hereafter invented, including photocopying and recording, or in any information storage or retrieval system, without permission in writing from the publishers.

Trademark notice: Product or corporate names may be trademarks or registered trademarks, and are used only for identification and explanation without intent to infringe.

British Library Cataloguing in Publication Data
A catalogue record for this book is available from the British Library

ISBN: 978-0-367-49869-6 (Set)
ISBN: 978-1-00-308009-1 (Set) (ebk)
ISBN: 978-0-367-50335-2 (Volume 3) (hbk)
ISBN: 978-1-00-304953-1 (Volume 3) (ebk)

Publisher's Note
The publisher has gone to great lengths to ensure the quality of this reprint but points out that some imperfections in the original copies may be apparent.

Disclaimer
The publisher has made every effort to trace copyright holders and would welcome correspondence from those they have been unable to trace.

Introduction to the 2020 Reissue

In the past decades there has been a proliferation of scholarly literature about 19th and 20th century racial ideologies and policies. Significant studies document the global scale of immigration restriction based upon the power of race hierarchies.

These works include: *The Gods of the Upper Air*, by Charles King, (Doubleday, 2019); *Defending the Master Race*, by Jonathan Spiro, (University of Vermont Press, 2009); *Drawing the Global Colour Line*, by Marilyn Lake and Henry Reynold, (Cambridge, 2008); *The Science and Politics of Racial Research*, by William Tucker, (University of Illinois Press, 1996); *The Color of Empire: Race and American Foreign Relations*, by Michael L. Krenn, (Potomac Books, 2006).

The Politics of Ethnic Pressure probes one national aspect of the American restriction movement against so-called undesirable immigrants. This study would be best viewed as part of the powerful and multifaceted global forces of racial ideologies and opposition to them. By the late 19th Century, white nations regarded themselves as progressive, scientifically-based societies built on a Darwinian survival of the fittest and a hierarchical ordained order of races. Racism gave itself a scientific name—eugenics—and provided a robust body of bogus thought built on prejudice in order to restrict immigration and sustain segregation. Racism, prized in Anglo-Saxon white cultures, was frequently mixed with prevailing Christian religious beliefs and wrapped, in many countries, in the cloak of new democratic ideals and practices. The racists, hoarding the benefits of democracy for themselves, were in battle against the perceived inferior, primitive peoples.

Judith S. Goldstein, March 2020

THE POLITICS OF ETHNIC PRESSURE

•

The American Jewish Committee Fight Against Immigration Restriction, 1906–1917

•

Judith S. Goldstein

GARLAND PUBLISHING • NEW YORK & LONDON • 1990

The last chapter of this volume appeared as "Ethnic Politics" in the *American Jewish Historical Quarterly* 65:1 (September 1975), pp. 36–58.

Copyright © 1990 by Judith S. Goldstein
All Rights Reserved

Library of Congress Cataloging-in-Publication Data

Politics of ethnic pressure: the American Jewish Committee fight against immigration restriction, 1906–1917/ Judith S. Goldstein
p. cm.—(European immigrants and American society)
Includes bibliographical references.
Thesis (Ph. D.)—Columbia University, 1972.
ISBN 0-8240-0244-X (alk. paper)
1. American Jewish Committee. 2. Jews—United States—Politics and government. 3. Emigration and immigration law—United States. 4. United States—Emigration and immigration. 5. United States—Ethnic relations.
I. Title. II. Series.
E184.J5G634   1990
323.1'1924073—dc20   90-3488

●

Printed on acid-free, 250-year-life paper.
Manufactured in the United States of America

Design by
Julie Threlkeld

TABLE OF CONTENTS

	Page
INTRODUCTION.	1
Chapter	
I. THE NEED FOR ORGANIZATION	12
II. THE SPEAKER PREVAILS.	66
III. THE HOLLOW VICTORY.	135
IV. THE DEFIANT TAFT.	184
V. WILSON TRIUMPHS	247
VI. VICTORIES AMID DEFEATS.	280
CONCLUSION.	327
BIBLIOGRAPHY.	340

INTRODUCTION

In 1906 several self-appointed leaders of the American Jewish community--the established, "uptown" Jews of German origin--were deeply concerned about the welfare and fate of Russian Jewry. These men, the most outstanding of whom were Jacob H. Schiff, Louis Marshall, and Oscar S. Straus, confronted two specific problems: the outbreak of a series of pogroms against the Jews in Russia and the campaign of the restrictionists in the United States who sought to impede the entry of the "new immigrants" from eastern and southern Europe. Therefore these leaders and several others from cities throughout the United States formed the American Jewish Committee which subsequently developed policies on political issues affecting American and Russian Jews and lobbied with Congress and Presidents Theodore Roosevelt, William Howard Taft, and Woodrow Wilson.

The purpose of this doctoral study is to examine and evaluate the lobbying activities of the AJC from 1906 to 1917 with respect to the related issues of the restrictive literacy test and American-Russian relations. In the past political scientists and historians of lobbying have concentrated on the techniques and activities of sundry groups:

peace societies, temperance groups, trade and agricultural associations, unions, and business and church organizations. They have tended, however, to ignore the efforts of ethnic groups who lobbied with Congressmen on domestic and foreign matters, especially in the period prior to the administrations of Woodrow Wilson.[1] This lack of attention and scholarly work would have satisfied the leaders of the AJC, for even though they never denied directly that they were lobbyists, they avoided public identification of their role and intent--to affect the writing of legislation.

In their view the AJC's political interests concerned idealistic issues: morality in American-Russian policy, the sanctity of American citizenship, and the continuation of the tradition of open immigration. The AJC associated lobbying with less lofty commercial enterprises and dishonorable practices, which were to be distinguished from its work.

---

[1] Three major studies of lobbying that ignore ethnic groups are: Grant McConnell, *Private Power and American Democracy* (New York, 1967); E. Pendelton Herring, *Group Representation Before Congress* (Baltimore, 1929); and David B. Truman, *The Governmental Process* (New York, 1951). Three studies concerning ethnic lobbying during the Wilson period are: Louis L. Gerson, *Woodrow Wilson and the Rebirth of Poland, 1914-1920: A Study in the Influence on American Policy of Minority Groups of Foreign Origin* (New Haven, 1953); Frank E. Manuel, *The Realities of American-Palestine Relations* (Washington, D.C., 1949); and Joseph P. O'Grady, *The Immigrants' Influence on Wilson's Peace Policies* (Lexington, Ky., 1967).

Other lobbyists had a sullied reputation in the Progressive period because of scandals exposing the corrupt connections between some legislators, on the one hand, and the insurance industry and certain men interested in tariff legislation, on the other. Furthermore, the AJC escaped exposure and public scrutiny because it never paid prominent intermediaries to represent the organization in Washington, D.C. and because there was no federal legislation (in fact, none until 1946) calling for the registration of lobbyists, regulating their work, and affecting the taxes that they paid and the contributions that they received.

Schiff, Marshall, and their small group of associates, who controlled the AJC for many years, were men who had become remarkably successful in their professional careers, benefiting from American educational institutions, extraordinary hard work, and the fluidity of America's social and economic order. They were grateful for the success that they had achieved in the past, outspoken in their appreciation of the opportunities afforded them in the United States, and optimistic about the future for themselves and other American Jews. And possibly because most of the leaders of the AJC were immigrants or the sons of immigrants, they enthusiastically identified with and sought to sustain America's ideals of liberty, religious freedom, the separation of church and state, and humanitarian diplomacy.

The AJC leaders regarded their American identity and Jewish identity with equal and non-conflicting respect. "Americans of the Jewish faith" was the way that Jacob H. Schiff preferred to describe himself and his Jewish brethren.[1] Since they regarded themselves as Jews by faith and not by race, Schiff, Louis Marshall, and Oscar S. Straus found no difficulty in seriously practicing their religious beliefs and honoring their duties as citizens. Although their integration into American life was incomplete because some prejudice still existed against the Jews, Schiff and his friends regarded the United States as their permanent home and not as a place of exile or temporary asylum, as did some American Zionists.[2] Emphasizing that Jewish ideals and American ideals reinforced one another, the leaders of the AJC proudly pointed to a striking similarity between reform Judaism, to which they adhered, and America's political tradition. Both sanctified liberty and acknowledged a mission to set an example for the rest of the world. Jews "have something precious, of high value to mankind, in our keeping," Schiff wrote in

---

[1] Jacob H. Schiff, *Jacob H. Schiff: His Life and Letters*, ed. by Cyrus Adler (Garden City, N.Y., 1929), I, 297.

[2] *Ibid.*, I, 165, 167.

the spirit of Progressive America. "Our mission in the world continues, and with it our responsibility of one for the other. Because of this our destiny is among the nations, as part and parcel of the nations."[1]

This sense of responsibility "one for the other" prompted Schiff and his associates to lobby with Presidents and Congress on behalf of Jews in Russia and Russian-Jewish immigrants in the United States. Although there were significant cultural, economic, and religious differences between the American-Jews of German origin and those from Russia, the AJC leaders always believed that the Russian-Jews should have the opportunity and would have the ability to adapt to American life. Therefore the leaders of the AJC urged the Russian immigrants to assimilate by learning English, working hard, and participating in elections and patriotic endeavors.

In its fight on behalf of the Russian immigrants, the AJC clashed with the majority of Congress year after year and fought against a widespread public sentiment which was hostile to the continuation of Russian-Jewish immigration. From 1906 to 1917 the United States faced the critical task of absorbing approximately ten million immigrants

---

[1] Ibid., I, 166.

from all parts of the world but predominantly from eastern and southern Europe. Fearful of the effects of this influx, restrictionists worked for the adoption of a literacy test, a proposed entry requirement for every immigrant except those from China and Japan. The literacy test campaigns evolved into four major battles between restrictionists and anti-restrictionists, until Congress finally passed the test over President Wilson's veto in 1917.

The AJC was the most active and important anti-restrictionist lobbying group in each of the fights. It allied with Italian, German, and Scandinavian groups but none of them displayed the interest, knowledge, and sophistication on the immigration issue that characterized the AJC effort. In each of the legislative battles the AJC sought to delay consideration of the test bills and to block their passage; as a last resort, the AJC sought to soften the effect of the test on the Russian-Jewish immigrants.

The AJC's lobbying activities should be viewed within the context of criticism made by political scientists such as Grant McConnell who object to the narrow, partisan views and activities of American lobbying groups. Critics have decried the sacrifice of a national point of view and national goals to the selfish concerns of vested interests.[1]

---

[1]McConnell, op. cit., Chapter x; Herring, op. cit., Chapter xiv; E. E. Schattschneider, Politics, Pressures and

But if faced with such a charge of partisanship and overriding self-interest--a charge which the leaders of the AJC were eager to avoid--they would have defended themselves by stating that they espoused the ideal, national point of view and that they were upholding the great American tradition which valued individual immigrants, irrespective of their origins and religious beliefs.

In their anti-restrictionist campaign, Jewish spokesmen glorified the long-time policy of open immigration and the practice of "cosmopolitan nationality."[1] They extolled the virtues of a nation built by immigrants, a rich industrial nation whose continued growth depended on unskilled European labor. Furthermore, they maintained that America's moral power and mission in the world were intimately connected with the idea that Americans had established a refuge and haven for those who had left--or would leave--the religious and political oppression and the economic deprivations of the old world. These anti-restrictionists contended that nativism and xenophobia had attended every previous wave

---

the Tariff: A Study of Free Private Enterprise in Pressure Politics, as Shown in the 1929-1930 Revision of the Tariff (New York, 1935), pp. 283-93.

[1] John Higham, Strangers in the Land: Patterns of American Nativism, 1860-1925 (New York, 1966), p. 119.

of immigration and that the new immigrants would be assimilated just as the earlier ones had been. Finally, they emphatically denied that literacy was a fair test either of a man's worth or of his potential value as an American citizen.

The AJC's concern with Russian-Jewish immigration not only led to the consideration of the deplorable conditions that caused mass emigration from Russia, but also to an extensive lobbying effort in the area of foreign policy. Although the AJC leaders welcomed the immigrants to the United States, it was obvious that ending the pogroms and improving the conditions in Russia would lessen the need and volume of Jewish immigration. For the Russian immigrants constituted the overwhelming majority of Jewish immigrants year after year: in 1906 alone, 125,234 out of the 153,748 Jewish immigrants originated from some place within the Russian Empire.[1] Reducing the number of Jewish immigrants was desirable not because the German Jews wanted to keep out the Russian Jews--as is popularly but erroneously thought--but because the AJC recognized that some day the restrictionists would succeed in blocking the entry of a significant number of Jewish immigrants. Solving the Jewish problem in

---

[1] Samuel Joseph, *Jewish Immigration to the United States: From 1881-1910* (New York, 1914), p. 164.

Russia meant avoiding the damaging effects of a reversal of America's open immigration policy.

Therefore, the AJC sought to pressure the United States government to design its foreign policy to force Russia to improve the economic and political conditions of Russian Jewry. From 1906 through 1917 the men who ran the AJC lobbied--sometimes through the AJC and sometimes through non-organizational channels--with three Presidents, with Congress, and with the American business community to devise diplomatic and economic policies which would solve the Russian-Jewish problem. They focused on a few specific issues in American-Russian relations: America's reaction to the pogroms in 1905 and 1906; a campaign in 1910 and 1911 to abrogate the commercial Treaty of 1832 between Russia and the United States; the writing of a new treaty in 1916; and, from 1905 through 1917, the blocking of American investments in Russia.

The AJC was both a surrogate group and an oligarchy. It was, as Grant McConnell has accused many lobbying organizations of being, an undemocratic, élite organization.[1] Despite its assumed mandate from Russian Jews in America--the large constituency for whom the organization claimed to speak--

---

[1] McConnell, op. cit., p. 339.

the AJC almost completely excluded Russian Jews from its ranks. Therefore other Jews deeply resented the AJC, although it held exactly the same position on immigration matters and Russian-American treaty relations as did the Yiddish press and most Russian-Jewish organizations. Ultimately, the inconsistency between the AJC's humane goals and the discriminatory organizational structure led to recriminations, disputes, and finally to a schism within the American-Jewish community during the First World War.

Much historical interest has centered upon the differences and tensions between German and Russian Jews in America. Unfortunately, an emphasis upon the snobbish, domineering, exclusive attitude and practices of the German Jews towards the impoverished Russian-Jewish immigrants has distorted perspective and clouded knowledge of the uptown Jews' deep involvement with Russian Jewry. Despite the myths, the historical record reveals that the leaders of the AJC used their impressive financial resources, their social status, and the resulting access to men in government to try to solve the Jewish problem in Russia and to fight the restrictionist movement in the United States.

Why did these American-Jewish leaders of German descent care about the Russian problem? How did they view their place in American society? How did they affect the course of the literacy test struggle and America's Russian policy? How did they lobby on behalf of their Jewish interests? These are the issues that are presented and evaluated in this study--a study of an ethnic minority in the Progressive period which had rising expectations, rising fears, and an increasing sophistication in dealing with the executive and legislative branches of government.

CHAPTER I

THE NEED FOR ORGANIZATION

Between 1903 and 1906 approximately three hundred pogroms sent waves of despair and panic through the Jewish community in Russia and caused the departure of hundreds of thousands of Jews for England, Palestine, South Africa, and in most cases, the eastern cities of the United States.[1] The pogroms and the dreadful Russian-Jewish conditions out of which these violent acts developed, altered the attitudes, interests, and organization of American Jewry. Before 1903 American Jewish leaders--the uptown or German-Jews--were not deeply interested in the problems of Russian Jewry and sometimes even resented the influx of the poor, illiterate, and culturally strange Russian immigrants. After 1903, however, these same American-Jewish leaders became knowledgeable about Russian Jewry and mindful of the political voice of the Jewish immigrants who significantly increased the Jewish population in the United States.

---

[1] Cyrus Adler and Aaron M. Margalith, With Firmness in the Right: American Diplomatic Action Affecting Jews, 1840-1945 (New York, 1946), p. 276. "From Kishinev to Byelstok: A Table of Pogroms," The American Jewish Yearbook (Philadelphia, 1906), 5667, pp. 34-89.

With the outbreak of the pogroms, the unofficial American-Jewish leaders assumed the obligation of giving philanthropic aid to the victims as well as exerting pressure on the Russian government to change its anti-Semitic policies. In the latter effort they directly sought the aid of President Theodore Roosevelt. Although lacking a Jewish organization that could apply political pressure, Jacob H. Schiff and Oscar S. Straus, as spokesmen for American Jews, urged Roosevelt in 1905 and 1906 to intervene in Russia's affairs to stop the pogroms. Roosevelt, however, would not accede to the impassioned demands of an ethnic minority, refusing to antagonize the Russians and make an international issue of the pogroms.

Frustration over their inability to change Roosevelt's Russian policies as well as the expectation that more pogroms would soon occur were two factors which led Schiff and several of his associates to organize the American Jewish Committee in November, 1906. Although the AJC concentrated power in the hands of a few German-Jews, it projected itself as a guardian of Russian Jewry and as the official spokesman on certain political matters for the Russian-Jewish immigrants in the United States. Its founders intended for the AJC to watch closely over legislative and diplomatic matters of interest to American-Jews and to convey to the President,

State Department, and Congress, requests, information, and if need be, political threats. The AJC leaders also expected the organization to lobby discreetly without isolating American Jewry as a manipulative, political pressure group. Thus conflicting pressures and interests involving its basis of representation and lobbying techniques affected the AJC from its formative stages throughout its many battles on behalf of Russian Jewry and the Russian-Jewish immigrants.

I

"Five million people cannot emigrate," wrote Jacob H. Schiff sadly but realistically, "and no matter how many Jews may leave Russia, five millions [sic] will always remain there."[1] The thought of those five million remaining there in Russia was painful for Schiff because by 1903 he and other American-Jewish leaders were fully aware of the numerous pogroms and the dire demographic, economic, and educational conditions that formed the pattern of Jewish life in Russia. From 1800 to 1905 the Russian-Jewish population increased from 1,500,000 to 6,060,415, constituting 3.7 percent of the total Russian population as well as one-half of world Jewry.[2] With the exception of a few privileged

---

[1] Schiff, op. cit., II, 122.

[2] The American Jewish Yearbook (Philadelphia, 1914), 5675, p. 337.

classes of Jews, the Russian government subjected the Jewish population to severe geographical restrictions which confined residence to the twenty-five provinces in Russia and Russian-Poland called the Pale of Jewish Settlement. 93.3 percent of the Jews lived within the Pale, consisting of Congress Poland, Lithuania, Byelorussia, and the Ukraine, while 6.07 percent lived illegally or with temporary dispensations in some part of the Empire outside the Pale.[1] But even within the Pale itself, the government prohibited residence in certain rural areas, villages, and cities.

The Jews were further hampered by restrictions on their occupational and professional pursuits. Small quotas were set to limit Jewish representation in municipal governing bodies and public corporations. Russian laws also prohibited Jewish employment in state agencies; therefore, only a handful of Jews worked in the state-run railroad or liquor industries and none in the post office.[2] The majority of Jews worked as small-scale tradesmen, many were artisans and factory workers, and a large group lived on "philanthropic

---

[1] The Jewish Encyclopedia, X (1925), 529.

[2] Lucien Wolf, ed., The Legal Sufferings of the Jews in Russia: A Survey of their Present Situation, and a Summary of Laws (London, 1912), p. 10.

relief."[1] By law they were also required to serve in the army for longer periods than other minority groups. To be sure, there were exceptions to the laws designed to deny Jews wealth and influence in Russian life, as exemplified by the high proportion of Russian-Jewish barristers.[2] Nevertheless, it was estimated that 90 percent of the Jewish population lived in poverty at the turn of the century because of the geographical and economic restrictions as well as the undeveloped nature of the Russian economy.[3]

The pattern of educational restriction for the Jews had particularly serious implications because American restrictionists supported the literacy test as the principal barrier against immigration from eastern and southern Europe. Illiteracy rates were extremely high for the entire Russian population because of poverty and the inefficient Russian bureaucracy. The American Ambassador to Russia, George von

---

[1] Michael T. Florinsky, ed., McGraw-Hill Encyclopedia of Russia and the Soviet Union (New York, 1961), p. 258.

[2] William Rockhill to Philander C. Knox, Apr. 20, 1910, in Knox Papers (Library of Congress, Washington, D.C.), Box 41. Cited hereafter as Knox Papers.

[3] U.S., Congress, Senate, Report of the Immigration Commission, 61st Cong., 3d sess., 1911, Rept. 748, IV, 332. Cited hereafter as RIC. The term poverty was defined in the following way: "In the broader sense of a person with an insufficient income, a person unable to make any savings and forced to live from hand to mouth. . . ." Ibid.

Lengerke Meyer, estimated in 1905 that 99 million Russians were illiterate and, according to the Russian census of 1897, only 21.1 percent of the population was literate.[1] In addition to the obstacles of poverty and the bureaucracy, the Jews had to contend with educational quotas which prohibited Jewish students from filling more than 10 percent of the places in the primary and secondary level government schools. It is possible that these quotas were not strictly observed, as William Rockhill, the American Ambassador to Russia in 1910 maintained.[2] The government was probably as inefficient and corrupt in the practice of its educational quota system as it was in other facets of its operations. Therefore, many Jews must have tried to get around the restrictions imposed upon them, and in some cases they must have succeeded. But clearly the Jews were not as free to use the schools as were other Russians, nor could the Jews afford to organize a system of their own which would teach non-religious subjects.

The combination of poverty, demographic pressures, and government hostility made it inevitable for the Jews to

---

[1] Mark Anthony DeWolfe Howe, George von Lengerke Meyer: His Life and Public Services (New York, 1920), p. 196; Florinsky, op. cit., p. 150.

[2] Rockhill to Knox, Apr. 20, 1910, in Knox Papers, Box 41.

have a high illiteracy rate. According to official United States government statistics between 25.1 percent and 26 percent of the Russian-Jewish immigrants were illiterate. In 1913 the National Jewish Immigration Council studied the levels of Jewish immigrant illiteracy in order to determine the accuracy of the Immigration Bureau's statistics. After making three independent studies the Council supported the Bureau's findings, stating that 15 percent of the male immigrants and 39 percent of the female immigrants were illiterate.[1]

Female illiteracy was significant because of the large number of unaccompanied female Jewish immigrants; in fact, the proportion of females was far larger than among other immigrant groups. From 1899 to 1910 women constituted 43.4 percent of the total Jewish immigration, in comparison to 30.4 percent of all other immigrant groups. In each of the literacy test fights from 1906 through 1917, the restrictionists exempted illiterate females who accompanied literate husbands or fathers. The Council study suggested, however, that the exemption would not help the Jewish female

---

[1] The Immigration Bureau established Jewish female illiteracy at 40 percent. U.S., Congress, Senate, <u>Jewish Immigration: Report of a Special Committee of the National Jewish Immigration Council Appointed to Examine into the Question of Illiteracy Among Jewish Immigrants and Its Causes</u>, 63d Cong., 2d sess., 1914, S. Doc. 611, p. 5.

immigrants: "An exemption in the literacy test in regard to Jewish females coming to certain specified near relations would not be a material counterweighing influence because of the fact that the bulk of the female Jewish immigrants come without having parent or husband here."[1]

Driven by pogroms and demographic and economic pressures, the Russian Jews constantly moved in a "mass flight from poverty" from place to place within the Pale, through Europe, and across the Atlantic.[2] Although Russian policy prohibited emigration from the Empire there were a few official exceptions to the rules.[3] One involved Jewish orphans and those Jews who left in whole families including fathers, mothers, unmarried daughters, and sons. The government promulgated this rule in 1892 after negotiating with the Baron de Hirsch Jewish Colonization Association. According to the agreement, the Jews whose families had fulfilled their military obligations, who had no criminal records, and who promised to leave Russian territory forever were entitled

---

[1] Ibid., p. 10.

[2] Moses Rischin, The Promised City: New York's Jews, 1870-1914 (Cambridge, 1962), p. 24.

[3] In 1907 over 100,000 Jews crossed the border illegally, according to a special commission study made by the Russian government. Rockhill to Knox, Feb. 22, 1910, in Knox Papers, Box 41.

to receive their exit permits without cost.[1]

Many Jewish emigrés, however, paid for the expensive exit permits required by the Russian government. A common but costly practice involved paying the steamship company from which transatlantic passage had been bought to obtain the necessary exit papers. If these methods failed, as they frequently did, emigrés could forgo the formalities and bribe border officials or sneak across the unwatched sectors of the frontier.

Russian-Jewish immigrants who arrived in America bore the marks of deprivation in Russia, the costly and often illegal departure from home, the difficult journey through Europe, and a trying three weeks at sea. (The latter experience was particularly agonizing for the large numbers of Jews who observed religious dietary laws.) They were poor: 50,720 had $50 or less in their possession upon arrival in 1906. They also arrived in large families with a great number of dependents: out of a total of 153,748 Jewish immigrants who arrived in 1906, 43,620 were fourteen years or under, and 8,253 were forty-five years or older. These figures are most meaningful in comparison with those for the 240,528 southern Italian immigrants: among them only 26,546

---

[1] RIC, IV, 260-61.

were fourteen years or under, and only 11,094 were forty-five years or older.[1]

No matter how difficult the process of assimilation was in the United States and no matter how great the tensions were between Gentile and Jew, German-Jew and Russian-Jew, few Jewish immigrants ever returned to the deplorable conditions in Russia. From 1908 to 1924 the number of permanent Jewish immigrants actually outnumbered other immigrant groups from Italy, Germany, and Great Britain, as only 52,294 foreign Jews emigrated from the United States.[2] Approximately 956,000 Jewish immigrants remained as compared to 945,000 Italians, 644,000 Germans, and 648,000 from the British Isles. From 1908 to 1943 the Jewish emigration rate from the United States to Europe was only 4.6 percent compared to 34.4 percent for all other immigrant groups.[3] Thus

---

[1] Frank P. Sargent, *Report of the Commissioner-General of Immigration* (Washington, D.C., 1906), p. 486. For a study of the traumatic journey see Oscar Handlin, *The Uprooted: The Epic Story of the Great Migrations that Made the American People* (Boston, 1951), Chapter ii.

[2] Harry E. Hull, *Annual Report of the Commissioner General of Immigration: For the Fiscal Year Ended June 30, 1925* (Washington, D.C., 1925), p. 125. During the years 1908 to 1925, 1,012,768 southern Italians re-emigrated. *Ibid.*

[3] L. Hersch, "Jewish Migrations During the Last Hundred Years," *The Jewish People Past and Present* (New York, 1946), I, 421.

the Russian-Jewish immigrants stayed in the United States, forming distinct social, economic, and political patterns which drastically changed their lives and greatly affected the assimilation process of America's German-Jewish population as well.

At first, the arrival of the poor and illiterate Russian-Jews was an unpleasant shock to the German-Jews, many of whom were immigrants themselves or first generation Americans. Not only were they generally unconcerned about the plight of Russian Jewry, but during the 1880's, which saw the first influx of Russian-Jewish immigrants, many American Jews had actually acted in a frightened and inhospitable manner. They had disliked the unenlightened Orthodox Jewish immigrants and had tried ineffectually to discourage their coming.[1] Nevertheless, a program of financial responsibility for the immigrants, if not a sympathetic attitude, eventually prevailed by the turn of the century as American-Jews established numerous philanthropic services such as hospitals, settlement houses, religious organizations, and immigrant aid societies for the Russian-Jews.

In part, the philanthropic activity was needed to carry out an agreement made in 1892 between Jewish leaders

---

[1] Rischin, *op. cit.*, Chapter vi.

and the Secretary of the Treasury, Charles Foster, regarding the entry of impoverished Jews who upon arrival in the United States received financial aid from charitable organizations. The agreement, negotiated by Simon Wolf, a leader of B'nai B'rith, provided that the Jewish community would take financial responsibility for the impoverished Jewish immigrants. Thus the American Jews would prevent the immigrants from becoming public charges and help to disperse them from the eastern cities. On its part, the Immigration Bureau (in the Treasury Department) promised to give a liberal interpretation to the 1891 immigration law which prohibited the entry of those likely to become public charges.

"You declare the readiness . . . to give the Government in all cases a satisfactory bond guaranteeing that none of these refugee immigrants shall become a public charge," Foster wrote to Simon Wolf. If the immigrants leave the cities, Foster went on to declare, and do not irritate industrial conditions "no worthy immigrant . . . should be excluded from the country because, through the action of others, he is for the time being homeless and without property."[1] This understanding between Wolf, the Jews he

---

[1] Simon Wolf, *The Presidents I Have Known from 1860-1918* (Washington, D.C., 1918), pp. 160-61.

represented, and the government remained operative throughout the early years of the twentieth century.[1]

American-Jewish leaders took one step when they responded generously to the immigrants already in America; they took another when they tried to affect the Jewish situation in Russia itself. Their moment of awakening to the need to improve the lives of the Jews in Russia occurred as a result of the Kishinev pogrom in April, 1903. A violent outburst directed against Jews with the semi-official sanction of the Czar's government, the pogrom left many dead and wounded and thousands homeless. Kishinev struck the American-Jewish public as an act of uncommon barbarity reminiscent of the cruel practices of the Middle Ages. Numerous rallies were held in cities throughout the United States, and thousands of Jews and non-Jews signed a petition of protest which President Roosevelt sent to the Russian government. His was a symbolic gesture, however, since the President accurately predicted that the Russians would refuse to accept the petition. American-Jews also raised $100,000 for the relief of the Russian victims and thereby started a flow

---

[1]Statistics of the Immigration Bureau showed that Jewish immigrants were indeed public charges in 1914. Simon Wolf to Jacob H. Schiff, Feb. 9, 1914, in Hebrew Sheltering and Immigrants Aid Society of America Papers (HIAS), (Yivo Institute for Jewish Research, New York).

of money from America to Europe to parallel the traditional pattern whereby European philanthropic organizations, such as the Baron de Hirsch Fund and the Alliance Israelite, provided aid for Jewish immigrants in America.

After Kishinev the uptown Jews were deeply involved in political events in Russia. They protested the pogroms; they studied the many changes of governments; and they rejoiced at each challenge to the Czar's authority, as did the Russian-Jewish immigrants who kept abreast of events in Russia through the Yiddish press in New York.

It was Jacob H. Schiff, the most powerful man in organized Jewish life in America, who went further, seeking directly to weaken the autocratic Russian government. Schiff, a decisive, uncompromising, and stern man, felt an intense sense of responsibility, stemming from his strong religious beliefs, for the welfare of Jews in the United States and eastern Europe. A comfortable immigrant from Frankfurt, he arrived in the United States in 1865 at the age of eighteen. Thirty-five years later, Schiff had become one of the élite of American bankers, with intimate ties to the major railroad corporations, insurance companies, utilities, and the international banking community.[1] Because of

---

[1] From the Civil War to the first decade of the twentieth century "the growth of American financial capitalism

the fortune he made as a partner of Kuhn, Loeb, & Co., Schiff had direct access to the most powerful men in government and in the financial community, access which he used continually to benefit Jewish interests. Because of his fortune and his concern for those needing help, he was able to distribute between $50 million and $100 million in charitable contributions to a remarkable number of Jewish and non-sectarian institutions: the Red Cross, the Montefiore Hospital, the Henry Street Settlement House, the Semitic Museum at Harvard, the Jewish Division at the New York Public Library, the Joint Distribution Committee, and the Galveston plan--to name but a few.[1] With discretion and kindness Schiff gave to those men and causes that he thought merited his help.

Now in response to Kishinev, Schiff rigorously sought to punish Russia by closing off the American money market to the Russian government. To further weaken the Russians he underwrote a multi-million dollar loan to the

---

. . . was the work of no more than six firms and hardly 12 men--and of these Jacob Schiff was the only one not a descendant of New England, Puritan stock." Barry E. Supple, "A Business Elite: German-Jewish Financiers in Nineteenth-Century New York," Business History Review, XXXI (Summer, 1957), 171.

[1] Stephen Birmingham, "Our Crowd": The Great Jewish Families of New York (New York, 1967), p. 326.

Japanese government during the Russo-Japanese War and he even paid for the distribution of revolutionary literature to Russian prisoners of war held by the Japanese. Many years later in April, 1917, George Kennan, author of <u>Siberia and the Exile System</u> and a leader of the Friends of Russian Freedom, remembered and praised Schiff's effort: "It was fruitful in good results, because it was the support of the army that enabled the Duma to overthrow the Government of the Czar, and you helped to enlighten the army."[1]

Schiff even defended and financed the activities of some Jewish radicals in Russia.[2] "The claim that among the ranks of those who in Russia are seeking to undermine governmental authority there are considerable numbers of Jews, may be true," Schiff wrote to Sergei Yulievich Witte, Russia's chief negotiator at the Portsmouth Peace Conference. "In

---

[1] George Kennan to Jacob H. Schiff, Apr. 11, 1917, in Jacob H. Schiff Papers (American Jewish Archives, Cincinnati, Ohio). Cited hereafter as Schiff Papers.

[2] Zosa Szajkowski,"Paul Nathan, Lucien Wolf, Jacob H. Schiff and the Jewish Revolutionary Movements in Eastern Europe (1903-1917)," <u>Jewish Social Studies</u>, XXIX (Jan., 1967), 14. Unfortunately, most of Schiff's papers were destroyed in a fire at the Jewish Theological Seminary in 1966. No large collection of his papers is available for the years before 1914. Therefore, it has been necessary to rely heavily upon published letters in books and articles that reproduced some of those previously found in the Seminary's archives.

fact," he added, "it would be rather surprising if some of those so terribly afflicted by persecution and exceptional laws should not at last have turned against their merciless oppressors."[1]

Thus, by means of a financial boycott, by aiding Russia's enemy, and by supporting radicals and revolutionaries, Schiff vented his anger against Russian anti-Semitism. Now, in 1905 and 1906, with the outbreak of new pogroms, Schiff pursued one other approach: using his access to the President and Secretary of State to persuade them to aid the Jews in Russia. His appeals, however, were made difficult by the President, who held a sophisticated and detached view of Russian-American relations and carefully weighed American public opinion against the pressure of an ethnic minority.

II

A heated dialogue between Theodore Roosevelt and several American Jewish leaders regarding Russia's Jewish policies took place in 1905 and 1906 when Russia, which was weakened by defeat in her war with Japan, seemed on the verge of monumental political and social change. The Jews,

---

[1] Schiff, op. cit., II, 131. The letter was co-signed by Isaac N. Seligman, Oscar S. Straus, Adolph Lewisohn, and Adolf Kraus.

along with other Americans interested in Russian affairs, oscillated between optimism and pessimism over the possibilities for fundamental changes. The revolutionary events stirred the hope that the autocratic regime would lose its grip and the barriers against the Jews would fall.

George von Lengerke Meyer, the American Ambassador to Russia, felt a surge of optimism when he reported to President Roosevelt about the Czar's Ukase on religious freedom "granting practically religious freedom to all sects, except the Jews." It "makes a great concession to the party of reform," Meyer wrote, "and if carried out in all its completeness, the greatest concession to individual liberty since the liberation of the serfs."[1] Schiff was hopeful that the Jews would receive "full rights" in the "revolution which is taking place." He continued to recommend the absorption of Russian Jews by "civilized nations," particularly the United States, if conditions in Russia failed to improve. "But I hope things will not happen so and I still hold fast to the belief that the Russian pale of settlement and the restrictive legislation against the Jews are a thing of the past."[2]

---

[1] Howe, op. cit., p. 149.

[2] Szajkowski, op. cit., p. 23.

Unfortunately, the same revolutionary events that led to the Ukase and the calling of the Duma also led to the outbreak of new pogroms in the summer and fall of 1905 and the spring of 1906, and to an intense series of communications among Roosevelt, Schiff, and Oscar S. Straus.

Of the two Jews, Straus was closest to Roosevelt and was used by the President as his advocate in the Jewish community. Straus had been a partner in his family's successful firm of L. Straus & Company, which merged with R. H. Macy's, and had served also under President Cleveland as the American Ambassador to Turkey. An ambitious man, who now wanted to continue his career of public service through appointive or elective office, he valued his close relationship to the President. Because he was a committed Republican, a great admirer of the President, and an outstanding Jewish leader, Roosevelt would later appoint Straus to his Cabinet as Secretary of Commerce and Labor.

In contrast to Straus, Schiff was neither a politician nor a trusted associate of the President's, but one who gained recognition from the President because of his importance in the financial world and his position as the unofficial leader of American Jewry. Schiff was a Republican too, but one who often criticized and opposed the President on his Russian policies as well as his corporate and monetary positions.

Roosevelt's highly publicized campaign against the trusts and unregulated business operations might have been more shadow than substance.[1] Nevertheless, Roosevelt's drive deeply concerned Schiff who was a member of numerous interlocking directorates which tied him to insurance companies, banks, and major industrial concerns. As the senior partner of Kuhn, Loeb, & Co., Schiff was deeply involved in the financing of several major railroad lines such as the Pennsylvania and the Union Pacific Railroads. Therefore, when Roosevelt moved against the Northern Securities Company in 1902, he broke up one of Schiff's creations. A few years later, when the President called for an Interstate Commerce Commission investigation of the Union Pacific Railroad, he scrutinized the activities of one of Schiff's major clients. Eventually, Schiff was so displeased by Roosevelt's corporate and monetary policies that on one occasion he boldly criticized the President to his face. Schiff directly accused Roosevelt of having a "stern and uncompromising attitude in important questions," as shown by "the manner in which changes in economic conditions, which in your opinion had become necessary, are forced upon the country and upon

---

[1] Richard Hofstadter, *The American Political Tradition: And the Men Who Made It* (New York, 1951), p. 228.

the interests involved."[1]

Now in November, 1905, Straus, the friend, and Schiff, the critic, pleaded for Roosevelt's help, turning to the President as the only one who could exert pressure on the Russian government. But Roosevelt responded to their pleas on a typical note of "heated righteousness."[2] The President's letters to his Jewish correspondents were testy and replete with his customary lectures on his conception of America's role in world affairs. He tried, with only limited success, however, to convince the Jews that the United States government was unable to stop the pogroms. He explained that he could not intervene in Russian affairs to help the Jews any more than he could help the Armenians in Turkey or the Negroes in Portuguese South Africa and the Congo Free State. The "professional hysteria crowd" and the "very worthy people of limited knowledge and hysterical habit of mind," was the way Roosevelt characterized those who sought help for the Russian Jews, Armenians, and African Negroes.[3]

---

[1] Schiff, op. cit., I, 47.

[2] John Morton Blum, The Republican Roosevelt (New York, 1965), p. 2.

[3] Roosevelt to Curtis Guild, Apr. 2, 1906, in Theodore Roosevelt Papers (Library of Congress, Washington, D.C.), Series II, 62. Cited hereafter as Roosevelt Papers.

Although Roosevelt was eager for the United States to play an important diplomatic role by maintaining a stable world order as well as by spreading her Christian and democratic values, he was cautious and realistic in his Russian policy. He refused to build a crisis, at the prompting of American Jewry, where, in his view, none seemed to exist. Because of four factors--his overriding concern with domestic matters, his information about Russian affairs, his sense of the limitations of American power, and finally, his support of the literacy test and restriction movement-- Roosevelt would not take any daring initiative vis-à-vis the Russians. He carefully avoided making himself vulnerable before American and world opinion, which did not regard the Russian-Jewish issue as a pressing matter.

After the end of the Russo-Japanese War, Roosevelt was primarily concerned with domestic politics. His interest centered on legislation such as the Hepburn bill and the pure food and drug bill as well as the Congressional elections of 1906. From time to time, however, important foreign policy matters intruded upon him. This was the case with the disorders in Cuba in 1906, the intense diplomatic negotiations with the Japanese over immigration to the West Coast, and the sending of the American fleet away from its home in the Atlantic to Japan and around the world.

Although his interest was mainly directed to domestic and other foreign matters, Roosevelt did show a lively concern and thorough knowledge of Russian affairs. This involvement in Russian events stemmed from the time that he mediated the settlement of the Russo-Japanese War. Perceiving that Russia's policies would determine whether Europe and Asia would remain at peace, he said, "There is no nation in the world which more than Russia holds in its hands the fate of the coming years. . . ."[1] The President also felt that the Russian government could not be trusted, characterizing it as "treacherous," "insincere," and most damaging of all, lacking knowledge of its own strengths and weaknesses.[2]

In March, 1905, Roosevelt assigned George Meyer, then the American Ambassador to Italy, to St. Petersburg, which he described to Meyer as "the only Embassy at which I do want work done just at present."[3] Roosevelt was eager for Meyer, a wealthy merchant from Boston who had been active in Massachusetts and Republican politics, to provide trustworthy information on the Russo-Japanese War and internal Russian political developments. In his letter to Meyer

---

[1] Blum, op. cit., p. 135

[2] Edward Charles Wagenknecht, The Seven Worlds of Theodore Roosevelt (New York, 1958), p. 240.

[3] Howe, op. cit., p. 111.

announcing the appointment, Roosevelt emphasized the significance of placing an able diplomat in Russia: "The trouble with our Ambassadors in stations of real importance is that they totally fail to give us real help and real information, and seem to think that the life work of our Ambassador is a kind of glorified pink tea-party. Now, at St. Petersburg I want some work done, and you are the man to do it."[1]

Meyer proved to be a capable and astute diplomat who would hardly have called his life in Russia "a glorified pink tea-party." He worked hard and displayed skill at the intricate maneuvers that resulted in the Portsmouth Peace Conference and the successful conclusion of peace terms. With the end of the War, however, his diplomatic activities became less pressing, and Meyer began to think that his presence in Russia was of limited value to himself and the President.[2] In fact, Meyer was quite eager throughout 1906 to return to Washington to a Cabinet position which Roosevelt had promised him, and which he obtained in March, 1907 as Postmaster-General.

---

[1] Ibid.

[2] George Meyer to Henry Cabot Lodge, Jan. 19, 1906, in Henry Cabot Lodge Papers (Massachusetts Historical Society, Boston).

Meyer wrote Roosevelt frequently about the revolutionary events that challenged the Czar's authority: the massive civil disorders, economic unrest, terrorist bombings, and the calling of the Duma. Throughout his term, Meyer also reported to Roosevelt about the Russian government's attitude towards the Jews and their emigation from Russia to the United States. In one such report Meyer wrote:

> To understand the feeling towards the Jews here among the Russians and even among the peasants, it is necessary to realize that it is quite as bitter and unreasonable as that of [Senator Ben] Tillman concerning the political rights of the Negro. Many of the Jews are active leaders in the revolutionary movement, which tends to increase the antipathy among the reactionists. The Jews are also feared for their ability to earn a living and make money under most adverse circumstances.[1]

A month later, Meyer recalled a conversation that he had had with the military Governor of Odessa, a city where 150,000 Jews lived: "I asked about the class of Jews that were to sail shortly for America. He smiled and replied that they had seven million in Russia that we were welcome to."[2]

Meyer's correspondence indicated that the United States government would be unable to alter the internal Russian-Jewish situation, should it ever wish to do so.

---

[1] Meyer to Theodore Roosevelt, Sept. 21, 1906, in Roosevelt Papers, Series I, Box 111.

[2] Meyer to Roosevelt, Oct. 28, 1906, in Roosevelt Papers, Series I, Box 113.

He stated this opinion when discussing some abortive plans for liberalizing Jewish occupational and residential restrictions. Some representatives in the first Duma had proposed that Jews who completed their military training should be allowed to live anywhere outside the Pale, although they would be allowed to own land only within the Pale itself. Reaction against this plan was intense and ultimately successful in blocking any liberalization. "The Jewish problem will not be settled by intervention or suggestion of foreign powers which the Government resents and refuses to listen to, but by financial necessities," Meyer observed. "The foreign bankers hold the cards, and great influence can be brought to bear on Russia through financial channels which I believe will eventually be most instrumental in forcing the Government to give the needed and proper reforms and privileges to the Russian Jews."[1]

Had he wanted, Roosevelt could have disregarded Meyer's advice and maintained that the United States had a special interest in Russian-Jewish conditions. He could have acted as the moral spokesman for civilized humanity by objecting to the barbaric treatment of the Russian Jews.

---

[1] Meyer to Roosevelt, Nov. 26, 1906, in Roosevelt Papers, Series I, Box 114.

Or, he could have maintained that Russia's treatment of the Jews caused an unnecessary wave of immigration which was detrimental to America's welfare. Roosevelt had two important precedents for the latter course of action. One was contained in President Benjamin Harrison's Message to Congress in December, 1891, which called upon the Russian government to improve the conditions of the Jews to reduce the causes of emigation. The second precedent in 1902 was contained in a note from Secretary of State John Hay to the Rumanian government, written in response to a request from Schiff, Oscar S. Straus, and Representative Lucius Littauer, a Republican from New York. This note linked America's concern for the deprivations sustained by Rumanian Jews with the heavy Jewish immigration to the United States, that stemmed from unsatisfactory living conditions. "It behooves the State to scrutinize most jealously the character of the immigration from a foreign land, and, if it be obnoxious to objection, to examine the causes which render it so. Should those causes originate in the act of another Sovereign State, to the detriment of its neighbors, it is the prerogative of an injured State to point out the evil and to make remonstrances."[1]

---

[1] Adler and Margalith, op. cit, p. 123. For a discussion of Jewish lobbying in this matter see Naomi Wiener Cohen, A Dual Heritage: The Public Career of Oscar S. Straus (Philadelphia, 1969), pp. 123-26.

When Roosevelt formulated his policies towards the pogroms, he did so, in part, because Russia, the largest and one of the most powerful nations in Europe, refused to respond positively to criticism on the Jewish issue from other nations. The Russian government had informed other European governments and the United States that objecting to the conditions of Russian Jewry would have but one result--to antagonize the government. Russia regarded the Jewish problem as an internal matter and not subject to censure from abroad.

The Roosevelt Administration could not join with friendly nations such as England and France in a direct appeal to the Russians, because these two countries were allied with Russia, France since 1894 and England finally in 1907. Preserving good relations with Russia was infinitely more important to France and England than improving the condition of Russian Jewry. They refused to press the irritating Jewish issue when other matters were at stake--matters which concerned territorial aggrandizement in Africa, the Middle East and the Far East; and the relative military power of European nations. Roosevelt, who was quite sensitive to both the importance and fragility of the alliance structure, was not about to force a potentially divisive issue on friendly nations, or to wage an isolated campaign against Russia's discriminatory practices.

The Roosevelt Administration, however, was willing to voice its concern for Moroccan Jewry at the same time that the Russian government protected itself from diplomatic interference concerning its Jewish question. In January, 1906, Secretary of State Elihu Root asked Henry White, America's representative at the Algeciras Conference, to raise the issue of Morocco's discrimination against the Jews. Root wanted "to restrain the spirit of intolerance and preclude the development of its effects into antagonism between all Mohammedans and non-Mohammedans." His instructions to White also contained a letter from Schiff describing Moroccan-Jewish conditions. The Conference supported a recommendation, proposed by White, expressing an interest in the "welfare of the Jews in Morocco."[1] The United States government was able to make this request on behalf of the Jews because the European powers at the Conference were deciding the economic and political fate of Morocco. Therefore, they could touch upon any internal subject of interest to them.

Instead of making futile and irksome diplomatic efforts to stop Russia's discrimination against the Jews, Roosevelt favored an alternative solution to the immigration problem, which stemmed from Russian-Jewish conditions.

---

[1] Adler and Margalith, op. cit., pp. 37-40.

Through restrictive legislation he sought to protect the United States from illiterate and impoverished Russian immigrants whom he regarded as undesirable. By supporting the literacy test, Roosevelt hoped to build a barrier between the United States and Russia and the other eastern and southern European countries that produced large numbers of emigrés, without troubling those countries about the unsatisfactory internal conditions which caused emigration.

Clearly, Russia was not directly concerned with Roosevelt's attempts to restrict immigration from Europe. This position was strikingly different from that of the Japanese government which had taken an active role in negotiations with the State Department to prevent the United States from singling out the Japanese immigrants as undesirable. Japan regarded the discrimination against her immigrants on the West Coast as an affront to her national dignity. Therefore, the two countries effected the Gentlemen's Agreement by which Japan herself stopped the immigration of unskilled laborers to the United States. But unlike Japan, no single eastern or southern European country felt insulted by the hostility towards the new immigrants; no European country, in fact, took a deep interest in the immigrants who settled in the United States. What this actually meant to Roosevelt was that Russia and other European nations would not interfere in the evolution of America's restrictive policy when it centered on the literacy test.

Now in November, 1905, when Meyer was home for a visit after the arduous months of work over the Portsmouth negotiations, the conflict between the American-Jewish leaders and the Republican administration emerged. According to Meyer, Secretary of State Elihu Root personally asked him upon his return to St. Petersburg to discuss the pogroms with Count Sergei Witte, previously Russia's representative at the Portsmouth Conference, and now president of the Council of Ministers. Witte had learned at first hand of American Jewry's deep concern for its Russian brethren when he had conferred with Schiff and several other Jews during his stay in the United States. Thus Root hoped that Witte would now say "something that would assure the Jewish element and quiet public sentiment." Meyer added in his diary that Root believed "that it was a delicate matter for us to interfere in any way and that certain Jews in America were merely striving for notoriety."[1]

The pogroms that broke out in the late fall of 1905 amidst general civil disorders in Russia were a direct result of the trials of the Russo-Japanese War and the

---

[1] Howe, op. cit., p. 222.

identification of specific Russian Jews with radical and reformist elements. In response to the new crisis, Schiff, Straus, and Cyrus L. Sulzberger headed the National Committee for the Relief of Sufferers by Russian Massacres. Rallies were held to express outrage at the pogroms and American Jews raised $1,200,000 from thousands of contributors.[1]

Not content with public demonstrations and fund raising, in December Schiff wrote an impassioned plea to Roosevelt about the pogroms. Suggesting that it was "the duty of the civilized world to intervene," Schiff asked Roosevelt to speak for the Jews on behalf of humanity, as he had once done for the Cubans in 1898. Schiff recommended that the President express his concern for the Russian Jews in a message to Congress and direct the United States to cooperate with other nations in an effort to pressure the Russians. He justified his request by stating that a message from Roosevelt would "rally self-respect in Russia" and allow for the establishment of a law-abiding government which would protect the Jews.[2]

---

[1] The committee spent all but $190,000 of the funds. In 1913, the AJC, represented by Benjamin Cardozo, received permission from the New York Supreme Court to transfer the remaining funds to the AJC, to be used for emergencies but never for the expenses incurred in running the AJC.

[2] Schiff, op. cit., II, 137-38.

Roosevelt, feeling that Schiff had become "hysterical" about the possibilities for Presidential action in response to the "dreadful atrocities," maintained that there was no way for him to implement these requests.[1] Therefore, he wrote Schiff that these proposals "would make the United States government ridiculous, and so far from helping the condition of the Jews would have hurt them in Russia and would have tended to hurt them here." Roosevelt firmly stated that the United States would not join a non-existent union of European states dedicated to helping the Russian Jews, nor would his Administration even promote such a union. "I sympathize thoroughly with your feelings, wrought up as they are and ought to be by the dreadful outrages committed on the Jews in Russia," Roosevelt wrote in his one conciliatory passage. He would do what he could but he would not "threaten aimlessly and thereby do harm."[2]

Straus, who was familiar with the correspondence between Roosevelt and Schiff, felt completely sympathetic to the President's view that the United States was powerless in this matter. He wrote the President, saying that he had

---

[1] Roosevelt to Oscar S. Straus, Dec. 14, 1905, in Roosevelt Papers, Series II, 60.

[2] Roosevelt to Schiff, Dec. 14, 1905, in Roosevelt Papers, Series II, 60.

come to Roosevelt's aid by further explaining to Schiff and other Jews that the President's hands were tied. Straus then indicated that some other form of Presidential action designed to please American Jews might be desirable. He wrote about the Jews who were arriving in America as a result of the pogroms and suggested that Roosevelt sometime in the future state publicly "that humanity and the spirit of our history and development alike, dictate that we should not give a grudging welcome to the refugees from religious persecution. . . ."[1]

The pogrom issue abated until April, 1906, when Schiff and Straus learned from European Jewish sources that new pogroms would occur during the Russian Easter. Straus asked the President to speak with Baron Roman Romanovich Rosen, Russia's Ambassador in Washington, as well as to direct Meyer to make inquiries of the Russian government in St. Petersburg; he wanted Roosevelt and Meyer to express America's concern and disapproval in advance of any pogroms.[2] Therefore Assistant Secretary of State Robert Bacon instructed Meyer to approach the Foreign Minister in a discreet manner

---

[1] Straus to Roosevelt, Dec. 15, 1905, in Roosevelt Papers, Series I, Box 101.

[2] Straus to Roosevelt, Apr. 1, 1906, in Roosevelt Papers, Series I, Box 104.

about the "grave apprehensions" in America over new pogroms. Meyer was asked to consult with the British and to get information about Russia's efforts to prevent the pogroms as well. Consequently, he received assurances from Count Witte, the President of the Council of Ministers, that the government would prevent the outbreak of Easter pogroms.[1]

Roosevelt, for his part, spoke with Rosen and received the same assurances. In relating this news to Straus on April 10, Roosevelt took the opportunity to express his displeasure with Schiff's approach to the Russian-Jewish issue. "Baron Rosen spoke very warmly of your courtesy and consideration," Roosevelt informed Straus. But "I am bound to add that he stated that another prominent Jewish gentleman in New York City had prejudiced Witte against the cause for which he was pleading by his attitude."[2] The President agreed to make public the fact that the United States had made the April inquiries, but Roosevelt was eager to convey

---

[1] Robert Bacon to Meyer, Apr. 9, 1906, in General Records of the State Department: Russia, Political Relations with the United States (National Archives, Washington, D.C.). Cited hereafter as SDF. Meyer to Straus, Apr. 9, 1906, in Oscar S. Straus Papers (Library of Congress, Washington, D.C.), Box 4. Cited hereafter as Straus Papers. Meyer to Straus, Apr. 10, 1906, in Roosevelt Papers, Series I, Box 104.

[2] Roosevelt to Straus, Apr. 10, 1906, in Roosevelt Papers, Series II, 62.

the impression that no "pressures" had been applied to get a favorable response.[1]

As the Russian government promised, no violence occurred at Easter, but two months later, during a period of large-scale agrarian unrest, a frightful pogrom took place at Bialystok. Again Schiff and Straus urgently asked Roosevelt to protest to the Russian government. But this time Schiff conceded to the President that the United States government could not prevent the outbreak of pogroms: "I do know in advance that unfortunately nothing can be done by our Government, but I have felt that I should at least more fully acquaint you with the terrible situation which has unfortunately developed in the faint hope that possibly you and also Secretary Root might be able to see some way in which pressure can be brought upon the Russian Government. . . ."[2]

Root instructed Meyer to consult informally with the Russian government to learn if local officials were partly responsible for the pogrom. A few hours after receiving the request Meyer met with Russian Minister of Foreign Affairs

---

[1] Roosevelt to Straus, Apr. 13, 1906, in Roosevelt Papers, Series II, 63.

[2] Schiff, op. cit., II, 139.

Alexandr Izvolsky but the Minister categorically refused to discuss the matter with Meyer or with the British Ambassador when he tried to raise the same subject. The meeting was particularly frustrating for Meyer not only because Izvolsky refused to hear his message, but also because it was clear that the Minister already knew its contents, the Russian government having deciphered the State Department code.[1] He also embarrassed the protesting British and American Ambassadors by telling the German Ambassador about the rebuff. Meyer learned of this disclosure while playing polo with the Counsellor of the Austrian Embassy: "I hear you and the English Ambassador received a refusal at the Foreign Office," to which Meyer replied, "Where did you get that idea?" Not only was it bad form, Meyer wrote in his diary, but "it would be bad for public sentiment if it got into the American papers."[2]

Roosevelt also regarded the June initiative as a secretive and delicate probe. "I do not wish to say to anyone as yet what was done," he wrote Schiff. "The efficacy of anything that is done depends largely upon there being no

---

[1] Meyer to Elihu Root, June 27, 1906, in SDF, no. 551.
[2] Howe, op. cit., p. 294.

symptom of offense to the Russian authorities."[1] Trying to do what Schiff suggested, Roosevelt later wrote, the United States was on the "verge of receiving a rebuff" that would have placed it "in a very undignified and unpleasant position. . . ."[2] Root expressed the same cautious view when he wrote Roosevelt that public knowledge of America's actions would "prevent the Russian Government from acting." It would, he said, "increase the anti-Jewish feeling," and "make further massacres more probable."[3]

While Root and Roosevelt were inhibited and frustrated by diplomatic constraints, it was easy for Congress, which had no direct responsibility in the matter, to pass a resolution of sympathy for the victims of the pogroms. The resolution, introduced by Senator Anselm M. McLaurin of

---

[1] Roosevelt to Schiff, June 22, 1906, in Roosevelt Papers, Series II, 64. Little has changed in the tone of official Presidential statements about the Russian-Jewish situation. For example, during the last week in December, 1970 the United States government made a discreet appeal to the Russian government to commute the death sentences of certain Russian-Jewish hijackers. "Both the White House and State Department refused to discuss actions by the Nixon Administration for fear that public criticism would only harden Moscow's attitude and provide an angry rejection of American appeals." The New York Times, Dec. 29, 1970, p. 1.

[2] Roosevelt to Schiff, June 26, 1906, in Roosevelt Papers, Series II, 65.

[3] Elihu Root to Roosevelt, June 23, 1906, in Roosevelt Papers, Series I, Box 106.

Mississippi and signed by Roosevelt on June 26, stated: "That the people of the United States are horrified by the reports of the massacres of Hebrews in Russia on account of their race and religion and that those bereaved thereby have the hearty sympathy of the people of this country."[1]

Jewish leaders continued to make appeals to the President throughout late June and early July in the wake of the Bialystok pogrom. Schiff suggested to Roosevelt that the United States send warships or ordinary steamers to pick up Russian refugees. Roosevelt rejected this course of action on the grounds that "it would be wholly impracticable to take it if more than a few score people were to try to take advantage of asylum."[2]

The President became impatient with those who demanded that he change a situation which was beyond his power, for both diplomatic and domestic reasons. He became piqued at the constant pressure the Jews brought to bear on him and the State Department and expressed his anger and frustration over the issue in a letter to Nathan Bijur, a prominent New York lawyer also concerned about Russian-Jewish conditions.

---

[1] U.S., *Congressional Record*, 59th Cong., 1st sess., 1906, XL, Part 9, 8919.

[2] Roosevelt to Schiff, July 26, 1906, in Roosevelt Papers, Series II, 65.

In this letter the President reaffirmed that the United States government could do nothing more for the Russian Jews; at the same time he promised that he would inform the Jewish leaders, through Straus, of diplomatic developments: "But the truth is that most of the public action on this side on behalf of the Russian Jews, including almost all of it that relates to action by the Government, represents not an effective purpose to do good to those who are suffering in Russia, but to exploit, in the interests of entirely selfish individuals, the Jewish vote in America."[1]

Although Roosevelt was sympathetic to the plight of Russian Jewry, he felt that he could not change those conditions and did not want to embarrass himself and the government in useless attempts at intervention. He refused to make strong public statements or threats, thereby denying that the Russian-Jewish issue affected the basic interests of the United States or presented a moral problem for the American public. Roosevelt was willing to please his Jewish constituents, but only if he could do so without antagonizing the Russian government. This was the case in April, 1906 when Easter pogroms were threatened, but this was not

---

[1] Roosevelt to Nathan Bijur, July 11, 1906, in Roosevelt Papers, Series II, 65.

so in December, 1905 nor June, 1906 after the outbreak of atrocities.

Roosevelt, however, was wrong to assume that the agitation on the part of the Jewish community stemmed from opportunism or the desire to garner votes. Schiff and Straus were truly outraged by the pogroms and eager to use the power and prestige of the President and State Department. They were operating in the tradition of Hofjuden--court Jews--by carrying on a discreet, personal dialogue with the President and State Department, but they failed in their efforts to influence decisively American foreign policy on behalf of American and Russian Jewry. They confronted a President who told them bluntly of the limits of their power and of his own. Roosevelt left no doubts in their minds of how little he could or would do to ameliorate the conditions of Russian Jewry.

III

The disappointing and meager results gained from the sporadic activity of unofficial spokesmen on Jewish issues came at a trying time for American Jewry. The pogroms had evoked an intense emotional feeling while at the same time heavy immigration, stimulated by the pogroms and depressed conditions in Russia, had brought additional economic, social, and political problems to the American-Jewish community.

Therefore, during the period from February to November, 1906, a group of established German-Jewish leaders--Schiff, Straus, Louis Marshall, Cyrus Adler, Judge Mayer Sulzberger, Cyrus L. Sulzberger, Judge Julian Mack, Judge Samuel Greenbaum, and Nathan Bijur--established the AJC.[1] They needed this organization to adopt policies on many Jewish-oriented issues, to lobby on various levels of government, and to increase the force of their individual pleas for help.[2]

Despite the recognized need to provide emergency aid for the next pogroms and to fight the restriction movement, the founders were ambivalent about forming this organization because they feared jeopardizing their status in American society. They brooded about the propriety and wisdom of organizing. Upon what should they base representation? What justification did Jews have for lobbying with the executive

---

[1] Adler was Assistant Secretary of the Smithsonian Institution, Judge Sulzberger served on the Philadelphia Court of Common Pleas, Cyrus L. Sulzberger was a merchant in New York City, Judge Mack sat on the Circuit Court of Cook County, Illinois, and Judge Greenbaum served on the New York State Supreme Court.

[2] Schiff maintained that "to a considerable extent, the Committee was formed at my suggestion, in order that my friends and I should not have to bear the whole responsibility in serious and weighty problems as has so often happened in recent years." Schiff, op. cit., II, 160. Unfortunately, no good work on the formation of the AJC exists.

and legislative branches? Would their political demands isolate the Jews as a political pressure group and threaten their well-being in the United States?

Louis Marshall, the man who would be the AJC's major strategist and most active lobbyist, was deeply troubled by these specific questions. The son of a poor and barely literate German immigrant, Marshall was born in 1856 in Syracuse, New York. After attending Columbia Law School and spending his first years of practice in Syracuse, he moved in 1894 to New York City where he joined the firm of Guggenheim, Untermyer, and Marshall. Soon he established the reputation of being a brilliant, hard-working, and unflamboyant litigator. In 1895 he married Florence Lowenstein, one of Samuel Untermyer's New York cousins and within a short time Marshall easily entered the upper reaches of New York's German-Jewish society.[1] Within the next few decades he became a generous contributor to Jewish, non-sectarian, and Republican party causes and also developed into one of American Jewry's most forceful and sensitive spokesmen.[2]

---

[1] Untermyer proved to be quite helpful to Marshall over the years in his AJC work. Although Untermyer was not a member of the organization, he used his influence with Democratic politicians when Marshall asked him to do so.

[2] As an adult, Marshall learned Yiddish to better understand and communicate with the Russian-Jewish immigrants. Lucy S. Dawidowicz, "Louis Marshall's Yiddish

Now in January, 1906, Marshall described some of his thoughts about Jewish identity and organization: "What I am trying to avoid more than anything else is, the creation of a political organization, one which will be looked upon as indicative of a purpose on the part of Jews to recognize that they have interests different from those of other American citizens."[1] Although he maintained that there were only two justifiable reasons for organizing--for religious and philanthropic purposes--Marshall nevertheless added a third category: it would be possible, he stated, for American Jews to organize to aid other Jews who were suffering from persecution and discrimination.[2] He failed to recognize or acknowledge, however, that achieving this last goal would necessarily involve the use of a political organization--a lobbying group--and one which would inevitably promote "interests different from those of other Americans."

Despite his paradoxical thoughts and ambivalent feelings, ones which Marshall shared with many German Jews, he and Nathan Bijur sent out notices to fifty-eight Jewish

---

Newspaper, the *Jewish World*: A Study in Contrasts," *Jewish Social Studies*, XXV (Apr., 1963), 102-32.

[1] Charles Reznikoff, *Louis Marshall: Champion of Liberty* (Philadelphia, 1957), I, 22.

[2] *Ibid.*

leaders throughout the country to gather in New York on February 3 and 4 to discuss setting up a permanent, philanthropic and politically oriented Jewish organization. Thirty-four men convened on those two days and started seriously to discuss Jewish lobbying. In the early negotiations several men questioned the propriety of having a Jewish group consult with men in the legislative and executive branches. The position which Oscar S. Straus took convinced the majority of participants: American Jews were best informed about European-Jewish conditions and therefore could provide relevant information to the United States government. The most serious discussion focused on whether future members should be democratically elected representatives of religious congregations or appointed by a small founding coterie. Marshall consistently argued that the organization should draw a large membership from religious congregations to emphasize the religious and democratic rather than the political and oligarchic connection between members.

No final decision was made at the February meetings. There was, however, a consensus that the organization should be small, consisting of an executive committee of fifteen which would then appoint an additional forty-five members. This idea was approved at a subsequent meeting on May 19, when Marshall's proposal for congregational ties was finally voted down. Despite his defeat Marshall still affirmed that American Jews should concern themselves with "the specific religious interests of the Jews of this country" in the same fashion as did Episcopalians and Methodists about their co-religionists. At this May meeting the participants made a firm decision to organize the AJC and empowered a committee of five to select a small executive committee which would then appoint approximately fifty general members.[1]

On November 11, 1906, the AJC, consisting of fifty-seven general members, convened its first annual meeting. Although the great majority of members came from New York, Chicago, and Philadelphia, the AJC also gained support from men in numerous cities throughout the country--from Kansas City, Missouri; Richmond, Virginia; Nashville, Tennessee; Galveston, Texas; Omaha, Nebraska; Wichita, Kansas; Greenboro, North Carolina; and Meridian, Mississippi. The membership adopted a constitution which declared:

> The purpose of this committee is to prevent infringement of the civil and religious rights of Jews, and to alleviate the consequences of persecution. In the event of a threatened or actual denial or invasion of such rights, or when conditions calling for relief from calamities affecting Jews exist anywhere, correspondence may be

---

[1] Minutes of the Executive Committee, Feb. 3, 4, 1906, May 19, 1906, American Jewish Committee, New York (in the files of the AJC). Cited hereafter as Minutes, AJC.

entered into with those familiar with the situation, and if the persons on the spot feel themselves able to cope with the situation, no action need be taken; if, on the other hand, they request aid, steps shall be taken to furnish it.[1]

At the time of this meeting the AJC's organizational structure was clearly outlined but not fully functioning. It consisted of an executive committee of thirteen men-- among them were Schiff, Marshall, Adler, Mayer Sulzberger, and Nathan Bijur. The thirteen directed the operations of the entire organization and acted on behalf of the general committee members who met once a year in a general meeting. The members were drawn from twelve districts throughout the country and the number of representatives per district was based upon the number of Jews within each district. The districts contributed a percentage of the cost of running the AJC which would average between $10,000 and $12,500 over the next few years.

In addition to district members who made up the general committee, it was proposed that each district maintain an advisory council consisting of ten members per district representative on the general committee. The advisory councils, devised to allow the AJC to reach the "entire Jewish

---

[1] *Annual Report of the American Jewish Committee* (New York, 1907), p. 4.

community," were supposed to make recommendations to the general committee and to elect the district's general committee members.[1] The executive committee, however, was responsible for approving the selection of all advisory members. Therefore, despite the structural apparatus which gave the appearance of a broadly based Jewish organization, real power was permanently lodged in the executive committee, especially in the hands of Schiff and Marshall. From its formative stages through 1914 the AJC was a cohesive, oligarchic organization, dominated by a few men from New York.

The men who formed the AJC regarded themselves as an élite that was ready for leadership on a national scale. They were enormously confident about their capacity to lead the American-Jewish community and they were accustomed to working closely together in philanthropic, religious, and fraternal organizations. What were the criteria for membership in the AJC in 1906? A German-Jewish background; professional success usually in banking, trade, and law; the habit of giving philanthropic aid to American Jewry; a past association or acquaintanceship with the organizers of the AJC; a concern for the welfare of Russian Jewry; a willingness to deal with politicians concerning Jewish questions; and last

---

[1]Reznikoff, op. cit., I, 25.

but not least, a fearful attitude about sharing power with the Russian-Jewish immigrants and jeopardizing the status of German Jews in American society.[1]

The formation of the AJC constituted a power play by self-appointed leaders who wished to make themselves the single, proper spokesmen on political matters for American Jewry. The issue was one of power and style. Louis Marshall made this clear when he asserted that his coterie of friends took the initiative in creating a lobbying organization "in order to avoid mischief" and to prevent less moderate men from attaining power.[2] Marshall and Schiff wanted to impress their political attitudes and lobbying techniques on the Jewish community because they believed in rapid assimilation rather than separatism, in reform rather than radical change, and in quiet persuasion through direct access to men in government rather than public rallies and mass action.

They were jealous and fearful of other Jewish leaders, Zionists or Russian-Jewish labor leaders, whatever

---

[1] Although the most influential German-Jewish group was concentrated in New York, its activities were representative of AJC members who came from other cities. Uptown Jewry, and therefore the AJC's Jewry, was, in the words of Stephen Birmingham, "a citadel of privilege, power, philanthropy, and family pride." Birmingham, op. cit., p. 7.

[2] Reznikoff, op. cit., I, 20.

their constituencies or causes. They feared that others would upset the dignified, discreet tone of the uptown style of pressure politics--expressed in the name of the AJC as well as through individual requests--and would spoil the facade of German-Jewish assimilation and the fragile appearance of German and Russian-Jewish unity. This latter concern was particularly important because the AJC's German-Jewish élite created the impression that it spoke for and perhaps controlled the Jewish immigrant voters who were regarded by a number of politicians as an important factor in certain local, state, and national elections. In the future, in fact, the AJC's political clout would partially rest upon this widely held belief.

Not surprisingly, there was resentment and hostility between the Germans and the Russians who, in 1906, made up the great majority of the 1,418,013 Jews in America.[1] The antagonistic relationship between the two groups stemmed in part from the class conflict between the Russian-Jewish garment workers and their many German-Jewish employers. Social tensions existed as well because the German Jews followed the

---

[1] The American Jewish Yearbook, 5667, 128. In 1914, there were 1,335,000 Jews in New York City of whom 10 percent were German Jews. Arthur A. Goren, New York Jews and the Quest for Community: The Kehillah Experiment, 1908-1922 (New York, 1970), p. 17.

contemporary model of the Gentile community by excluding the Russian Jews from their clubs, schools, and leadership positions in the AJC and other German-Jewish organizations.

The German and Russian Jews embodied different traditions. There was a language barrier between the Yiddish and Russian speaking and the German-and English-speaking Jews. There were religious differences between Orthodox, as well as non-practicing Russian Jews, and the reform German Jews. Economic and political differences separated capitalists from socialists and anarchists; political disputes divided American assimilationists from Zionists. But most important was the psychological gap between the powerful and the powerless, the givers of charity and the suppliants, between the satisfied, successful, and relatively secure German Jews and the poor, awkward, and frightened Russian-Jewish immigrants. Eventually these differences and the power imbalance that resulted from them would result in an open conflict in the Jewish community during the First World War and in a long fight over the formation of an American Jewish Congress.

Still, in 1906 while these German-Jewish leaders were assertive and confident vis-à-vis the Russian-Jewish immigrants, they were also concerned about the increasing signs of American anti-Semitism. Therefore, they promoted the AJC's inconspicuous, behind-the-scenes contacts with politicians as a way of avoiding criticism from non-Jewish political groups. Schiff told the organizing meeting of the AJC in February, 1906, that he and his friends needed a committee that would be powerful but discreet, one that would deal with "Jewish questions" without creating a "Jewish question."[1] He was fearful of substantiating the assumption prevalent in the 1890's that Jews were controlling invisible financial empires and secretly directing governments of many nations.

In fact, a curious and paradoxical array of stereotypes were still associated with Jews in Progressive America. They were characterized as greedy, financially domineering, part of an international gold conspiracy, cowardly, physically broken down, and as socialist and anarchist radicals.[2] Together the Russian and German Jews helped to create the impression that cities such as New York and Chicago were alien and sinister--dirty, disease-ridden, morally and politically corrupt, divided ethnically and economically--but also mysteriously rich and powerful.

In addition to the stereotypes, the German and Russian Jews actually encountered social and economic

---

[1] Minutes, AJC, Feb. 3, 1906.

[2] Higham, op. cit., pp. 92-94.

discrimination. Since the 1870's the American-Jewish community had become the object of an increasing number of restrictive practices established by the Gentile community. In areas such as housing, resorts, private clubs, and schools, the community-at-large had restricted the choices of American Jews.[1] The massive influx of Russian Jews exacerbated the social vulnerability of the first and second generation German Jews and the more established Jews of Spanish and Portuguese descent. Subsequently the Gentile community often failed to make distinctions between the strange new Jewish immigrants and the wealthy German Jews, some of whom tried to enter the Gentile establishment or at least gain social recognition from it. Thus American nativists reacted to the Russian-Jewish immigrants through the restriction movement and to the German Jews through social discrimination.[2]

---

[1] John Higham, "Social Discrimination Against Jews in America: 1830-1930," *Publications of the American Jewish Historical Society*, XLVII (Sept., 1957), 1-33.

[2] "The same impulse propelled the movement to check immigration and the discriminatory drive to limit internal mobility and opportunity. Both types of restriction resulted from fear of being invaded and overrun. Both sought to stabilize a society caught up in bewildering flux." John Higham, "American Anti-Semitism Historically Reconsidered," in *Jews in the Mind of America*, ed. by Herbert Stember (New York, 1966), p. 251.

In 1906 the AJC knew what it needed to do in regard to these two types of discrimination. First, oppose the restrictionists and also work to improve the condition of Russian Jewry without isolating and exposing itself as an ethnic pressure group; second, represent and guide the Russian-Jewish immigrants on many political matters without letting them share power and forcefully promote their type of pressure politics. Then, within two months of its founding, the AJC faced its first test of strength and purpose during the first Progressive period fight over the literacy test.

CHAPTER II

THE SPEAKER PREVAILS

Americans, wrote Jacob H. Schiff, "must do nothing which renders emigration to this country more difficult to those of our persecuted and oppressed co-religionists who wish to improve their lot." He never wished the Russians to say that Americans considered the Jews as "undesirable" or unwanted.[1] Unfortunately for Schiff, by 1906 the American Federation of Labor, the Immigration Restriction League, and many restrictionist politicians had concluded that immigrants from eastern and southern Europe, including those from Russia, were undesirable and should be excluded by means of a literacy test.

In the course of the fight over the literacy test--actually the second phase of the battle--the AJC directly confronted the depth of the opposition to the new immigrants, whom restrictionists accused of causing disturbing changes in the nation's economic, social, and political life. In lobbying against the literacy test, the AJC preferred to

---

[1] Schiff, op. cit., II, p. 122.

avoid the forum of public opinion and to concentrate instead on making direct contacts with Congressmen and important politicians. Privately, and in idealistic tones, the leaders of the AJC pleaded their case for the Russian-Jewish immigrants.

For their part, the restrictionists gave the appearance of being an unbeatable opponent. They exploited certain popular fears about the life-styles of the new immigrants while also basing their campaign upon specific idealistic expectations which were part of Progressive thinking. They forthrightly asked the public to face one vital question: could the United States continue to assimilate millions of southern and eastern European immigrants? In contrast to the AJC, the restrictionists confidently courted public support for the literacy test and successfully gained the backing of President Roosevelt and a majority of Congressmen. Impressive as this coalition was, it could not succeed in 1906 without the support of the all-powerful Speaker of the House of Representatives, Joseph Cannon. Despite the flurry of activity in Congress and the White House concerning the literacy test, despite the agitation of the restrictionists and the AJC, the fate of the test depended entirely upon Cannon.

When the battle was over and the restrictionists were defeated, the AJC, like most lobbying organizations, exaggerated the importance of its role and distorted the history of events. In fact, while the AJC's interest in the fight was very great, its role was actually not very significant. Therefore, to evaluate the AJC's activities and lobbying techniques it is necessary to describe those of its opponents and allies and to focus on the legislative maneuvers of the opposing forces in Congress.

I.

The appeals in the Progressive period to retard or to cut off the flow of new immigrants were firm and persistent, but such appeals were hardly new. American nativism, defined by John Higham as "an intense opposition to an internal minority on the grounds of its foreign (i.e., 'un-American') connections," had had a long and intricate history which reached back as far as the 1790's and the 1850's.[1] Nativist feeling erupted again as a forceful issue in the 1880's and 1890's with Catholics, foreign radicals, and cheap immigrant labor the targets.[2]

---

[1] Higham, *Strangers in the Land*, p. 4.
[2] *Ibid.*, pp. 4-9.

It was during the latter period that restrictionists first proposed that all non-Asian immigrants over a certain age be required to pass a literacy test (in one of several languages) before being admitted to the United States. Henry Cabot Lodge of Massachusetts introduced the test in the House of Representatives in 1891 and then successfully brought it to passage in the Republican Congress in 1897. His six-year effort, however, came to naught when President Grover Cleveland vetoed the test as an unfair and discriminatory measure, and the Senate refused to override the veto.

Lodge introduced the test after Edward W. Bemis, an economics professor, proposed the idea in the *Andover Review* in 1888. In his article Bemis suggested that Congress could build a formidable barrier against the entry of undesirable immigrants. Bemis argued that immigrants from Poland, Hungary, southern Italy, western Ireland, and the German borderlands with Poland and Austria lowered America's standard of living. They increased the rate of unemployment, committed violent crimes, populated the insane asylums, and provided the votes that allowed corrupt political machines to remain in office.

These new immigrants, Bemis insisted, were so different from the old and so dangerous as to justify ending the long tradition of open immigration. Bemis preferred making it prohibitive for poor immigrants to enter the country, by imposing a $50 per capita head tax. But, calculating that the literacy test would stand the best chance of passage by Congress, he proposed it instead.

Bemis acknowledged that a test barring illiterate male and female immigrants over sixteen years of age might seem to be a questionable way of maintaining the high quality of American citizenship. He assured his readers, however, that the literacy test would favor immigrants capable of maintaining a high standard of living. It would halve the number of immigrants from southern Italy, Hungary, and Poland and, according to Bemis' estimate, it would reduce by at least 30 percent the total number of new immigrants. But most important, the 30 percent would be immigrants from eastern and southern Europe, not the highly desirable ones from northern and western Europe.[1]

The Bemis literacy test gained popularity because many Americans were fearful of the new immigrants but were

---

[1] Edward W. Bemis, "Restriction of Immigration," The Andover Review, IX (March, 1888), 251-63. In the late 1880's and early 1890's the Irish immigrants were disliked as much as the immigrants from eastern and southern Europe. By the turn of the century, however, the Irish were accepted into the Anglo-Saxon tradition and no longer were considered undesirable. Barbara Soloman, Ancestors and Immigrants: A Changing New England Tradition (Cambridge, Mass., 1956), pp. 153-55.

not yet willing to end all immigration from eastern and
southern Europe. Some restrictionists argued that the literacy test would merely add another category to those established in the immigration laws of 1882, 1885, 1891, 1893,
and 1903 which prohibited the entry of immigrants suffering
from contagious diseases, those likely to become public
charges, those who espoused anarchy, and those who practiced polygamy or prostitution. The literacy test, however,
meant more than just including another selective category,
as both restrictionists and anti-restrictionists recognized:
adoption of the test would constitute the first significant
step in the effort to reduce drastically and discriminate
against the immigrants from eastern and southern Europe.

Unquestionably, the new immigrants presented serious
problems for Progressive America. A few statistics drawn
from the Report of the Commissioner-General of Immigration
for the year beginning July, 1905 to June, 1906 give the
best account of the dimensions of the problem. These figures
reveal the kinds of cultural and economic liabilities that
the new immigrants were weaving into the fabric of American
life.

Total admissions for the year were 1,100,735, an
increase of 106,598 over the previous year. Among them were
136,273 immigrants fourteen years and under, many of whom

would have to be educated in public and parochial schools. There were 913,955 immigrants between the ages of fourteen and forty-four, many of whom put pressure on the labor market which fluctuated between booms and recessions and gyrated under the pressure of labor-employer disputes.[1] In fact, the impact of these immigrant laborers was so great that by 1909 they formed, according to John Higham, "a third or more of the entire labor force of the principal industries of the country."[2] The remaining 50,507 immigrants were forty-five years of age or older, men and women past their prime in health and productive capabilities who would severely tax limited welfare facilities and philanthropic services.

    The obvious penury of the immigrants was frightening to a country with an increasingly high standard of living. There were 698,401 immigrants who entered the country possessing $50 or less. The literacy rates were also appalling to a nation that prided itself on its form of popular government and comparatively high standard of living. Among the immigrants fourteen years and older, 265,068 could

---

[1]Sargent, op. cit., pp. 486-87.

[2]Higham, Strangers in the Land, p. 114.

neither read nor write.[1] The average rates of immigrant illiteracy for the period 1899 to 1910 are even more revealing of the problem: 26 percent of the Jews fourteen years and older, 53.9 percent of the southern Italians, and 38.4 percent of the non-Jewish Russians were illiterate. In contrast, only 1 percent of the English, 5.2 percent of the Germans, .4 percent of the Scandinavians, and 2.6 percent of the Irish were illiterate.[2]

As far as the restrictionists were concerned, the most significant set of statistics concerned the rate of immigration for new and old immigrants. The federal government kept count of each immigrant by identifying his racial and national classification, a practice which the Immigration Bureau had started in 1899, and which Congress had in 1903 written into law. According to the statistics, in 1906 the "old" immigrants from England, Scotland, and Ireland

---

[1] Sargent, op. cit., pp. 486-87.

[2] Joseph, op. cit., pp. 193-94. The statistics used in Sargent's report as well as in Joseph's book were taken from the forms which each immigrant was required to fill out upon entering the country. If there is reason to question the accuracy of the figures on illiteracy one might suggest that they are too low. Immigrants might have stated that they were literate when they were not, but surely not the reverse. In any case, the official figures must be accepted, as they were in the Progressive period, in the absence of other information.

made up only 9.3 percent of the total immigration, those from Germany less than 8 percent, and those from Scandinavia 5 percent. By contrast, the "new" immigrants from eastern and southern Europe comprised 67 percent of the total, the Jews contributing 14 percent and the southern Italians 22 percent.[1]

The overwhelming influx of new immigrants was most important because of the racial attitudes of the Progressive period. Although it may be clear to us today that ethnic-racial classifications are stereotypes wrapped in pseudo-scientific garb by anthropologists, sociologists, and eugenicists, such stereotypes were meaningful to Progressive America. With astounding ease, in view of the fact that no one knew what constituted a race or how many there were in America and Europe, many Americans identified themselves and determined their value as human beings on a racial scale.

Hostility towards Asian immigrants and Negroes was particularly strong during this period. Racism underlay the continuation of the Chinese Exclusion laws, the simmering anti-Japanese feeling on the West Coast, and the nearly universal acceptance of the South's Jim Crow laws. Now, many

---

[1] Sargent, op. cit., p. 536.

people in Progressive America followed the example of the
Immigration Bureau, defining each ethnic and national group
as a racial group and perpetuating the use of racial stereotypes that were degrading for the new immigrants themselves.[1]
Eventually the racial tensions were sufficiently strong to
give legitimacy to the eugenics movement which studied
America's racial make-up, heredity, and the comparative
birth rates of the new and old immigrants. Underlying these
studies was the fear that Anglo-Saxon America was committing
racial suicide; the new immigrants would engulf the old
immigrants and native Americans, through immigration and a
high birth rate. According to John Higham, these fears
constituted a "minor national phobia" in the Progressive
period.[2]

    The yearly flood of immigration caused many soci-
ologists such as Edward A. Ross and Jeremiah Jenks, economists
such as Edward W. Bemis, Francis A. Walker, John R. Commons,
Richard T. Ely, and William Ripley, and eugenicists such as
Madison Grant and Charles B. Davenport to dread the unfavorable imbalance between old and new immigrants. These men
used government statistics to indict the new immigrants for

---

[1] Higham, Strangers in the Land, pp. 88-94.

[2] Ibid., p. 147.

bringing poverty, illiteracy, disease, unfair labor competition, violent crime, and immoral practices into the United States. They argued that the new immigrants would destroy the primacy of Protestant institutions and values, for by the sheer force of their numbers the new immigrants increased the power of the Catholic Church and gave the Jewish community a greater claim than ever before to recognition by American religious and political institutions.

The combination of religious and ethnic origins, poverty, and illiteracy proved to many Americans that the new immigrants could never be assimilated into American life. The Commissioner-General of Immigration, Frank P. Sargent, was one who subscribed to this view. In his annual Report for 1906 he recommended the adoption of the literacy test to protect the nation from racial subversion from within. His discussion summarizes the popular apprehensive attitude towards the new immigrants:

> In former years--that is, more particularly in decades preceding the present--we were obtaining English, Irish, Scotch, Scandinavian, and German allies, people whose racial characteristics and ideals in the main agree with our own, and whom, therefore, we could assimilate, racially and politically, in the course of a few years. . . . We cannot correctly hold the view that, because the Germans, Scandinavians, English, Scotch, and Irish heretofore landed on our shores have become valuable citizens within a few years, the aliens now coming that belong to distinctly different stocks can be added to our race with the same degree of success. The difference between the

origin and the history of those races and our own is too great and has extended through too many ages to be overcome, even in several generations, unless under the most favorable conditions. Do not the statistics of recent years on this subject point unmistakably to the conclusion that we, as a race, are endeavoring to assimilate a large mass of almost if not quite unassimilable material?[1]

In addition to the individual restrictionists, there were two important organizations which lobbied for restriction. The A.F.L., under Samuel Gompers' leadership, was one of the most active groups. Among its members the restriction issue was popular, although many of them, like Gompers, had been immigrants themselves. With some justification, the A.F.L. looked upon the new immigrants as ignorant, strike-breaking tools of the employers. Labor regarded the immigrants as unfair competition since they would work for lower pay and accept poorer working conditions than the established labor force. Spurred by the economic depression of 1893 to 1897, official labor policy came to favor the literacy test as the best means of ending open immigration.[2]

The years 1905 and 1906 had been bad for Gompers' organization because the Socialists and the Industrial Workers of the World mounted a militant and radical challenge to the

---

[1] Sargent, op. cit., pp. 535-36.

[2] Higham, Strangers in the Land, pp. 49-50, 71-72.

A.F.L. Employers also campaigned against the A.F.L. through the use of injunctions and open shop campaigns with the result that its dues and membership began to fall off.[1] Feeling the need for a vigorous and popular campaign, the A.F.L. reversed Gompers' old policy and decided to move into the political arena and battle Congressmen on such issues as the eight-hour day, an anti-injunction law, a strict interpretation of the Chinese exclusion laws, and the adoption of a literacy test.[2] Therefore, in 1906 the A.F.L. actively, but unsuccessfully, campaigned against Representative Nathaniel Littlefield of Maine, an arch foe of labor on the House Judiciary Committee, and against Speaker Joseph Cannon of Illinois, who was outspokenly unsympathetic to "Labor's Bill of Grievances."

The A.F.L.'s support of the literacy test was important to a number of Congressmen, even though the organization represented only a small portion of the American labor force in 1906 and the literacy test was but one of its many demands. Ironically, the literacy test fight provided the

---

[1] Marc Karson, *American Labor Unions and Politics: 1900-1918* (Carbondale, Ill., 1958), pp. 33-35; David B. Truman, *The Governmental Process: Political Interests and Public Opinion* (New York, 1951), p. 70.

[2] Karson, *op. cit.*, p. 29.

opportunity for New England restrictionists like Republican Senator Henry Cabot Lodge, who was rarely in labor's camp, to make new friends.

The Immigration Restriction League joined with the A.F.L. in actively pressing for the literacy test in 1906. Robert DeCourcy Ward and Prescott F. Hall, two scions of old-line New England families, had helped to found the League in 1894. The League propagated its views through public speaking campaigns, newspaper and magazine articles, and the founding of chapter groups throughout the country. Within two years of its founding, the League claimed 670 members.[1] It established alliances with unions and patriotic societies and in time assembled a group of well-known and influential supporters: Lodge, Theodore Roosevelt, Franklin MacVeagh, Taft's Secretary of the Treasury, A. Lawrence Lowell, President of Harvard University, David Starr Jordan, President of Stanford University, and Joseph Lee, President of the Massachusetts Civic League.

The League provided a steady pressure on Congress, a plenitude of arguments, and a crusading fervor that made it the most noticeable, although not the most politically

---

[1] Soloman, op. cit., p. 104.

powerful, force for restriction.[1] Ward, a lawyer, and Hall, a climatologist at Harvard, were the League's most active members. They employed all of the restrictionist arguments to demonstrate the need for the literacy test; the need to help labor, the need to maintain Anglo-Saxon supremacy, and the Progressives' need to improve the political process. But most of the time, Ward and Hall emphasized the social problems resulting from the presence of the poor, the insane, and the crime-oriented immigrant population.

Both the A.F.L. and the League were fortunate to find important new allies in the South and West in 1906. The intermingling of America's Asian and Negro problems with the European immigration problem helped bring the literacy test to life again. In 1906, California was obsessed with the desire to reduce the number of Japanese and Indian immigrants; whenever the House and Senate engaged in debate

---

[1] For a discussion of some of the League's arguments see Robert DeCourcy Ward, "Immigration and the South," Atlantic Monthly, XCVI (Nov., 1905), 611-17; Prescott F. Hall, "The Future of American Ideals," North American Review, CXCV (Jan., 1912), 94-102; Robert DeC. Ward, "National Eugenics in Relation to Immigration," North American Review, CXCII (July, 1910), 56-67; Robert DeC. Ward, "Agricultural Distribution of Immigrants," Popular Science Monthly, LXVI (Dec., 1904), 166-75; Joseph Lee, "Democracy and the Illiteracy Test," Survey, XXIX (Jan. 18, 1913), 497-99.

over eastern and southern European immigration, western
Congressmen seized the opportunity to propose more stringent
laws against Asian immigrants. Many southern Congressmen,
for their part, began to accept the racial arguments about
European immigrants as northern restrictionists maintained
that the country, and the South in particular, could not
handle another racial problem.[1] This southern restrictionist response, evident in 1906, would be particularly valuable after the Democratic victories in 1910 and 1912 when
southern Democrats would head the House and Senate immigration committees.

In the first decades of the twentieth century many
areas in the South encouraged the importation of white
immigrants to counterbalance the Negro population and to
lessen white reliance on Negro labor. But even in the
southern states which established immigration agencies, the
new immigrants were not welcomed. The often explicit but
usually implicit assumption was that only the old immigrants
from northern and western Europe were compatible with the
southern way of life. A 1904 South Carolina law, for
example, expressed the discriminatory attitude towards the

---

[1] Higham, *Strangers in the Land*, pp. 167-68.

new immigrants. The law created a State Department of Agriculture, Commerce, and Immigration, and required that the immigrants recruited by the state's agency "shall be confined to white citizens of the United States, citizens of Ireland, Scotland, Switzerland, France, and all other foreigners of Saxon origin."[1]

The A.F.L., the League, and the restrictionists in the South and West, however, did not have to build their arguments exclusively on defending labor's needs, on the Anglo-Saxon tradition, or even on narrow prejudices. They could also appeal to broader and more positive impulses in the Progressive period since to many contemporaries restriction seemed to be an enlightened proposal. According to this viewpoint, restriction might help to improve the quality of American life and maintain the educational level necessary for an industrial society.

Thus the restriction movement had deep roots in what Roland Berthoff has called the "conservative counterrevolution" which sought to lessen the antagonism between unions and employers, to control corporate empires, and to protect the natural environment through conservation. For

---

[1] U.S., *Congressional Record*, 59th Cong., 2d sess., 1907, XLI, Part 3, 2946.

many Americans a series of disturbing social and economic experiences had created "social disorder": the westward movement, the industrial revolution, the urban explosion, and the influx of millions upon millions of immigrants.[1]

Therefore, many people looked to the federal government to impose order on the corporate world, to defend the interests of the consumer, to protect natural resources, and to refine the pattern of immigration. Now the government might also reduce the number of entering immigrants, and thereby provide one immediate and feasible way of reducing the tensions in the society as a whole.

The humanitarian urge to improve the conditions of the immigrants who had already arrived in America might also have led to a restrictionist position because many Progressives were deeply ashamed of the misery which they discovered in the urban slums. Some struggled to help the immigrants improve their standard of living as was the case for Robert Woods of Boston's East End House, and Joseph Lee, a pioneer in establishing playgrounds and recreation areas in slums and ghettoes. These men held the view that the problems the immigrants faced--the struggle to earn a living,

---

[1] Roland Berthoff, "The American Social Order: A Conservative Hypothesis," *The American Historical Review*, LXV (Apr., 1960), 507, 510.

deplorable living conditions, epidemics of contagious diseases, prostitution, and alcoholism--could best be dealt with by holding the immigrant population at its current level. Furthermore, many Progressives feared that a social revolution would result if nothing were done to improve these deplorable conditions.[1]

The restrictionists also appealed to positive aspirations in the field of education and political life. During the latter part of the nineteenth century, both the private and public school system had expanded and by 1900 almost all northern and western states required compulsory primary education.[2] Americans had made this effort to adjust to the industrial society as well as to promote

---

[1] John Joseph Carey, "Progressives and the Immigrants" (unpublished Ph.D. dissertation, University of Connecticut, 1968), pp. 93, 98. Not all socially minded Progressives, however, held a restrictionist point of view. In fact, restriction was a divisive issue for the social workers. Jane Addams, Frances Kellor, Emily Balch, Lillian Wald, and Grace Abbot lent their full support to the anti-restrictionist campaign. They denied the premise that heredity determined the value of the individual, arguing that the new immigrants, with their different but rich traditions, could contribute much of value to American life. And they insisted that the new immigrants could assimilate when allowed remunerative employment, good housing, and schooling. *Ibid.*, p. 18.

[2] Robert Wiebe, *The Search for Order* (New York, 1967), p. 119.

enlightened political participation. Through the mechanisms of direct primaries, the popular election of Senators, initiative, referendum, and recall, the Progressives now were calling on Americans to have a greater involvement in the political process. Progressives promoted these reforms to clean up the corrupt practices of the political machines and to create greater cohesion in the body politic, an effort which seemed to be frustrated by the new immigrants. They were outsiders--culturally and politically alienated-- for at least the first few years after arriving in the United States. They accepted any work that was offered, in the factories, the mines, and the streets, as all of their efforts centered on feeding themselves and their families. Interest in political life, at least as Progressives conceived of it, was a luxury which the new immigrants could not immediately afford.

Alienation was one part of the problem, the patterns of political life which the immigrants eventually developed was another. The new immigrants reinforced and perpetuated the power of the big city bosses because the machines provided the immigrants with employment, patronage, and, if need be, protection from the police.[1] Probably even more

---

[1] Richard Hofstadter, The Age of Reform: From Bryan to F.D.R. (New York, 1960), p. 182.

frightening to the Progressives was the fact that many of the new immigrants advocated radical European doctrines such as socialism and anarchism.

The restrictionist emphasis on education and political participation, however, often involved a degree of prejudice. For how could the restrictionists use the literacy test as a means of pre-testing and pre-judging the new immigrants when high rates of illiteracy prevailed in many parts of the country? This was particularly true in the increasingly nativist South. It is curious and revealing that southern proponents of the literacy test did not feel threatened by southern illiterates; instead, they sympathetically regarded them as victims of the deprivations endured since the Civil War days. This attitude contrasts sharply with the lack of sympathy for those living in the repressive atmosphere of Russia.

According to the restrictionists, the southern illiterates made good citizens because of the subtle but instructive political ambiance of the South which taught her illiterate citizens to respect the American (and Southern) political and economic system. Democratic Senator Furnifold M. Simmons of North Carolina exemplified this trusting spirit when he described the process of political education in the South:

Happily under our system of government, with our churches open to all, with our courts, with our hustings discussions and debates, with the absence of class distinctions, bringing the unlettered man in constant contact and association with the best intelligence of his community, by association and absorption, the American citizen, without being educated, without school advantages, becomes an intelligent citizen, not only capable of the highest thrift, but capable of understanding the duties and responsibilities and of exercising the privileges of citizenship in a country where the people govern.[1]

One of the most serious indictments against the new immigrants was that they would not settle on farms or in small towns, as did the old immigrants. Therefore, many Americans, such as Simmons, had the impression that the new immigrants knew nothing of American agrarian ideals and ways of life. Instead, the new immigrants voluntarily became prisoners of an eastern or mid-western city which George Mowry has described as "a veritable pressure cooker in which racial, economic, and psychic tensions bubbled and boiled to the consternation of the older American population."[2] By associating the new immigrants with the pernicious cities, the centers of financial domination, political corruption,

---

[1] U.S., Congressional Record, 59th Cong., 1st sess., 1906, XL, Part 8, 7295.

[2] George E. Mowry, The Era of Theodore Roosevelt and the Birth of Modern America: 1900-1912 (New York, 1958), p. 14.

crime, and disease, the restrictionists most effectively condemned the new immigrants. The restrictionists thereby reinforced the assumption that the immigrants in the festering ghettoes, who had much to learn about American democracy and much work to do to raise themselves from poverty, could not adapt to the American way of life.

There is, however, an irony and contradiction to be found in this attitude too. The new immigrants were scorned for isolating themselves in the eastern ghettoes, but when they did on occasion leave the cities to settle in the South and West, they only increased the restrictionist fervor. The mere presence of the new immigrants--dark-skinned, foreign speaking, poor, and Catholic or Jewish--upset the tenuous patterns of racial adjustment and accommodation in areas outside of the Northeast and increased the strength of the restrictionists.[1]

II.

Now in the spring of 1906 the restrictionists led by President Roosevelt and Senator Henry Cabot Lodge had every reason to believe that Congress finally would adopt the literacy test. In fact, the restrictionist gained the first

---

[1] Higham, *Strangers in the Land*, p. 173.

and only success of their campaign in the Senate in May, 1906. During the first session of the 59th Congress, the Senate Committee on Immigration had considered numerous bills aimed at amending the 1903 immigration law. Among the law's notable provisions were the exclusion of idiots, insane persons, persons likely to become public charges, professional beggars, those with contagious diseases, prostitutes and those who procured for prostitutes, persons convicted of a felony or crime of moral turpitude, polygamists, anarchists, those who advocated the violent overthrow of the government and the assassination of public officials, and those whose transatlantic passage was paid for by others--except in those instances when money was sent by a friend or relative already in the United States. In addition, each immigrant paid a $2 head tax. These provisions were enforced not only by rejecting at the ports of entry those immigrants who came under the above categories, but also by fining and punishing the steamship companies which transported the immigrants with the knowledge that they were unfit for entry.[1]

On May 22, Republican Senator William Dillingham of Vermont, Chairman of the Senate Committee on Immigration,

---

[1] RIC, XXXIX, 102-10.

opened debate on his Committee's bill. The bill did not include a literacy test. Dillingham, who at the time was most interested in increasing the head tax and excluding those with frail physical appearances, recommended the following changes: increase the head tax from $2 to $5; exclude all those specified in the 1903 law along with imbeciles, feeble-minded persons, consumptives, those with a history of insanity, "persons who are found to be and are certified by the examining surgeon as being mentally or physically defective, such mental or physical defect being of a nature which may affect the ability to earn a living . . ."; [1] extend from two to three years the period during which immigrants who entered the country in violation of the law and/or became public charges would be subject to deportation; stiffen the penalties against steamship companies for transporting immigrants ineligible for entry; and create a Bureau of Information designed to alleviate urban congestion. [2]

The Senate debate was short, tepid, and generally of little interest to the Senate as a whole. The senior Senator from North Carolina, Democrat Furnifold M. Simmons,

---

[1] U.S., Congress, Senate, Committee on Immigration, Immigration of Aliens into the United States, 59th Cong., 1st sess., Mar. 29, 1906, S. Rept. 2186 to accompany S4403.

[2] Ibid.

presented the first literacy test amendment during the debate. It excluded all adult males who could not read or write in some language and also required that each literate male immigrant possess $25 plus $10 for each member of the family under twenty-one years of age.[1]

Simmons specifically wanted to exclude those Greeks, Poles, Hungarians, and Italians whom he regarded as unfit "for the high duties and responsibilities of American citizenship" by their "heredity and training." The majority of new immigrants, he went on to say, "are so ignorant, not to say sinister, as to preclude the hope of their becoming good and desirable citizens in the future."[2] Simmons further asserted that because of the new immigrants, the tradition of open immigration no longer worked to America's advantage, as it had done in the past. He justified the practical value of the literacy test by contrasting the low illiteracy rates of the old immigrants with the high rates of the new ones.

Then Senator Lodge, a fervent supporter of the literacy test since the 1890's, presented his own test amendment in which he refined Simmons' amendment by separating the

___

[1] U.S., *Congressional Record*, 59th Cong., 1st sess., 1906, XL, Part 8, 7293.

[2] *Ibid.*, p. 7295.

issue of money from literacy. The Lodge amendment stipulated that every immigrant "physically capable of reading" who was sixteen years or older would be refused entry if he could not read parts of the United States Constitution in English or "some other language." A qualified immigrant could "bring in or send for his wife, his children under 18 years of age, and his parents or grandparents over 50 years of age, if they are otherwise admissible, whether they are so able to read or not."[1] If he were rejected, however, the steamship company which brought him over would be financially responsible for returning him to his country of last origin.

The Senate quickly passed the Lodge amendment by a voice vote. The following day it approved, without further amendment or a division vote, the entire immigration bill.

This bill, popularly called the Dillingham bill, then went to the House where it was referred to the House Committee on Immigration and Naturalization. The Committee had already considered numerous bills and issued several reports. Finally, it reported an amended version of the Dillingham bill which called for a literacy test in "English or some other language or dialect." Furthermore, literate immigrants could bring in illiterate wives, mothers,

---

[1] Ibid., p. 7298.

grandmothers, fathers and grandfathers over fifty-five years of age, as well as sons eighteen years or younger and daughters twenty-one years or younger. Another change provided for the rejection of immigrants "who are dependent for their support upon their own physical exertions and who are certified by the examining medical officer to be of low vitality or poor physique such as would incapacitate them for such work."[1]

Representative Augustus P. Gardner, a Republican from Massachusetts who was Lodge's son-in-law, presented the Committee's report to the House on June 11. At the time, Gardner was concerned about how the test would fare in the House because Speaker Cannon refused to divulge his position before the debate began. His silence encouraged both the restrictionists, led by Roosevelt, Lodge, and Gardner, and the anti-restrictionists, led by Oscar S. Straus and the National Liberal Immigration League, to lobby for their respective positions. Therefore, Roosevelt tried to influence Cannon, and Straus tried to influence Roosevelt.

---

[1]U.S., Congress, House, Committee on Immigration and Naturalization, *Immigration of Aliens into the United States*, 59th Cong., 1st sess., June 11, 1906, H. Rept. 4912 to accompany S4403. Sometime after the Senate passed the literacy test and before S4403 was printed and sent to the House the word "dialect" was added.

But Cannon, who held the power over the House and the literacy test, kept his position secret.

Cannon's silence in no way indicated an ambivalence towards the test; rather it was a function of his domineering, powerful style of leadership and of his crusty personality. At the height of his power in 1906, Cannon was a shrewd practitioner of political manipulations as well as an idealistic preserver of America's traditional institutions. Therefore he brusquely killed the test without even revealing his reasons for doing so, despite strong bi-partisan support in the House for the measure. Only several years later, after he had lost his position as Speaker, did he explain his reasons for strongly disliking the literacy measure. Then, in 1912, he told his confreres in the House that he had perceived no economic or political justification for abandoning open immigration and ending America's hospitality to Europeans who wished to improve their lot. America had achieved and maintained her greatness because she attracted men who wanted to build prosperous lives, said Cannon. The immigrants posed no threat to America which was, in Cannon's words, "a hell of a success."[1] Furthermore,

---

[1] William Rea Gwinn, <u>Uncle Joe Cannon: Archfoe of Insurgency, A History of the Rise and Fall of Cannonism</u> (1957), p. 2.

generally reluctant to challenge the status quo, Cannon often said that "the devil was the first smasher of precedents."[1]

In the spring of 1906, Theodore Roosevelt, unaware of Cannon's opposition to the test, continued to support it as he had done during the preceding five years. In his Annual Message to Congress in 1901, for example, he called for the test "to decrease the sum of ignorance, so potent in producing the envy, suspicion, malignant passion, and hatred of order out of which anarchist sentiment mentally springs."[2] As America's moral and political leader, the President spoke about the disruptive effects of massive immigration: "congestion, and a lowering of the standard of living and of the standard of wages."[3]

---

[1]Blair Bolles, Tyrant from Illinois (New York, 1951), p. 21. Cannon consistently and strongly opposed the literacy test while he was in the House. For example, when President Taft was deliberating in February, 1913, over whether to sign or veto another literacy test bill, Cannon remarked to a journalist friend: "There are two things I'd like to see the President do before he goes out of office. I want to see him veto the immigration bill. . . . He could show his courage and the people of the United States would honor him for it. You can tell him I said so." Gus Karger Papers (American Jewish Archives, Cincinnati), Feb. 10, 1913. Cited hereafter as Karger Papers.

[2]U.S., Congressional Record, 59th Cong., 1st sess., 1906, XL, Part 8, 7294.

[3]Roosevelt to Cannon, June 13, 1906, in Roosevelt Papers, Series II, 64.

The President favored the literacy test as a workable mechanism for excluding the many new immigrants who would impair America's stability and her "national character." According to John M. Blum, Roosevelt defined that character as "the conglutinations that history prepared, the accepted traditions of political and social behavior by which people imposed order on themselves."[1] The President objected to the new immigrants because of their low standard of living, their low educational level, their exceedingly high birth rate, and their radical attitudes. At times, Roosevelt was even susceptible to the racist thinking that defined Negroes, Indians, and Asians as "ignorant and unprogressive" and southern and eastern Europeans as somewhat "inferior" to the Anglo-Saxons.[2] Still, despite his obvious prejudices, he was not as antagonistic to the new immigrants as were Lodge, Gardner, and the members of the Immigration Restriction League.

The President did not involve himself with the Senate's consideration of the literacy test because he expected it to pass without difficulty. But on the same day that the Senate approved the test, he began his efforts to

---

[1] Blum, op. cit., p. 108.

[2] Ibid., p. 28.

persuade Cannon to favor it. In a long letter, Roosevelt told Cannon that he was deeply concerned about the recent type of immigration because it lowered America's standard of living and depressed the wages of the working class. Roosevelt wanted to encourage immigration of only those men who possessed the "physical and mental fitness" required for good citizenship. "In other words, I want to see immigrants of such a character that we need not be afraid of their grandchildren intermingling with ours as their political, social, and industrial equals."[1]

Roosevelt also asserted that Cannon was wrong to think that Wall Street interests supported the test. According to Roosevelt, those interests were against the test because shipping and mining concerns profited from a large passenger traffic and from cheap labor in the mines. While Roosevelt conceded that certain German and Scandinavian groups were opposed to the test, he maintained that their opposition was not significant because these two groups would not be adversely affected by it.

"I wish you could see your way clear to support the bill; that is get Grosvenor, Payne, Dalzell, and Hepburn,

_____

[1]Roosevelt to Cannon, May 23, 1906, in Roosevelt Papers, Series II, 64.

any or all, interested in its passage," Roosevelt wrote Cannon concerning House strategy.[1] Then he expressed only one serious reservation about the test, that it was an insufficient measure for ending the flow of undesirable immigrants. Instead, Roosevelt wanted consular officials or officials of the Bureau of Immigration to conduct inspections abroad to "decline to allow any to come here who were not physically, morally and intellectually of a good type." But such a practice, he wrote, would be too expensive to undertake at the present time. Roosevelt also revealed that he favored the eradication of the steerage class on ships to make it impossible to bring over immigrants "save in comparatively small numbers and on good, big ships." Finally, in a postscript he wrote: "I understand the Pure Food bill and the Naturalization bill must be considered first. I earnestly favor both especially the Pure Food bill; but let us have all three."[2]

Cannon responded to Roosevelt's lengthy discourse in a noncommittal way as he made perfectly clear that the

---

[1] Ibid. Charles Grosvenor, Rep. Ohio; Sereno Elisha Payne, Rep. New York; John Dalzell, Rep. Pennsylvania; William Peters Hepburn, Rep. Iowa.

[2] Ibid.

President would have to wait patiently for the Speaker to act. Cannon's reply is most interesting for its tone which attempts to disguise the Speaker's power. It read, in part: "In reply I have to say that the Naturalization bill, the Immigration bill, and the Pure Food bill are all on the Calendar, and by the action of the House are privileged; and it is in the power of the majority of the House to consider any one of these bills on any day, and to continue consideration until completed."[1]

Roosevelt tried to influence Cannon not only out of personal conviction but also to satisfy his close friend Lodge. In several notes to the President, Lodge speculated on Cannon's position and asked Roosevelt to help persuade Cannon to support the test. In one note Lodge wrote Roosevelt that two-thirds of the House favored the test, but that Cannon appeared to be against it. In another note, Lodge wrote that Gardner had spent several hours in conference with Cannon and had gotten the Speaker's support for all of the major provisions of the bill--including the test. It seemed that the only question to be settled was when and how quickly the bill would be debated and passed. Lodge asked

---

[1] Cannon to William Loeb (Roosevelt's secretary), May 30, 1906, in Roosevelt Papers, Series I, Box 106.

the President to intervene with Cannon: "It might be well Gus [Gardner] thinks if you were to ask [Cannon] whether he had come to any understanding or arrangement with Gardner about Immigration bill without mentioning of course that you have had intimation from Gus about it."[1]

It is not clear whether Roosevelt spoke to Cannon about the test as Lodge asked him to do. He did, however, write another letter to Cannon in which he reported that he had recently heard from James Cardinal Gibbons of Baltimore, who strongly opposed the test. Roosevelt wrote that he thought it important to inform Cannon of the Cardinal's opposition, but Roosevelt was quick to add that he still favored the test.[2]

Although Roosevelt would concede nothing to the Cardinal, he wrote Cannon in the same letter that he would give up the test, if need be, for another reason. He had his own set of legislative priorities: he wanted the literacy test, to be sure; but even more he wanted Cannon to approve the pure food bill, which the Speaker was known to dislike. "I of course do not know the details of your

---

[1] Lodge to Roosevelt, June 3, 1906, Lodge to Roosevelt, May 29, 1906, in Roosevelt Papers, Series I, Box 106.

[2] Roosevelt to Cannon, June 13, 1906, in Roosevelt Papers, Series II, 64.

arrangements, and as I told you before, I would not do anything that would interfere with the pure food bill, which is another measure which I think imperatively called for."[1] Whether this qualification had any effect on Cannon is debatable. There is little reason to believe that Cannon would have felt compelled to support the test, even if Roosevelt had showed unrelenting interest in it. Roosevelt's new position, however, did indicate that failure to pass the test would not deeply antagonize the President--provided that Cannon allowed the pure food bill to pass.

Precisely at the time that Roosevelt was encouraging Cannon to favor the test, Oscar S. Straus tried to persuade Roosevelt to abandon the restrictionist cause. Still deeply involved in organizing the AJC, Marshall, Adler, and Schiff relied upon Straus, who was the one among them with the closest ties to the President, to make their opposition known.

Straus and the people for whom he spoke, however, misled themselves in several ways. For a while they mistakenly thought that Roosevelt could be talked out of supporting the test. They also assumed that the President had the power to influence Cannon and to direct Congress to pass

---

[1] Ibid.

the test. Even more surprisingly, Adler, Straus, and Marshall did not yet know how the literacy test would affect Russian-Jewish immigrants. These men had never been involved in a legislative fight over an immigration bill and had not made any investigations of their own or of the government's statistics. They did not know, or acknowledge that they knew, that 26 percent of the Russian-Jewish immigrants were illiterate. Why then did they oppose the test at this stage? The answer probably lies in the fact that the Jewish leaders knew that the restrictionists wanted to exclude all new immigrants, a hostile attitude which the Jews resented and opposed. Therefore, the test in 1906 was the symbolic issue between those who defended the new immigrants and those who accused them of polluting American life.

Cyrus Adler, formerly a professor of Semitic languages and now Assistant Secretary of the Smithsonian Institution, regarded the Dillingham bill as "fair and not objectionable" except for the "absurd" test. "I am not prepared to say how far it will affect Jewish interests."[1] Straus was more specific, informing Adler that the test would jeopardize the entry of only 10 percent of the Jewish

---

[1] Cyrus Adler to Bijur, May 24, 1906, in Straus Papers, Box 4.

immigrants, but in his view, 10 percent was high enough to warrant opposition to the test. Straus also wrote Adler that he did not know how the President regarded the restriction issue, but that "we should not trouble him unless it becomes absolutely necessary."[1]

Within a few days, however, Straus advised Roosevelt of strong Jewish opposition to the literacy test. Roosevelt's secretary, William Loeb, responded for the President by saying that Roosevelt was indeed surprised to learn of Straus' position in view of the consensus in Washington supporting the restrictionists. Loeb reinforced this opinion by stating that ex-President Cleveland was now a restrictionist, having regretted vetoing the test in 1897. Straus, distressed by the news that Cleveland had switched his position, spoke with him and learned that he had not really changed his mind. Straus immediately wrote Roosevelt that the information about Cleveland's change of heart was wrong.[2]

---

[1] Straus to Adler, May 28, 1906, in Straus Papers, Box 4.

[2] Loeb to Straus, May 29, 1906, Straus to Loeb, June 4, 1906, in Straus Papers, Box 4. Roosevelt heard the story about Cleveland from his close friend General Leonard Wood, who was Governor of the Philippines. After Cleveland denied the story through Straus, Roosevelt asked Wood to give him the exact circumstances of Cleveland's reported change of heart. It seems that the President was encouraged

Straus also encouraged the anti-restrictionist lobbying of the Catholic Church. He wrote Cardinal Gibbons asking him to contact Cannon and Maryland Senator Isidor Raynor of Maryland, stressing that the passage of the test would imply America's cooperation with those autocratic governments that denied some subjects reasonable educational and economic opportunities. He pointed out that the test would be more damaging to the Italians, Hungarians, and Russians than it would be to the Jews since only 5 percent to 7 percent of the Jews were illiterate. Cardinal Gibbons, for his part, obliged Straus by writing the President and by asking him to defeat the "obnoxious immigration bill." A few days later, the Cardinal received Roosevelt's reply which stated that his position on the test could be found in many of his messages to Congress.[1]

Straus spoke directly with the President about the literacy test at a meeting in Washington on June 12. He

---

by the knowledge that although lacking a public precedent for signing a literacy test bill, the private ruminations of an ex-President proved that restriction was desirable. Roosevelt to Major General Leonard Wood, June 5, 1906, Series II, 64.

[1] Straus to James Cardinal Gibbons, June 4, 1906, Straus to Gibbons, June 6, 1906, in Straus Papers, Box 4; Gibbons to Roosevelt, June 7, 1906, in Roosevelt Papers, Series I, Box 103; Roosevelt to Gibbons, June 8, 1906, in Roosevelt Papers, Series II, 64.

left the meeting convinced that Roosevelt was committed to the test and would surely sign the Dillingham bill if it passed in the House. Now Straus shifted his hopes to Cannon whom he expected to realize that passage of the test would be "bad politics" for the Republicans.[1]

While most Jewish leaders were inactive in the spring of 1906, transatlantic shipping lines and certain railroad, steel, and mining concerns were lobbying against the test. They and the "business press" fought restriction because they saw the need for cheap labor.[2] Businessmen in the steel and shipping industries relied upon their personal contacts with Congressmen to oppose the test and, in addition, secretly paid for the lobbying activities of the non-sectarian, non-partisan National Liberal Immigration League. Until 1914 when Samuel Gompers exposed its ties with its business sponsors, the NLIL passed as a disinterested party in the restriction fight.

Nissim Behar, a French Jew who represented the Alliance Israélite Universelle in the United States, organized the NLIL in 1904, a few years before prominent

---

[1] Straus to Cyrus Sulzberger, June 14, 1906, in Straus Papers, Box 4.

[2] Higham, Strangers in the Land, pp. 115-16.

American Jews saw the need to lobby against restrictive legislation. Unfortunately, Behar's abrasive personality and his reliance on rallies and public demonstrations antagonized the leaders of the AJC; despite his repeated requests for aid, the AJC ignored Behar's organization. Marshall described his attitude towards the NLIL in a letter to Lillian Wald in 1911, telling her that the AJC's style of working in a "quiet and unobstrusive manner" was better than using the "blare of trumpets" and mass meetings. "I do not think that the general public can be very much stirred up on the subject. There is a strong and growing feeling in favor of immigration restriction, and I think that for every meeting that we can hold which will adopt resolutions against restriction, an equal number of meetings will be held by those in favor of it."[1]

The NLIL had little impact, especially after 1913 when it was in desperate financial straits. It was typical of organizations which spring up to combat a particular legislative evil and elicit the superficial support of aspiring politicians, academic leaders, and philanthropists. The most prominent supporters of the NLIL were Woodrow

---

[1] Marshall to Lillian Wald, Jan. 18, 1911, in Marshall Papers, AJA.

Wilson, Charles Eliot, and Andrew Carnegie. Basically, the NLIL provided a vehicle for non-Jewish politicians who wanted to associate themselves with the new immigrants. The organization and the politicians worked in a symbiotic way; the NLIL depended upon the politicians for legitimacy and, in some cases, for financial aid, while the politicians depended upon the organization for publicity and identification with the anti-restriction movement.[1] But from 1906 through 1917 the NLIL was an organization that mainly issued anti-restrictionist bulletins and petitions to ethnic organizations which in turn sent them to Congress and the White House as part of a public campaign against restrictive legislation.

When the House finally took up the literacy test on June 25, it was readily apparent that Cannon had decided,

---

[1] For example, in 1914 Cannon, who had been defeated for re-election, accepted the presidency of the NLEL at the prompting of William Bennet--who was also out of office. Cannon would do no work for the organization; when he went back to the House the following year he dropped his affiliation. Manoel Behar to Nissim Behar, Apr. 10, 1914, in National Liberal Immigration League Papers (Yivo Institute for Jewish Research, New York). Hereafter cited as NLIL Papers. In 1913 and 1914 the NLIL was in desperate financial condition and lived from week to week on donations made by Bennet. The connection between Bennet and the shipping industry was quite involved since he received a $5,000 annual retainer from certain shipping companies to lobby for them in Washington. Manoel Behar to Nissim Behar, Mar. 13, 1914, in NLIL Papers.

for reasons that have been previously discussed, to throw out the test. Cannon, who had become Speaker in 1903, was riding at the peak of his power, flouting the wishes of a Republican President, the Senate, and the House. He achieved his firm control because he simultaneously held the two crucial positions of Speaker and Chairman of the Rules Committee. Since he handed out the coveted positions of committee chairmen, he controlled the hierarchy in the House.[1] With the aid of these chairmen who were deeply indebted to him, Cannon used his power to oppose his own Committee on Immigration and Naturalization and to force the House to conform to his views on the literacy test.

To insure victory, Cannon not only compelled the restrictionist majority in the House to accept a special rule limiting debate, but he also stepped down from the Speaker's Chair to cajole members and to cast his vote on the test and other provisions of the bill. Cannon arranged for Republican John Dalzell of Pennsylvania to propose a special rule--"one of those ukases disguised as a resolution."[2] The rule set three hours for debate and provided that Section 1, which aimed to increase the head tax to $5

---

[1] Bolles, op. cit., p. 64.

[2] Ibid., p. 54.

and Section 38, which sought to establish the literacy test, were the only provisions subject to amendment. This special rule foreclosed any general discussion of the bill as a whole and, for purely partisan reasons, two leading Democrats, John Sharp Williams of Mississippi and David De Armond of Missouri, voiced objections. Gardner also opposed the rule because he was eager to force a roll call vote on the test; yet the House easily adopted the rule by a vote of 151 to 52.

The debate on the two amendable sections was swift and conclusive. Cannon, by sitting with his House confreres, was able to manipulate the House into supporting his position on the crucial votes. He used extraordinarily persuasive methods to get the House to support him on the bill. What Cannon actually said to the recalcitrant members is not known, but he pulled men out of the smoking rooms to vote with him when necessary, and, according to Samuel Gompers, he "even pulled one man up by his collar and ordered him to pass between the tellers."[1]

The first vote concerned the head tax which was set at $5 by the House Committee. An amendment was offered to reduce the amount back to the 1903 level of $2. In the

---

[1] Samuel Gompers, *Seventy Years of Life and Labor* (New York, 1925), II, 171.

voice vote that followed, the nays were in the majority. A division vote was called; the House reversed itself by voting 73 to 67. For the final vote, tellers were ordered and the House agreed to lower the tax by a vote of 94 to 79.

Then Lucius Littauer, a Republican from New York and a good friend of Cannon's, offered an amendment to Section 1. He proposed to exempt thousands of Russian-Jewish immigrants from the "public charge" provision:

> That an immigrant who proves that he is seeking admission to this country to avoid persecution or punishment on religious or political grounds, for an offense of a political character, or persecution involving danger of imprisonment or danger to life and limb on account of religious belief, shall not be deported because of want of means or the probability of his being unable to earn a livelihood.[1]

Several Representatives objected to the amendment on the grounds that it would permit the entry of large numbers of undesirable immigrants. Gardner expressed displeasure with the exemption as it pertained to the public charge clause, but said that he would favor a more tightly framed version if it were attached to the literacy test. Gardner suggested, and Littauer agreed, to add the word "solely"--"solely to avoid religious persecution"--to the exemption.[2] When the

---

[1] U.S., Congressional Record, 59th Cong., 1st sess., 1906, XL, Part 10, 9164.

[2] Ibid.

vote took place Cannon again rallied his forces; in the initial vote, House sentiment was against Littauer as the vote was 66 to 79, but the reversal came under Cannon's prodding with the teller vote and the amendment passed 92 to 69.

The House then took up the literacy test. Charles Grosvenor, a Republican from Ohio and a close associate of Cannon's, offered an amendment that called for dropping the test and substituting a commission study of the entire immigration problem.[1] He proposed that three Representatives, two Senators, and two appointees of the President investigate the immigration controversy. Before voting on the commission proposal, the House agreed to add the complete Littauer exemption clause to the literacy test, but this vote meant little at the time because the House proceeded to drop the test entirely. The vote was 123 to 136 on the amendment to substitute the study for the test. On the

---

[1] According to Representative James Watson, a strong restrictionist who was close to Cannon, Roosevelt asked him to withdraw his sponsorship of the literacy test and to let it die in committee because "high-up Church dignitaries" had made it clear that the President could not risk passage of the test in an election year. Watson wrote that he conceded to Roosevelt's demand by substituting the commission study for the test. It is difficult, however, to rely on Watson's information; in the first place, he gives no dates for the conversations that took place long before he wrote his account of the episode; secondly, it is evident that Roosevelt was quite unhappy about the commission idea. James E. Watson, *As I Knew Them* (Indianapolis, 1936), p. 79.

final vote, however, Cannon won again as the House reversed itself by voting 128 to 116 for the substitution.

With the votes on the two sections completed to Cannon's liking, the Speaker went back to his Chair. The House then passed the immigration bill without a division vote. The new House version replaced the literacy test with a commission study, decreased the head tax to $2, and inserted the Littauer amendment. The bill also included the provision to exclude immigrants of "low vitality."

Cannon tasted one more fruit of victory when he appointed Republicans William Bennet of New York and Benjamin Howell of New Jersey and Democrat Jacob Ruppert of New York to the House-Senate conference committee. Bennet and Ruppert, both first term Representatives, were two members of the Committee on Immigration and Naturalization who had filed a minority report against the head tax and the literacy test. Howell, Chairman of the Committee and a restrictionist, was, nevertheless, expected to adhere to the sentiment of the House when he met with the Senate conferees.[1]

Thus Cannon presented Roosevelt, Lodge, Dillingham and Gardner with stinging defeats on the test, head tax, and the public charge clauses. The President was particularly

---

[1]Bolles, op. cit., p. 74.

annoyed by the commission proposal which he regarded as a delaying tactic of the anti-restrictionists. Therefore, he proposed to Cannon that if an investigation were undertaken, it should be handled by the President's Immigration and Labor Commissioners Frank P. Sargent and Charles P. Neill. Roosevelt described both men as "experts" in the "intricate" immigration field. Both men were also strong restrictionists. But without waiting to hear from Cannon, Roosevelt directed the two men to work on their own investigations, calling on them to make an exhaustive but confidential study of the immigration situation as quickly as possible.[1] Roosevelt's hope was that the existence of a detailed report would make it possible for the House-Senate conference committee to drop the House demand for a Congressional investigation.

During the summer and fall months that followed Cannon's victory, Roosevelt played down the Republican party's advocacy of the literacy test. He did not wish to antagonize needlessly the ethnic vote--the German, Italian, and Jewish vote--which opposed the test; nor did he want to undermine Republican support in such an important

---

[1] Roosevelt to Cannon, June 27, 1906, in Roosevelt Papers, Series II, 65; Roosevelt to Frank P. Sargent, June 28, 1906, in Roosevelt Papers, Series II, 65.

election as the New York gubernatorial fight between William Randolph Hearst and Charles Evans Hughes. Therefore, Roosevelt advised against mentioning his support of the literacy test in the Watson letter, a Republican position paper designed to help Republican Congressional candidates. He wrote Lodge about the literacy test and the letter:

> I did all I could for the immigration bill because I thought it would be of benefit to the country. I did not think it would be an advantage politically. On the contrary, I thought it would probably be a disadvantage. Such being the case, it does not seem to me expedient to make any mention of it in a document which is intended to influence votes for Congress rather than to influence Congress.[1]

Roosevelt even tried to ingratiate himself and his party with Jewish voters in the heated contest between Hughes and Hearst. To this end, he appointed Straus, his good friend and spokesman in the Jewish community, as Secretary of Commerce and Labor (the Department which controlled the Immigration Bureau). The appointment was officially made in September in fulfillment of a promise made to Straus in January, 1906. The President wrote Straus that one reason for his selection was to dramatize the differences between the democratic system in America and the

---

[1] Roosevelt to Lodge, Aug. 15, 1906, in Roosevelt Papers, Series II, 66.

autocratic one in Russia.[1] But Roosevelt also wanted to insure Republican control over his home state by cutting into Hearst's popularity on the Lower East Side. "I did all I could to help out the campaign by announcing the selection of Oscar Straus for my Cabinet," Roosevelt wrote Jacob Riis before the election.[2]

Roosevelt was the first President to appoint a Jew to his Cabinet. Whatever his motives, the appointment gave the American Jewish community a real as well as a symbolic stake in the political world in Washington. The selection came at an important time, for Roosevelt and the restrictionists in Congress still threatened to end the policy of open immigration which was so advantageous to the Russian Jews and of such great concern to the AJC.

III.

Once the elections were over and the Republican party was free of the threat of defections by pivotal ethnic groups, attention was once again directed to the conflicting immigration bills. The AJC, now a functioning organization,

---

[1] Roosevelt to Straus, Jan. 13, 1906, in Roosevelt Papers, Series II, 60; Roosevelt to Straus, Sept. 6, 1906, in Straus Papers, Box 4.

[2] Roosevelt to Jacob Riis, Oct. 28, 1906, in Roosevelt Papers, Series IVa, Box 3.

was ready to make its first effort to defeat the restrictionists. The issue seemed far from being resolved as speculation centered on whether any immigration bill would be reported out of the conference committee. At Cannon's insistence, the House conferees would not adopt the literacy test supported by the Senate conferees Lodge, Dillingham, and Anselm M. McLaurin. Adopting dilatory practices, the House members forced an examination of every sentence in the long bills, a technique that was particularly time-consuming and annoying for Senator Lodge.[1]

By the time that the 2nd Session of the 59th Congress had opened, there were important new elements in the immigration fight. A national and international dispute over Japanese immigration to the West Coast had developed. First, Japanese immigrants were continuing to settle in California despite the Japanese government's policy of refusing passports to laborers headed directly for the United States. Second, this influx was resulting in acts of violence against individual Japanese aliens and against their property. Reflecting this hostile sentiment, the San Francisco school board decided in October, 1906 to implement a

---

[1] William Bennet, Columbia University Oral History Project, p. 36.

decision made the previous year to segregate Japanese school children with other Asian children. The crux of the issue was not school segregation but Japanese immigration and Japanese land holdings.[1]

Roosevelt assumed the responsibility for settling the school and immigration conflicts, despite objections from several politicians who thought these were purely local issues. The President, nevertheless, became involved because the Japanese government protested the discrimination against its people in the United States. Through his intervention the President sought to reduce the danger of injury to the immigrants, to prevent the segregation of the Japanese school children, and ultimately, to work out a settlement which would put an end to the immigration of Japanese laborers to the United States.

At first Roosevelt wanted to solve the dispute within the framework of the European-oriented immigration bill which the Senate had passed. He favored a restrictive

---

[1] For a full discussion of the Japanese crisis see Charles E. Neu, An Uncertain Friendship: Theodore Roosevelt and Japan, 1906-1909 (Cambridge, Mass., 1967); Thomas A. Bailey, Theodore Roosevelt and the Japanese-American Crisis (Stanford, Cal., 1934); and Roger Daniels, "The Politics of Prejudice: The Anti-Japanese Movement in California and the Struggle for Japanese Exclusion," University of California Publications in History, LXXI (Berkeley, Cal., 1962).

bill that would affect both Japanese and eastern and southern European immigration. Such a measure, he said, would "keep out all people who have difficulty in assimilating with our own" without "giving offense to any one nation."[1] But Cannon remained firmly opposed to the literacy test and Roosevelt found it impossible to achieve his goals.

In contrast to his earlier behavior, Roosevelt now approached Cannon cautiously, making no new effort to persuade the Speaker to support the test. In fact, in his December Annual Message to Congress, delivered at the moment when Congress was considering the test, Roosevelt failed even to mention and endorse it as he had done in his previous Annual Messages. Roosevelt's Message was otherwise highly controversial because he proposed far-reaching business reforms and criticized the rude and hostile behavior of the Californians in regard to the Japanese. By calling on Congress to pass a law to allow the Japanese to become naturalized citizens--a right no immigrant from Asia enjoyed --Roosevelt further inflamed the California-Japanese dispute.

Roosevelt never offered his reasons for failing to recommend the literacy test, but clearly he was most

---

[1] Roosevelt to John St. Loe Strachey, Dec. 21, 1906, in Roosevelt Papers, Series II, 69.

concerned with the Japanese immigration problem. In addition, his apprehensions about the new immigrants were not strong enough to justify a public fight with Cannon over the test. Nor did the President want to aggravate the differences that already existed between Cannon and himself over federal control of corporations. He was not willing to crusade throughout the country to arouse public support on the immigration issue, as he had done for the Hepburn bill and as he threatened to do for the pure food bill.

Still, Roosevelt wanted Congress to pass an immigration bill. Therefore, he reversed his earlier position and suddenly recognized the value of a commission study. The President asked Cannon to support the study when he realized that it would provide the justification for proposing restrictive legislation in the future: "I would want a commission which would enable me . . . to put before the Congress a plan which would amount to a definite solution of this immigration business, which would provide for keeping out the unfit, physically, morally, or mentally. . . ."[1]

Roosevelt also sought to comfort his restrictionist friends, writing Robert DeC. Ward, publicist for the Immigration Restriction League, to assure him that he was doing

---

[1] Roosevelt to Cannon, Jan. 12, 1907, in Roosevelt Papers, Series II, 69.

everything possible to pass an immigration bill. But the opposition, he said, was overwhelming: "You would be astounded at the amount of genuine misconception that exists on the subject, and of the intensity of the hostility aroused among very good people who really ought to be with us."[1]

While Roosevelt was trying to settle the Japanese controversy and support his restrictionist friends, the AJC embarked on an intense campaign to shape the immigration bills to their liking. The prospects for some immigration legislation changed continually throughout January and February, according to Congressional sources who supplied a steady flow of sometimes erroneous information to the AJC. In early January, Adler and Marshall learned that an immigration bill--without the literacy test--would pass. Therefore, the AJC sent out an urgent bulletin to all general committee members calling on them to persuade their Congressmen to oppose the immigration bill--especially the low-vitality clause.

Individual leaders of the AJC started to lobby actively. Adler, based in Washington at the Smithsonian

---

[1] Roosevelt to Robert DeCourcy Ward, Jan. 29, 1907, in Roosevelt Papers, Series II, 70.

Institution, was head of the AJC's Washington office, established to gather "information on Jewish matters."[1] Adler made great efforts, for example, to convince the Pennsylvania Congressional delegation to oppose the bills, calling on A. Leo Weil, a corporate lawyer in Pittsburgh, to get in touch with Representative Dalzell and the two Republican Senators Philander C. Knox and Boies Penrose. Adler also asked for help from Isador Sobel of Erie, a former President of the Pennsylvania League of Republican Clubs and Postmaster of Erie from 1898 to 1914. Adler described Sobel as having more political experience than any other American Jew. Still, when Sobel offered to go to Washington during the deliberations over the immigration bill, Adler was afraid that Sobel's actions might be recognized as lobbying and might put the AJC in a bad position.[2]

As part of the same campaign, Straus, now Secretary of Commerce and Labor, met with Cannon and advised him that at the moment there was no need to revise the 1903 immigration law. Straus told the Speaker that the waves of immigration were not hurting the country economically and that,

---

[1] Minutes, AJC, Nov. 25, 1906.

[2] Adler to Herbert Friedenwald, Jan. 10, 1907, in Cyrus Adler Papers (American Jewish Committee, New York). Cited hereafter as Adler Papers.

in fact, they actually provided a sign of the country's vitality.[1]

Marshall waged his own intense and calculating campaign against the literacy test and low vitality clauses. Seeking out men who could put pressure on important Congressmen, he wrote Jacob Wertheim, President of the United Cigar Manufacturers, who had a large plant in Benjamin Howell's New Jersey Congressional district. Marshall asked Wertheim to contact Howell, or friends of Howell's, to express displeasure with the test and support for the commission study. He wrote directly to Senators Thomas H. Carter, a Republican from Montana, Isidor Raynor, a Democrat from Maryland and also to ex-Governor Carroll S. Page of Vermont who he hoped would influence Senator Dillingham.[2] Furthermore, Marshall wrote Daniel Guggenheim, president of the American Smelting and Refining Corporation, to ask for help in reaching Republican Senator Nelson Aldrich of Rhode Island and supplied a letter which Guggenheim might use for

---

[1] Diary of Oscar S. Straus, Jan. 10, 1907, in Straus Papers, Box 22. Straus dropped his official affiliation with the AJC when he entered the Cabinet.

[2] Marshall to Wertheim, Feb. 2, 1907, in Marshall Papers (American Jewish Historical Society, Brandeis University, Waltham, Mass.). Cited hereafter as Marshall Papers, AJHS. Marshall to Edward Lauterbach, Feb. 9, 1907, Marshall Papers, AJA; Reznikoff, op. cit., I, 113-15.

this purpose. Marshall explained exactly why he wanted Guggenheim's help: "It occurs to me that your relations to Senator Aldrich, who is a great power in the Senate, are such that he will heed your wishes and prevent the passage of a law which would be most cruel in its operation."[1]

Despite the fact that they were Republicans, Marshall and Schiff even lobbied with important Democrats. They conferred with Judge Alton B. Parker, the Democratic nominee for President in 1904, convincing him to wire Representative John Sharp Williams of Mississippi to express opposition to the literacy test. Marshall also enlisted the aid of John Fox, President of the National Democratic Club, who in turn wrote Representative David De Armond of Missouri, an important figure on the Rules Committee, in support of the commission study.[2] Marshall had been able to reach Fox through New York Supreme Court Judge M. Warley Platzek, who was a close friend of Fox's. Marshall's letter to Platzek reveals his desire to see the AJC's lobbying effort carried out in the most careful way. His instructions were the

---

[1] Marshall to Daniel Guggenheim, Feb. 9, 1907, in Marshall Papers, AJHS.

[2] Marshall to Adler, Feb. 6, 1907, in Marshall Papers, AJA; Marshall to M. Warley Platzek, Feb. 4, 1907, in Marshall Papers, AJA; John Fox to David De Armond, Feb. 5, 1907, in Marshall Papers, AJHS.

following: "Mr. Fox, signing himself as President of the Democratic Club for purposes of identification, should telegraph to Congressman De Armond, saying in substance, that in his opinion and in that of many of his friends it would be considered as a great economic blunder as well as an act un-American in its nature, if the Restrictive Immigration Bill . . . be enacted."[1] Marshall, however, was extremely careful not to get any Democratic clubs involved in the lobbying, contrary to a suggestion made by Platzek, fearing that a partisan campaign would antagonize the most important anti-restrictionist of all--Speaker Cannon.

Just as Marshall was afraid to get involved in partisan politics, some of the other AJC members feared that the public would accuse them of belonging to a politically active organization. Two examples illustrate this apprehensive attitude. In January, Mayer Sulzberger, president of the AJC, issued a call to all members to oppose the immigration bills but he requested that the members make their appeals to politicians without mentioning their affiliation with the AJC. In the second instance, Herbert Friedenwald, secretary of the AJC, rebuked a fellow member in Portland, Oregon, who had disregarded Sulzberger's request.

---

[1] Marshall to Platzek, Feb. 5, 1907, in Marshall Papers, AJA.

The member actually had passed on an official AJC communication on the immigration issue to a local politician. Thus Friedenwald wrote, "In view of the danger that the Jews may be accused of being organized for a political purpose I think great caution ought to be observed by the members . . . in the utilization of the information sent out to them."[1]

On February 6, Marshall felt that his efforts were proving successful: "It seems to me," he wrote Adler, "that we have killed the bill, yet it may be only scotched."[2] Three days later, however, Marshall suddenly recognized the need for some "hedging" because he expected Cannon to approve an immigration bill. Marshall cautiously set priorities based upon his erroneous idea of the level of Jewish illiteracy, which was actually 26 percent. Thus the low vitality clause, not the literacy test, became the principal target of opposition. Marshall described this new objective to Edward Lauterbach, a New York lawyer who was formerly

___

[1] Friedenwald to Mayer Sulzberger, Feb. 6, 1907, in Mayer Sulzberger Papers (American Jewish Committee, New York). Cited hereafter as Sulzberger Papers. Mayer Sulzberger to AJC members, Jan. 15, 1907, in Sulzberger Papers.

[2] Marshall to Adler, Feb. 6, 1907, in Marshall Papers, AJA.

chairman of the New York Republican County Committee and now a leader of the NLIL. Marshall wrote Lauterbach because he was under the impression that New York Senators Thomas Platt and Chauncey Depew, both Republicans, had great personal "obligations" to him.

> In all likelihood the illiteracy provision will be dropped, but inasmuch as that does not affect our Russian Jewish immigrants very seriously, since probably ninety-eight per cent of the men can read and write in some language (in the case of the women the percentage is however much lower), it is important that something at least should be done for the purpose of modifying the rigor of the low vitality clause.[1]

In early February, unbeknownst to the AJC leaders, Roosevelt, Root, and Lodge were pushing the Japanese and European immigration issues towards a climax. During the second week in February, Roosevelt summoned the Mayor and the entire San Francisco school board to Washington to persuade them to accept his terms of settlement, those which Lodge had first suggested.[2] Roosevelt recommended that the school board rescind its segregation order and thereby appease the Japanese government. To appease the Californians, in turn, Roosevelt suggested that Congress pass an immigration bill which would empower the President to deny entry

---

[1] Marshall to Lauterbach, Feb. 9, 1907, in Marshall Papers, AJA.

[2] Neu, op. cit., p. 67.

to Japanese immigrants who held passports for Hawaii and Mexico, but who intended to remain in the United States. The settlement was extremely attractive to Roosevelt and Root, who regarded it as the first step towards ending all Japanese immigration to the United States.

While Roosevelt negotiated with the school board, Root met with the conference committee considering the immigration bills. On February 12, Root conferred with the Republican members of the committee: Lodge, Howell, Bennet, and Dillingham and he strongly advised them to end their differences. If necessary, Root told the Senate conferees, the literacy test should be replaced by a commission study to solve the major problem at hand, namely, the Japanese dispute. Later, Bennet described the direct result of Root's intervention: "Well, we were patriotic Americans. We didn't want any war with Japan, and so we said all right."[1]

The Republicans followed Root's advice and the following day the conference committee accepted the compromise. (Marshall, hearing of this, belatedly recognized that "it is now quite possible that the Japanese embroglio will cut quite a figure in the ultimate shaping of the pending

---

[1] Bennet, op. cit., p. 37.

legislation. . . .")[1] The literacy test was dropped. The new bill allowed the President to deny entry to Japanese laborers from Hawaii and Mexico. The committee increased the head tax to $4; it deleted the "low vitality" clause but excluded those immigrants "found to be . . . mentally or physically defective, such mental or physical defect being of a nature which may affect the ability . . . to earn a living." (At the insistence of the Senate conferees, the Littauer exemption clause was dropped; it would have exempted the Russian Jews from the operation of the public charge provision.) The conferees also called for a commission study of the immigration problem: its membership would consist of three Representatives, three Senators, and three appointees of the President. A Bureau of Information was established, new specifications for steerage conditions were set, and finally, the bill empowered the President to appoint commissioners to negotiate with foreign governments about resolving the immigration problem.[2]

---

[1] Marshall to Schiff, Feb. 13, 1907, in Marshall Papers, AJA.

[2] U.S., Congress, House, Conference Report, Regulation of Immigration of Aliens into the United States, 59th Cong., 2d sess., Feb. 13, 1907, H. Rept. 7607 to accompany S4403.

Having worked out the compromise with the school board and the conference committee, Roosevelt and Lodge were now concerned about the fate of the bill because some southern Senators were raising objections to its contract labor provisions. The issue was a sectional one between the South and North; many southerners wanted a bill that would encourage skilled and unskilled white immigrant laborers to go to the southern states and thereby stimulate industrialization; many northern states, such as Massachusetts, were eager, however, to prevent the development of competing industries in the South, especially in the textile field.

After the passage of the 1903 immigration law, some southern states solicited abroad for immigrants. South Carolina, for example, established an agency to encourage the immigration of white Anglo-Saxon laborers. According to Charles Earl, Solicitor of the Department of Commerce and Labor, the South Carolina agency operated within the legal requirements of the 1903 law. But suddenly in 1907 certain southern Senators feared that the pending immigration legislation would reverse Earl's liberal interpretation. Straus met with some of the doubtful southern Senators and Governors and, on the strength of his assurances that the new bill would not harm southern interests, many of the Senators agreed to support the bill.[1]

Despite Straus' assurances, the Senate debate which began on February 13, was testy and long-winded owing to the dilatory tactics of Democratic southern Senators such as Augustus Bacon of Georgia and Benjamin Tillman of South Carolina. The southern labor problem was discussed at length, with Lodge and Bacon engaging in a series of sharp exchanges. Lodge, speaking for many northern interests, explained that he favored allowing a state government to solicit for immigrants, but that he would never agree to allow individual southerners to solicit and to pay for the transportation of immigrants. It was clear to both Lodge and Bacon that southern states, which had limited revenues, would never engage in expensive and prolonged efforts to attract immigrants. Tillman, an arch foe of the President's, not only objected to the interference of the President in a local issue on the West Coast, but also accused him of pressuring Congress to pass the immigration bill.

---

[1] Diary of Oscar S. Straus, Feb. 15, 1907, in Straus Papers, Box 22. On March 22, 1907 Weill informed Straus that he had been mistaken about the implications of the new law: southern interests would be seriously affected by it. Ibid., Mar. 12, 1907.

Reportedly, various Senators who opposed the bill were brought into line by the threat of withholding appropriations under a pending rivers and harbors bill. There were rumors, too, that if the immigration bill failed, Roosevelt would call a special session of Congress to deal with the Japanese dispute.[1] It is impossible to know whether these threats emanated directly from the President, but when the bill came up for the final vote on February 17, the Senate passed it on a voice vote.

The House debate on the bill was perfunctory, although, according to William Bennet, the compromise was unpopular because it left out the literacy test.[2] The debate echoed the concerns of the individual Representatives, sympathy for the plight of religious refugees from Russia and fears about the barbarization of the American stock. The House, which hardly could have rejected a bill supported by Cannon and the President, passed the compromise immigration bill by a vote of 143 to 101. Two days later, on February 20, Roosevelt signed it into law.

Thus Cannon's power, used to oppose the literacy test, frustrated Roosevelt and the restrictionists and

---

[1] Bailey, op. cit., p. 146; Lodge to Roosevelt, Feb. 13, 1907, in Roosevelt Papers, Series I, Box 116.

[2] Bennet, op. cit., p. 38.

delighted the AJC. Marshall termed the outcome "a scorching victory"; in fact, he said, "all of the provisions against which we fought have been eliminated."[1] The AJC leaders were also pleased with the way the fledgling organization had performed. The executive committee sent a note of thanks to its general members for not "wasting effort on public meetings or other forms of publicity, but in making their appeals direct" to Congressmen.[2]

In truth, the AJC's elation concerning its own role was not justified because it was Cannon who, independently of the AJC, had carried the day. Adler was the only one of the AJC leaders who recognized what had really happened; his realistic assessment came in a discussion of the Littauer exemption clause: "We did not give up the Littauer Amendment, it had to be given up. The fact is that the thing has gotten too big for any of us to handle; it has reached the stage of national and international politics and I doubt whether there is any use of our doing any more."[3]

In one respect, however, the resolution of the

---

[1] Friedenwald to Adler, Feb. 18, 1907, in Adler Papers.

[2] Minutes, AJC, Jan. 27, 1907.

[3] Adler to Friedenwald, Feb. 15, 1907, in Adler Papers.

Japanese dispute caused concern among AJC leaders as they considered another aspect of their immigration policy, namely, Russian-American relations. A new issue, similar to the pogroms, was beginning to arouse the American Jews. It involved Russia's refusal to allow native-born or naturalized American Jews to travel freely in Russia, despite the fact that they possessed American passports. According to Jewish leaders, this demeaning and offensive practice violated the existing commercial Treaty of 1832 between Russia and the United States.

The Japanese provision in the 1907 immigration law directed the President to withhold recognition of certain passports. But this was precisely the power exercised by the Russian government which so antagonized American Jews. Marshall, sensing the danger in the 1907 provision, wrote Mayer Sulzberger that the Japanese settlement

> constitutes only another of many precedents which will make it difficult for our government to agitate either for a recognition of its passports in Russia, or for intervention there or elsewhere on behalf of our brethren. When we are engaged in legislation of a discriminatory character against the subjects of friendly nations, and are pandering to the prejudices, intolerance and bigotry of our own citizens, any representations which our government may make to another, on alleged humanitarian grounds, will be rejected with the admonition that we first remove the beam from our own eyes before we undertake to operate on the optics of our neighbors.[1]

---

[1] Marshall to Mayer Sulzberger, Feb. 18, 1907, in Marshall Papers, AJA.

Despite this conclusion, Marshall and the AJC soon began to "agitate" on the passport issue. By 1911 they turned their grievances against the Russian and American governments into an impassioned campaign to abrogate the 1832 Treaty and thereby changed the course of Russian-American relations.

CHAPTER III

THE HOLLOW VICTORY

The AJC's crusade to abrogate the Russian-American commercial Treaty was the organization's most ambitious and confident attempt in the period from 1906 to 1917 to convince the President, the State Department, and Congress to use American foreign policy on behalf of Russian Jewry. Riding on the crest of an intense anti-Russian feeling that had been building up within the American-Jewish community since Kishinev, the AJC came to regard the passport dispute as the means of ending the oppression of Russian Jewry. Marshall and Schiff idealistically believed that abrogation would force Russia to end the Pale, to liberate Russian Jewry, and ultimately, to relieve the pressure for emigration.

Beyond the Russian-Jewish problem, the leaders of the AJC lobbied to gain something for themselves as well. The passport fight served as the means by which the AJC boldly asserted its power on the domestic political scene and its claim, for American Jews, to equal rights at home and abroad. By making an issue of the Treaty, the AJC declared its unwillingness to live with the inconsistency of lofty rhetoric about American equality and the reality of anti-Semitism in Progressive America. The AJC assumed that the rhetoric was meaningful and sought to force the President, Congress, and the American public to live up to their professed goals.

In striking contrast to the literacy test fight, the AJC adopted a different set of lobbying techniques: lavish expenditures of money, public speaking campaigns, extensive distribution of propaganda, and courting politicians by playing off Republicans against Democrats. In its first highly publicized venture into the public arena all of these lobbying devices were of value to the AJC. But of even greater significance was the timing of the campaign in which the AJC crusaded against an unpopular President during a period of political turmoil. President William Howard Taft was not willing to shape America's Russian policy around the needs of Russian Jewry and the desires of an ethnic minority at home. In this regard he closely followed Roosevelt's policy in 1905 and 1906 concerning the pogroms. Unfortunately for Taft, he failed to assert himself as the national spokesman who did not want to give in to the claims of a special interest group. The AJC, recognizing Taft's lack of astuteness and political strength, cleverly and boldly employed its network of national contacts to build public support for an ethnic minority and to ally with politicians who were hungry for votes in the 1911 and 1912 elections.

I

A prelude to the passport controversy was the Galveston project that was of great importance to Jacob Schiff. At the time of the literacy test fight in 1906, Schiff had become intrigued by the possibility of breaking the pattern of immigrant settlement in the urban areas of the East Coast. His immediate aim in 1906 was to attract 20,000 to 25,000 Russian-Jewish immigrants to Galveston, Texas and then to settle them in southern, northwestern, and Pacific states. The Galveston project was a significant venture because it raised Schiff's hopes about radically improving the Jewish immigration problem and because it embroiled him in a controversy with the Taft Administration.

Pledging $500,000 to fund the project, Schiff hoped to provide eventually for the settlement of two million immigrants in unpopulated western areas. The two million "if properly handled and distributed will be very welcome as well as useful to the country itself," wrote Schiff in August, 1906. "I believe that in government circles, as well as elsewhere, where the congestion of Russian immigrants in the Atlantic seaports is looked upon with a certain anxiety, such a movement will be regarded with great satisfaction and be given full moral support."[1] Eleven months later, Schiff was still optimistic about his idea: "I am definitely convinced that if it will be possible to stimulate further emigration to Galveston . . . public opinion will be profoundly influenced in favor of Russian Jewish immigration."[2]

Unfortunately for Schiff, the potentiality was never realized because the Galveston organization distributed only 2,000 immigrants between 1907 and 1910. The depression of 1907 reduced the flow of immigrants and caused a drop in the number of job opportunities. But it was the Department of Commerce and Labor that delivered the worst blow to the project by turning back, in the summer months of 1910, many Galveston-bound immigrants because they allegedly violated the 1907 immigration law. The government charged that the Galveston organization paid the transatlantic fares of some of the immigrants; other immigrants were judged to be so poor that they were likely to become public charges.

Schiff angrily denied that his organization paid the

---

[1] Szajkowski, op. cit., p. 24.

[2] Ibid., p. 25.

fares of the immigrants, in violation of the law. Furthermore, he argued that impoverished immigrants were entitled legally to receive, and temporarily depend upon, private charity to avoid becoming public charges. Schiff indignantly wrote Benjamin S. Cable, the Assistant Secretary of the Department, that a "considerable section of the American people" would blame the Taft Administration for the failure of the distribution scheme.[1] Cable replied that the Department would not change its policy unless directed to do so by the courts.[2] But when Schiff carried his appeal to Charles Nagel, Secretary of the Department of Commerce and Labor, and to President Taft, they directed Cable to stop interfering with the project. Unfortunately, despite an expenditure of $250,000 between 1906 and 1914, the Galveston plan failed because of the uncooperative attitude of the Immigration Bureau, the tightening of the job market in 1913 and 1914, and the drastic reduction in Russian-Jewish immigration during the First World War.[3]

In 1910, when Schiff was beginning to have difficulties

---

[1] Schiff, op. cit., II, 109.

[2] Minutes, AJC, Sept. 20, 1910.

[3] Financial Statement of Receipts and Disbursements, on Account of the Galveston Committee, 1907-1914, in Schiff Papers, AJA.

with his Galveston program, the AJC started its crusade to terminate the Treaty of 1832. Specifically, the AJC objected to Russia's interpretation of two articles in the Treaty. Article I stated, in part:

> There shall be between the territories of the high contracting parties a reciprocal liberty of commerce and navigation. The inhabitants of their respective States . . . shall be at liberty to sojourn and reside in all parts whatsoever of said territories, in order to attend to their affairs, and they shall enjoy, to that effect, the same security and protection as natives of the country wherein they reside, on condition of their submitting to the laws and ordinances there prevailing, and particularly to the regulations in force concerning commerce.[1]

Article X bound the United States to respect Russia's emigration laws and policies. Russia used these two articles to prohibit American Jews from visiting Russia for business or other reasons, although it granted the privilege to other American citizens.

In the unusual case when Russia did grant an American Jew the required visa for travel, the government subjected him to the same geographical restrictions which applied to Russian Jews. In a few instances, the Russian government even arrested naturalized American-Jewish citizens of Russian birth who were visiting Russia, charging desertion or violation of Russian emigration laws. Although in 1832

---

[1] Reznikoff, op. cit., I, 61.

both Russia and the United States had recognized the principle of indefeasible allegiance--the inability to change one's nationality--American policy changed during the middle decades of the nineteenth century. Thereafter, the United States made treaties with many European countries (but not Russia) which recognized its right to naturalize its immigrant population.[1]

On several occasions, beginning in the 1850's, the United States government publicly objected to Russia's interpretation of the Treaty. Secretaries of State Edward Everett and James G. Blaine maintained that American Jews in Russia should not be treated like their Russian brethren. Instead, they should have the same equality and freedom of movement that they found in the United States and, in the words of the Treaty, "the same security and protection as natives of the country wherein they reside." There was one outstanding instance, however, when the government accepted the Russian interpretation: in May, 1907, Secretary of State Root issued a circular announcing that the government would refuse

---

[1] The United States entered agreements with the North German Union in 1868, Belgium in 1868, Norway and Sweden in 1869, Great Britain in 1870, Austro-Hungary in 1870, and Denmark in 1872. Richard W. Flournoy, Jr. and Manley O. Hudson, eds., A Collection of Nationality Laws of Various Countries as Contained in Constitutions, Statutes and Treaties (New York, 1929), pp. 660-73.

to give passports to American Jews unless they first received the necessary visas from the Russians.[1] Marshall and other Jewish leaders were outraged by the announcement and in February, 1908 prevailed upon Root to withdraw his circular.

A few months later, the Roosevelt Administration expressed deep interest in negotiating a new understanding with the Russians, one which would recognize America's naturalization laws and would resolve the passport dispute. Both the Roosevelt and the succeeding Taft Administrations hoped that in time Russia would adopt a liberal attitude towards foreign and Russian Jews, but neither administration wanted to create a crisis with the Russians over the issue.

The AJC, for its part, was dissatisfied with the patient and flexible Russian policy of the two administrations. Instead, the AJC wanted the government to startle the Russians by abrogating the old Treaty and writing a new one, which would stipulate that the principle of religious equality would accompany the bearer of an American passport throughout the world, even in countries that practiced religious discrimination. According to the AJC leaders, something important would be gained from abrogation even if the

---

[1] *The American Jewish Yearbook* (Philadelphia, 1911), 5672, p. 23.

Russians refused to accede to American principles. Abrogation would embarrass the Russian government and censure its system of justice before the rest of the world. It also would demonstrate America's great moral strength and liberal principles.[1]

The AJC promoted abrogation for other reasons that were not publicized but were equally compelling.[2] For one, the AJC hoped to break the Pale and to end the misery of Russian Jewry. This could be done, the AJC assumed, because abrogation would change the policies of European countries which hitherto had completely accepted Russian discrimination against their Jewish populations. The United States was not part of the European alliance system in which Russia loomed so large; therefore, American Jews, unlike European Jews, could freely condemn Russia without infringing on any obvious national interests. The AJC expected that ultimately European nations would join the United States in the diplomatic effort to press Russia to allow foreign Jews to travel freely. Schiff told the AJC executive committee in May, 1910

---

[1] Reznikoff, op. cit., I, 88-89.

[2] For a detailed study of the abrogation fight see Naomi Wiener Cohen, "Abrogation of the Russo-American Treaty of 1832," Jewish Social Studies, XXV (Jan., 1963), 3-41.

that it should not enlist the aid of French and German Jews since they are "differently situated with regard to the manner in which they may approach their governments." Schiff went on to say that "those other governments will be compelled to respond to public opinion" after the United States abrogates its treaty with Russia.[1]

When both American and European Jews could travel in Russia, the AJC argument continued, their freedom of movement would liberate the Pale. Schiff explained to the executive committee in February, 1910 that "when Russia is compelled to admit foreign Jews into the country it will have to open the Pale."[2] He made the same point to Adolph S. Ochs, publisher of the New York Times, when he wrote that breaking the Pale was the heart of the passport matter: "You see, it is a large question, involving the most sacred of human rights, in the solution of which the United States should be only too eager and proud to take the first leading step."[3] Mayer Sulzberger held the same view, stating that Russia thought it ridiculous that the United States "should bother itself about Jews." The AJC's objective, according

---

[1] Minutes, AJC, May 29, 1910.

[2] Ibid., Feb. 20, 1910.

[3] Schiff, op. cit., II, 152.

to Sulzberger, was to force the United States to recognize the rights of its Jews which "would have some effects on the conditions of Russian Jews."[1]

Another important but obscure aim of the abrogation campaign was to redress an American grievance and to assert the power of American Jewry. In a period of religious liberalism and rising expectations for American Jews, the AJC claimed rights for Jews enjoyed by other Americans. As far as Jews were concerned, the passport matter reduced them to "second-class citizens."[2] This situation was humiliating and intolerable to the newly organized and highly articulate AJC leadership that wanted to prove its political power and importance to the Taft Administration and to the masses of Russian-Jewish immigrants in America.

This impatient assertive attitude in regard to the passport dispute was something new. Several years before, Marshall berated a journalist (writing in Yiddish) who had criticized President Roosevelt for failing to protect American Jews from Russia's discriminatory practices. Referring to the fact that the American-Jewish population was but a

---

[1] Minutes, AJC, Apr. 23, 1911.

[2] Schiff to Charles P. Bloom, June 22, 1916, in Schiff Papers.

small one, Marshall denied the right of the Jews to call upon the United States government to intervene in Russian problems. Marshall maintained that if the United States attacked other nations because of their domestic policies, then other nations would feel free to question this country's "treatment of the Negroes, the Chinese and Indians. . . ." Thus Marshall wrote that the "article has the vicious tendency of promoting discontent against the government with regard to a subject as to which the government is practically powerless to act."[1]

Now, in 1910, the AJC gave voice to a strong feeling of indignation about the Administration's immigration policies that were obstructing the Galveston project, and about Taft's friendly attitude towards the Russians. Jewish leaders offered discreet objections to Taft about Russian-American relations, but Taft maintained the traditional policy. In fact, despite inaction on the passport matter, the United States ratified a commercial agreement with Russia in 1909; it also granted minimum tariff rates to Russia under provision of the Payne-Aldrich Tariff Act of 1910.

Frustrated and angered by the failure of American Jews to influence Taft, Schiff told the AJC executive

---

[1] Dawidowicz, op. cit., p. 129.

committee in February, 1910 that Russian-born Jews in the United States would "revolt" if Taft did not force Russia to change her passport policy. The Jews were "licking the hands of the President." Any other group of citizens of equal size would have forced recognition of their demand but the problem with the Jews, Schiff said, was that they did not have enough self-respect. Finally, he predicted that the Jews would vote in a bloc in 1912 for the party that supported abrogation and that the vote would determine the outcome of the election.[1] Herbert Friedenwald shared the same burning resentment: "We have been played with for two years, and if we do not call a halt, I see no evidence that we will not be played with for as many years more."[2]

For the AJC the passport issue was of critical importance, but for Taft it was just another headache, and not a high priority matter, similar to such issues as Canadian reciprocity, dollar diplomacy in China and Latin America, and the arbitration treaties with England and France. Taft did, however, express sympathy for the Jewish cause when he gave a campaign pledge to a Brooklyn audience in October,

---

[1] Minutes, AJC, Feb. 20, 1910.

[2] Friedenwald to Mayer Sulzberger, Mar. 31, 1910, in Adler Papers.

1908 that he would try to "devise ways and means to make the American passport respected the world over."[1] Once in office, however, Taft and his Secretary of State Philander C. Knox decided to give Russia time to develop a less discriminatory policy toward Russian and American Jews. Caught between the pressure of the AJC leaders, with whom he conferred on several occasions, and the State Department, from whom he received his information about the Russian situation, Taft slowly evolved an anti-abrogation position between 1908 and 1910.

In June, 1909 Taft appointed William Rockhill, the American Ambassador to China and former Assistant Secretary of State, as American Ambassador to Russia. The State Department instructed Rockhill to report on Russia's disposition towards satisfying the demands of the American-Jewish community. Several months after his arrival in St. Petersburg, Rockhill presented a long memorandum on the Jewish question in which he concluded that the Russian government would not grant civil rights to the Jews. In fact, Russian officials refused to discuss the Jewish problem with Rockhill. He predicted, nonetheless, that future discussions between the United States and Russia might persuade the Russians to

---

[1] Reznikoff, op. cit., I, 66.

end the practice of asking the religious identity of each visa applicant.

Rockhill also reported that he had asked the German, French, and British Ambassadors to Russia whether they would formally object to Russia's policy of excluding European Jews from visiting Russia. All three Ambassadors concluded that any attempt to change the Russian policy would be fruitless and potentially upsetting to their respective countries. It was clear to Rockhill then that the United States government would get no support from European friends on the passport matter.[1]

In January, 1910 the AJC started applying pressure on Taft directly through Harry Cutler, a friend of Taft's, a member of the Rhode Island legislature, and an AJC member. At a meeting with the President, Cutler said that he had introduced a resolution calling for the equal treatment of American citizens in Russia. Taft, after hearing the resolution, maintained that it was drawn from the 1908 Republican party platform which Taft said he had written himself. After the discussion, Cutler reported to the AJC executive committee that Taft was working hard to settle the dispute, but Schiff and Cyrus Adler were far from satisfied with the

---

[1] Rockhill to Knox, Apr. 20, 1910, in Knox Papers, Box 41.

President's attitude. The discussion between Cutler, Schiff, and Adler now turned to a series of articles soon to be published in the conservative and Orthodox Jewish Daily News on the passport issue. Aided by Cutler's advice, Taft proposed to state his position on the matter; however, Schiff was eager to meet with Taft before the President published his views.

Soon after, Schiff and Mayer Sulzberger conferred with Taft on another matter, and in the course of the meeting touched briefly on the dispute. This discussion led to a conference in May, 1910 when Taft, Knox, Schiff, Sulzberger, and Adler talked at length about the passport matter. Basing his opinions and information upon the Rockhill memorandum, Taft explained that the Russian government regarded its passport regulations as an internal matter, and the AJC's anti-Russian campaign as an attempt to destroy the Pale--thinly disguised by the AJC's public rhetoric that spoke only of treaty obligations and religious equality in the United States. Taft informed his Jewish listeners that he disapproved of any attempt to interfere in Russia's internal affairs, especially when massacres might result. Although he was pessimistic about changing Russia's attitude, particularly since the United States would be acting alone, and he was wary of the AJC's objectives, Taft promised that the

State Department would make a complete study of the matter in the near future.[1]

Over the next few months Schiff continued to prod the President. When Taft congratulated the 2nd Session of the 61st Congress upon its adjournment in June, 1910 for fulfilling many Republican pledges made in the 1908 platform, Schiff sent a telegram to Taft commending the party too, but also reminding him that the passport dispute was still unresolved. Schiff, however, received no reply to his message. Two months later Benjamin S. Cable started his campaign, in Schiff's words, to "break up" the Galveston project.

Schiff immediately wrote Charles Norton, the President's secretary, to complain about Cable's unfriendly actions as well as to mention "another grievance," the passport dispute about which Taft and the Administration had been silent since May. Schiff predicted that if Taft did not resolve the dispute in a favorable manner, the President might lose the "goodwill of that section of the people for whom Mr. Schiff ventured to speak." Norton showed Schiff's letter to the President who decided to raise the matter at his next Cabinet meeting.[2]

---

[1] Minutes, AJC, May 29, 1910.

[2] Ibid., Sept. 26, 1910.

It was not until December, however, that Knox complied with Taft's May request and presented a fifty-four page memorandum on the dispute. Knox, who worked closely and harmoniously with the President, decisively influenced Taft with this anti-abrogation paper. Knox maintained that abrogation would have a pernicious effect on Russian Jewry and would lead to unsettled diplomatic and economic relations between the United States and Russia. His most important argument, however, was predicated upon America's immigration policies; he insisted that the United States could not punish Russia for refusing to accept American-Jewish visitors when the United States practiced such restrictions against the Chinese and Japanese. Knox concluded, in the strongest terms, that abrogation would damage the pending negotiations between the United States and Japan over renewing the bilateral treaty of 1894. According to him, abrogation would place the United States in a "morally indefensible position" with respect to the restriction of Asian immigrants.[1]

It is ironic that the State Department opposed abrogation mainly because it seemed to threaten America's restrictive immigration laws and practices. For the AJC, on its part, pressed the passport issue primarily to improve the

---

[1] Knox to Taft, Dec. 14, 1910, in SDF, 711.612/18.

condition of Russian Jewry and thereby relieve the pressure of Russian-Jewish immigration. Naturally, the AJC conceded the right of the United States to restrict immigration, but it argued that the passport issue raised the question of restricting temporary sojourners and not that of restricting immigration. By the end of 1910 Taft, the State Department, and the AJC were unwilling to make fine distinctions; by this time, they were not even arguing from the same reference points. Distinctions were ignored because a basic issue was at stake: should the United States promote friendly or hostile relations with Russia. Taft and the State Department recoiled from the unsettling effects of the abrogation fight, wanting to avoid a crisis in Russian-American relations. The AJC, for its part, resented the patient, compliant attitude of the Administration in regard to Russia's discrimination against American and Russian Jewry.

Frustration and desperation about the issue itself drove the leaders of the AJC to oppose Taft and the Treaty. In fact, the Jewish leaders were so convinced that abrogation was the right solution for the Russian problem that they were willing to risk temporarily making life more difficult for Russian Jews. Marshall told Simon Wolf that conditions could not get worse for the Jews in Russia and therefore he did not fear reprisals: "If there are to be more martyrs--harsh as it may seem to say so--the eventual result will be a triumph for humanity. The blood of the martyrs is not only the seed of the Church. Through it Judaism has been preserved through the ages."[1]

Now, with grand objectives and strong emotions, the leaders of the AJC discarded their hitherto quiet method of pressure politics. They deemed it ineffective and inappropriate for the abrogation campaign. Frustrated by their own impotence, they overestimated their lobbying skills in the recent literacy test fight, as Marshall made clear in a letter to Schiff in December, 1910:

> We have during the entire existence of the American Jewish Committee pursued the policy of silence with regard to the passport question. We can point to no triumphs as a result of this policy. In dealing with the immigration question we have pursued the contrary policy, and although conditions are not as satisfactory as we should like to see them, we have certainly during the last four years practically prevented restrictive legislation.[2]

Marshall greatly exaggerated the AJC's role in the literacy test fight to justify a new type of pressure politics through which American Jews would appeal to Congress and the public to oppose President Taft.

---

[1] Marshall to Simon Wolf, July 20, 1911, in Marshall Papers, AJA.

[2] Reznikoff, op. cit., I, 58.

II

In January, 1911 the AJC abandoned the traditional American-Jewish policy of discreet, private negotiations with the executive branch and appealed to Congressmen and other politicians for help in the abrogation campaign. The AJC needed prominent politicians to give the passport issue legitimacy, importance, and publicity, and so to convert an ethnic grievance into a public issue. Since Taft would not abrogate the Treaty on his own, the AJC turned to Congress to precipitate a crisis over the passport dispute and to force the President to act against his will.

Although Marshall and Schiff were Republicans, generous and interested in party causes, they too lashed out at Taft at a time when much of the American political community was criticizing him with abandon. In fact, the President's general difficulties gave the AJC the opportunity to ignite the abrogation controversy. Taft, as President, was a lonely, slow-working, and indecisive man who experienced, according to William Manners, one of his biographers, "general discomfort in the Presidency."[1] He sustained a personal blow when his wife suffered a stroke in May, 1909 which affected her speech and ability to walk; he was ravaged by controversies

---

[1] William Manners, TR and Will: A Friendship that Split the Republican Party (New York, 1969), p. 185.

such as the Ballinger-Pinchot affair and by disputes with his mentor Roosevelt and crucial segments of his own party. Roosevelt's biographer Edward Wagenknecht has best described Taft's situation in the White House: he "was not a bad President, he was a marvelously inept one. He had never really wanted the office and he never learned how to play the political game."[1]

Furthermore, Taft's own secretary Charles Norton, no longer in the President's favor because of the Roosevelt split, provided the AJC with the specific justification for starting its public campaign against the Treaty. Marshall decided to present the issue to the public only after Schiff learned from Norton that publicizing the AJC's point of view would help the President to make up his mind as to what to do.[2] It is certain, however, that the response would have been different had Schiff asked anyone else who was close to Taft and who was familiar with Taft's and the State Department's views on abrogation. Norton, a former Assistant Secretary of the Treasury, knew very little about the issue. He was primarily interested in the dispute between Taft and

---

[1] Wagenknecht, op. cit., p. 138.

[2] Reznikoff, op. cit., I, 59.

Roosevelt. In fact, at the time that Schiff spoke with him he was already looking for another job since he had made too many enemies to suit Taft.[1] Therefore, Norton probably cared little about the passport matter and probably never thought that the issue could embarrass the President.

Despite his ignorance and lack of forethought, Norton gave the AJC the signal to begin the fight. The public campaign to force the President to terminate the Treaty officially began on January 19, 1911 in New York City. On that day Marshall explained the reasons for the fight to representatives of the Union of American Hebrew Congregations in a speech which established the patriotic, even chauvinistic tone for the public fight. Marshall argued for such lofty American ideals as the "national sense of honor" and the "right of citizenship." He deplored the fact that the Russian government dishonored and rejected the American passport when an American Jew sought entry to Russia. He recalled that despite the objections of Presidents and Secretaries of State the Russians refused and would continue to refuse to abide by the Treaty. Finally, and most incisively, Marshall raised the Progressive banner against the sanctity of trade, finance, and dollar diplomacy. In pursuing abrogation, Marshall said, America should be willing to jeopardize

---

[1] Manners, op. cit., pp. 183-85.

the millions of American dollars invested in Russian trade and industry. End the Treaty "rather than have it said that our country rates the dollar higher than it does the man, that it esteems the volume of its trade more than its national dignity."[1]

Soon after Marshall made this indirect attack on Taft, the President accepted the AJC's challenge. He was beginning to feel uncomfortable because of Congressional pressure--pressure which Marshall was counting upon to break Taft's resistance. Representative Herbert Parsons, a Republican from New York City, had introduced an abrogation resolution in the House in February and twice met with Taft to promote the issue. Parsons, after one meeting with Taft, Knox, and five other members of the Cabinet, reported to Marshall that they all "seemed to think that Russia would do nothing if the Treaty was terminated."[2]

Taft did not suffer alone in his discomfort as the Parsons resolution greatly upset Rockhill, who was in St. Petersburg. The Ambassador wrote Taft several times, arguing that abrogation would jeopardize American investments in

---

[1] Reznikoff, op. cit., I, 59-71.

[2] Herbert Parsons to Marshall, Feb. 4, 1911; Parsons to Marshall, Jan. 27, 1911, in Marshall Papers, AJA.

Russia, that it would conflict with American interests in northern China by driving Japan and Russia closer together, and that it would aid Germany and hurt America's European friends, France and Russia.[1]

Therefore, on February 15, Taft invited several Jewish leaders, among them Schiff, Marshall, Democratic Congressman Henry M. Goldfogle of New York, and representatives of B'nai B'rith and the Union of American Hebrew Congregations to meet in his office. Taft explained that he would gladly terminate the Treaty and sacrifice the security of American investments in Russia that Rockhill estimated to be worth over $100 million, if abrogation would improve the Russian-Jewish situation. But abrogation, Taft insisted, "would accomplish nothing at all." He conceded that the controversy raised questions about the ability of the United States to offer equal protection to its citizens, but, he added, "ultimately as Russia grows better we shall secure recognition of the right. . . ."[2]

Charles Nagel, Taft's Secretary of Commerce and Labor, was the only Cabinet member present at the meeting. (Norton was there too.) Taft might have used Nagel's

---

[1] Rockhill to Knox, Jan. 21, 1911, in SDF 711.612/21.
[2] Reznikoff, op. cit., I, 79-87.

presence to emphasize that the passport controversy raised serious questions concerning America's immigration policies as far as Taft was concerned. "How much would this affect the real, that is, the great question," Taft said as he discussed the meaning of abrogation. "How much would this affect the Russian Jews who are coming to this country . . . and whom I am glad to welcome?" He answered his own question by predicting that abrogation would greatly antagonize the Russians and "change the normal flow" of immigration from Russia to the United States. Taft reaffirmed his liberal attitude towards Jewish immigrants by referring to the Galveston dispute and his earlier intervention aimed at allowing Jewish immigrants to disperse to western states. Finally, Taft said that he understood why the Jews, with a "justifiable pride of race," felt the "sense of outrageous injustice." Nevertheless, he concluded that he could not pursue a policy that would sacrifice larger American interests to satisfy the demands of an ethnic minority.[1]

Withdrawing from Taft's presence to confer together, the Jewish leaders expressed their disappointment and anger at Taft's wait-and-see attitude. When they returned to Taft, Schiff and Marshall spoke for the entire group. Schiff said

---

[1] Ibid.

that Russia's policy was a blow to America's honor; Marshall coolly and directly accused the President of placing commercial considerations above national pride and dividing American citizens into classes, some of whom were denied rights because of their religious identity. Taft then offered to make a public statement saying that the matter was still under consideration by the Administration, but Marshall and Schiff insisted that Taft take the same stand in public as he took with them in private.[1]

"This means war," the "indignant" Schiff said after the meeting, and he proceeded to pledge $25,000 to carry on the public campaign for abrogation.[2] Marshall remarked about Schiff's excited state: "I never knew Mr. Schiff to be so much worked up over anything."[3] A few days later Schiff wrote Taft to express once more his disappointment and dismay at the President's position and the "continuous insult" which the American people were subject to because of Russia's policy. He assured Taft that American public opinion would eventually force the government to "resent" Russia's position.[4]

---

[1] Minutes, AJC, Feb. 19, 1911.
[2] Reznikoff, op. cit., I, 79-87.
[3] Minutes, AJC, Feb. 19, 1911.
[4] Schiff, op. cit., II, 148.

After the battle lines were drawn between Taft and
the Jewish leaders, the AJC threw out the abrogation issue
to Taft's many political adversaries in Congress and without,
taking advantage of his dwindling popularity and support.
The President was already under attack by Roosevelt's supporters and the Democrats. Furthermore, the insurgents opposed him for his role in the fight against Speaker Cannon,
his support of the Payne-Aldrich tariff legislation, and his
patronage and campaign policies which he directed, somewhat
unsuccessfully, against them. In fact, in January, 1911
eight Republican Senators, six Governors, and many Congressmen formed the Progressive Republican League to oust Taft
from the leadership of the party. The Democrats, for their
part, took control of the House by a margin of over fifty
seats and gained eight Senate seats in the 1910 elections;
already they smelled the scent of a Presidential victory
in 1912.

In this unsettled political climate, the AJC skillfully sought out and rewarded politicians who needed the
Jewish vote in the 1911 and 1912 elections. The chief
figures in this group were Governor Woodrow Wilson of New
Jersey, William Gibbs McAdoo, Champ Clark of Missouri,
Speaker of the Democratic House, Representatives William
Sulzer and Francis Burton Harrison, Democrats from New York,

and Representative Herbert Parsons. These politicians recognized that abrogation provided a good foreign policy issue with which to build support among an important ethnic minority, as well as another issue, in addition to Canadian reciprocity, the arbitration pacts, and the Japanese negotiations, with which to trouble Taft.

These men endorsed the AJC campaign, spoke at abrogation rallies, corresponded with AJC leaders about strategy, and introduced abrogation resolutions in Congress. For his part, Marshall made clear that the Jewish voters would reward the party and politicians promoting abrogation. For example, Marshall wrote Parsons, who was running for re-election in New York City in 1911, that "I can assure you that when the time comes to afford practical evidence of my appreciation and that of my friends of your action, we will not be found wanting." Marshall had previously offered to print and distribute, at AJC expense, thousands of copies of one of Parsons' speeches favoring abrogation.[1]

For the Democrats, abrogation was a fine way to embarrass and undermine the President. Marshall was delighted to let them fight the President, but he was eager to avoid

---

[1] Marshall to Parsons, Apr. 21, 1911; Marshall to Parsons, Feb. 27, 1911, in Marshall Papers, AJA. Despite Marshall's good intentions, Parsons was defeated the same year.

associating the AJC with an attack on Taft, "a very obstinate man" who would "be more apt to become actively hostile, if he feels that we are attacking him, than he would otherwise be." Marshall described Taft as inactive and passive on the issue, "but he might if irritated exercise his great power with deadly force."[1]

The AJC did not welcome all of the political support that came its way, especially when it derived from the controversy between Taft and Roosevelt. In an article in Outlook, Roosevelt expressed his support for the abrogation campaign and agreed that the United States should not allow Russia to continue to violate the Treaty. Still, Roosevelt did not recommend abrogation, suggesting instead that the United States bring the passport dispute before the Hague International Tribunal.[2]

Roosevelt was not the first politician to propose the idea, for Taft had supported it in the summer of 1911. At that time Marshall strongly opposed it and now in the fall he regarded it as a diversionary tactic, one that could

---

[1] Marshall to Friedenwald, July 11, 1911, in Marshall Papers (American Jewish Committee, New York). Cited hereafter as Marshall Papers, AJC.

[2] Theodore Roosevelt, "A Proper Case for Arbitration," The Outlook, XCIX (Oct. 14, 1911), 365-66.

easily destroy the momentum for abrogation that was building up in Congress.[1] From Taft's point of view, Roosevelt's suggestion was particularly disturbing because Taft was certain that Roosevelt would soon begin a public fight to regain the leadership of the Republican party. The arbitration proposal was galling because Roosevelt strongly opposed the arbitration pacts with England and France which Taft was deeply committed to passing. (He even hoped to write an arbitration treaty with Russia.)[2] Much to Taft's dismay, his and Roosevelt's basic positions on arbitration were reversed: Taft, who strongly favored arbitration, was against employing it to settle the passport dispute; Roosevelt, who was vehemently opposed to the French and English pacts, promoted arbitration in this one instance.

Marshall directed the AJC in a skillful, uncompromising campaign to spread the abrogation message to politicians on the state and national levels. With a budget set at $25,000, the AJC worked openly and unabashedly to convince Congress and the public that the passport issue involved

---

[1] Marshall to Schiff, Oct. 17, 1911, in Marshall Papers, AJA.

[2] Taft to Curtis Guild, Aug. 10, 1911, in William Howard Taft Papers (Library of Congress, Washington, D.C.), Series III, File 47. Cited hereafter as Taft Papers.

national rights and power, in which the Jews just happened to be the catalyst. A series of anti-Russian, pro-abrogation articles for newspapers and magazines throughout the country was prepared. The AJC even accused the Associated Press of biased, unreliable, and anti-Semitic attitudes on the Russian-Jewish problem. In this connection, AJC leaders spoke privately with important members of the Associated Press and aided the inquiry of Oswald Garrison Villard by producing evidence of biased reporting. Although Villard agreed with the AJC charges, the Associated Press did not change its methods.[1]

The AJC also sent 35,000 copies of Marshall's January speech to the "creators and leaders of public opinion in every part of the country," to all newspapers with a circulation of over 2,200, to newspapers in home towns of federal judges, Democratic and Republican national committeemen, district attorneys, and Congressmen.[2] Around Thanksgiving time, the AJC wrote 50,000 ministers throughout the country, suggesting that they make the passport dispute the subject of their sermons. There was an attempt to get the Catholic

___

[1] Cohen, "Abrogation of the Russo-American Treaty of 1832," pp. 25-26.

[2] Ibid., p. 21.

Church behind the abrogation effort when A. Leo Weil spoke with Bishop J. F. Regis Canevin of Pittsburgh. The Bishop acknowledged that Catholic priests were excluded from Russia but he took the position, according to the minutes of the AJC's executive committee, that "the Church as such would not move on the matter."[1]

Jewish organizations and individuals prevailed upon fraternal organizations, unions, and state legislatures to pass abrogation resolutions. V. H. Kriegshaber of Atlanta was active in influencing the Georgia legislature to pass its resolution; Rabbi Abelson of Helene had similar results in Montana, as did other Jews in Illinois, Florida, Nevada, New York, and Washington.[2] Marshall, Schiff, Mayer Sulzberger, Harry Cutler, and Straus presented lengthy testimony before several House and Senate hearings which considered abrogation resolutions. (Their arguments were all the more impressive because no one ever testified against them.)

Finally, in December, 1911 the AJC staged an enormous abrogation rally in New York City which featured the appearance of two Presidential hopefuls, Woodrow Wilson and

---

[1] Minutes, AJC, Mar. 19, 1911.

[2] V. H. Kriegshaber to Marshall, Aug. 19, 1911, in Marshall Papers, AJC; Minutes, AJC, Apr. 23, 1911.

Champ Clark, Senators Boies Penrose of Pennsylvania and James O'Gorman of New York, William McAdoo, William Randolph Hearst, Andrew Dickson White, former Ambassador to Russia, and several Congressmen. McAdoo was the key man for the AJC in organizing the rally as it counted upon him to keep all the speakers in line, that is, for abrogation and against arbitration.[1]

All of the AJC's public efforts were aimed at persuading Congress to pass a joint resolution directing the President to terminate the Treaty. Attempts were made to get Oscar Underwood of Alabama, one of the two most powerful Democrats in the House, to support abrogation and, to this end, the AJC contacted friends in his district and concentrated on publicizing the issue at home. Felix Barth of Fort Worth met with Senator Charles Allen Culberson of Texas; Senator William J. Stone of Missouri suggested that the best way to interest Wisconsin Senator Robert M. LaFollette would be to organize a delegation of interested Wisconsin constituents who would speak with the Senator in Washington. Morris M. Cohen and Charles Jacobson of Little Rock, Arkansas tried

---

[1] Friedenwald to Marshall, Nov. 14, 1911, in Marshall Papers, AJC. McAdoo also offered to distribute 50,000 copies of a piece of abrogation literature. Marshall to Friedenwald, Dec. 1911, in Marshall Papers, AJC.

to influence Senators Augustus Bacon of Georgia and Jeff Davis of Arkansas. Marshall sought unsuccessfully to persuade Maryland Senator Isidor Raynor to take a seat on the Senate Foreign Relations Committee to press abrogation, but Raynor was not interested in obliging Marshall. The AJC also organized a large New York delegation to visit Senators O'Gorman and Elihu Root to get their firm support for abrogation. O'Gorman strongly supported the AJC, but Root equivocated; the AJC then printed and distributed 50,000 copies of their two replies.[1]

Because of all these efforts, the AJC made many abrogation friends in Congress, but among them William Sulzer was the most important. Sulzer, the chairman of the House Committee on Foreign Affairs, was well situated to push a joint resolution through the House, to the Senate and to the President Sulzer's intention to force Taft to change his policy was never in doubt: "I am going to abrogate the treaty," he wrote Marshall, "or Russia must recognize all American citizens without regard to race or religion."[2]

---

[1] Adler to Friedenwald, July 28, 1911; Friedenwald to Mayer Sulzberger, May 29, 1911; Adler to Friedenwald, Nov. 14, 1911; Friedenwald to Marshall, Nov. 15, 1911, in Adler Papers; Marshall to Friedenwald, Mar. 25, 1911, in Marshall Papers, AJC.

[2] Sulzer to Marshall, June 2, 1911, in Marshall Papers, AJC.

Marshall himself worked closely with Sulzer on his resolution.

Sulzer's interest in the issue and his strong support for the AJC stemmed in large part from the fact that he was an ambitious, aggressive politician who was not satisfied with staying in the House year after year. He had been there since 1895, and from 1898 to 1910 he had actively tried to obtain the Democratic nomination for Governor, an honor which Tammany Hall would not give him. In 1911 Sulzer was a Protestant Congressman in need of Jewish support to promote his candidacy for Governor and he desperately wanted an issue that would endear him to Jewish interests. Abrogation suited his needs perfectly. With the approval of Champ Clark and Oscar Underwood, who both had Presidential aspirations, Sulzer could easily promote his abrogation resolution. It was a safe issue since Taft and Knox, who had few allies in the Democratic House, were the only prominent figures who would oppose Sulzer.

Later, Sulzer would be rewarded by Tammany Hall, the leaders of the AJC, and New York's Jewish voters who helped to make him Governor. The abrogation fight made him immensely popular among the Jews and convinced Tammany Hall to give him the gubernatorial nomination in 1912 as the only one who could defeat the Progressive candidate, Oscar S. Straus. Sulzer's campaign slogan, "non-Jewish but pro-Jewish," incensed a few Jews but appealed to most.[1] Schiff defended Sulzer's campaign which emphasized his aid to the Jews, publicly endorsed him over Straus, and contributed $2,500 to the effort. (Before this endorsement Schiff had given Straus $1,000 which Straus later returned to him.)[2] Marshall, despite remaining a faithful Republican, spoke warmly of Sulzer throughout the campaign; later, in October, 1913, Marshall greatly aided Sulzer by representing the Governor during his impeachment proceedings.

III

Now in December, 1911 Sulzer brought the abrogation issue to a climax during the 2nd Session of the 62nd Congress. He seized the initiative by introducing a strongly worded joint resolution which called upon the President to terminate the Treaty--"the President is hereby charged with the duty of communicating such notice"--and also condemned the Russians for violating it. Senator Charles Allen Culberson of Texas introduced the identical resolution in the Senate

---

[1] Jacob Alexis Friedman, *The Impeachment of Governor William Sulzer* (New York, 1939), p. 27. The AJC executive committee even discussed spending $2,000 for a portrait of Sulzer which would then be given to him as a gift for his efforts on behalf of the AJC. Minutes, AJC, May 12, 1912.

[2] Cohen, *A Dual Heritage*, p. 219.

on December 5, which stated, in part:

> That the people of the United States assert as a fundamental principle that the rights of its citizens shall not be impaired at home or abroad because of race or religion; that the Government of the United States concludes its treaties for the equal protection of all classes of its citizens, without regard to race or religion; that the Government of the United States will not be a party to any treaty which discriminates, or which by one of the parties thereto is so construed as to discriminate, between American citizens on the ground of race or religion; that the Government of Russia has violated the treaty between the United States and Russia . . . refusing to honor American passports duly issued to American citizens, on account of race and religion. . . .[1]

As Taft watched Sulzer gain support in the House, he labored to keep some control over the abrogation issue. To this end, Taft announced in his message to Congress on foreign affairs on December 7, that Russia and the United States were seriously negotiating over their differences on the passport matter. Taft based his statement on a report from Curtis Guild, formerly Governor of Massachusetts and now Rockhill's replacement in St. Petersburg, that the Russian government would allow American-born Jews to have visas for commercial visits.[2]

---

[1] U.S., *Congressional Record*, 62d Cong., 2d sess., 1911, XLVIII, Part 1, 311.

[2] Taft to Otto Bannard, Nov. 13, 1911, in Taft Papers, Series VIII.

Both Taft and Knox were still strongly opposed to abrogation, believing that it would severely strain Russian-American relations and jeopardize America's restrictive immigration policies. "To no country in the world is this right of exclusion of more vital importance than to the United States; and no country has adopted . . . a policy more rigorous and far-reaching than our own," Knox informed Taft on November 28. Objecting strongly to the Sulzer resolution, he told Taft that ending "normal relations" with Russia because she excluded American Jews for the sake of her domestic policy would "stultify our traditional policy in the matter of immigration."[1]

Furthermore, Taft deeply resented the pressure that the AJC leaders were exerting. Writing to Otto Bannard, the Republican candidate for Mayor of New York City in 1909, Taft expressed his dismay about the controversy: "The trouble about this business is they [the Jews] have so much politics in it, and Jake Schiff and others are determined to use the political club, that I presume they will succeed in getting our country into a condition where the Jews will not be helped but where we shall be in an unpleasant situation."[2]

---

[1] Knox to Taft, Nov. 28, 1911, in SDF 711.612/61Gb.
[2] Taft to Bannard, loc. cit.

Taft felt trapped between a slow-moving and autocratic European power, supported by all other European powers on the passport dispute, and the American Jews, whom he called "an imperious crowd threatening 200,000 votes." Taft wrote Bannard that he would try to persuade Russia to change her interpretation of the Treaty, but that he really expected that abrogation would be forced upon him.[1]

In a letter to his brother Horace, Taft explained that Russia would start granting visas to American-born Jews to travel in Russia for commercial purposes, but not to naturalized Americans of Russian-Jewish origin. As far as Taft was concerned, the Russians would finally start to comply with their treaty obligations with this concession. Still, they refused to allow American Jews to travel freely throughout Russia, for fear that a reversal of this policy would necessarily apply to European as well as to American Jews. Taft concluded that there were "nice distinctions" in the dispute "all of which I think will be overlooked in the indignation of the Jews at Russia, and under the influence of the political power that they exercise in New York City and elsewhere throughout the country."[2]

---

[1] Ibid.

[2] Taft to Horace Taft, Nov. 25, 1911, in Taft Papers, Series VIII.

Taft was right to assume that the Russian concession concerning American-born Jews would not satisfy the AJC. It could never have ended the abrogation campaign because Russia decided to permit American-born Jews to visit Russia on a restricted basis. The AJC goal of establishing free travel throughout Russia as a means of breaking the Pale was too important to give up; furthermore, the proposed compromise would have meant political suicide for the AJC, since 75 percent of the American Jews were of Russian origin. Marshall feared that the AJC would be "hung in effigy" if it agreed to such an understanding with the Administration. "What account could we give to them [the Russian Jews] of our stewardship," Marshall asked, if the AJC accepted one set of regulations for the Russian Jews and another, more advantageous one for the American-born Jews.[1]

Although Taft asked Congress to withhold action on the Sulzer resolution until after the Christmas recess, the State Department in the first week in December decided to accept abrogation. Knox recognized that if Taft vetoed the resolution, Congress would simply repass it. Therefore, on December 6, Knox wrote the Russian Ambassador in Washington, Boris Bakhméteff, that the best way to avoid embarrassment

---

[1] Marshall to Julian Mack, Oct. 20, 1911, in Marshall Papers, AJA.

for both countries was to end the old Treaty and negotiate a new one.[1] Only seven days later, the House passed the Sulzer resolution by the resounding vote of 301 to 1, and the following day, the Senate agreed to consider the resolution no later than the 18th of December.

By this time it was clear to Taft that he should ask Congress to terminate the Treaty, not on Sulzer's terms but on his own. Taft wanted the official notice of abrogation to avoid any reference to Russia's internal affairs or to Russia's violations of the Treaty. Consequently, on December 18, the President told the Senate Foreign Relations Committee that he had informed Russia the previous day of the termination of the Treaty, to be effective on January 1, 1913. He told the Committee that termination was desirable because the Treaty was "no longer fully responsive in various respects to the needs of the political and material relations of the two countries, which grow constantly more important." The Treaty had "given rise from time to time to certain controversies equally regretted by both Governments," he added.[2]

---

[1] Knox to Boris Bakhmeteff, Dec. 6, 1911, in SDF 711.612a.

[2] U.S., *Congressional Record*, 62d Cong., 2d sess., 1911, XLVIII, Part 1, 453.

Three days before, Knox had instructed Guild to inform the Russian Foreign Minister Sergei Dimitrievich Sazonoff that the United States would terminate the Treaty. As soon as Guild received the news, he met with Sazonoff for what developed into a testy confrontation. Although Guild was strongly opposed to abrogation, he nevertheless declared that the Sulzer resolution represented a humanitarian concern for improving the conditions of Russian Jews by granting them freedom of movement. The House acted, Guild said, to stop Russia's discrimination against American and Russian Jews; "freedom of speech and freedom of movement," he advised, "appeared to be the best cure for treason and conspiracy by removing any possible grievance." But Sazonoff strongly disagreed, stating that Russia considered the Jews a menace and said, "seriously, that he was prepared to consider an arrangement by which the United States might cooperate for the transfer of all Jews from Russia to the United States."[1]

---

[1] Knox to Guild, Dec. 15, 1911, in SDF 711.612/62A; Guild to Knox, Dec. 16, 1911, in SDF 711.612/62. As an afterthought on the 15th Knox sent another telegram to Guild asking him to suggest that Russia and the United States agree that termination was mutually acceptable and that a new treaty would be negotiated soon. But Guild reported that the Russian government would not act under pressure, insisted that Russia had not violated the treaty, and would

Taft asked the Senate Committee to ratify his actions and to adopt his reasons for abrogation. But the Committee did not follow his specific request; instead, it maintained control over the issue, and assumed partial credit for abrogation, by amending the Sulzer resolution. Thus the new version declared that the Treaty was "no longer responsive in various respects to the political principles and commercial needs of the two countries . . . . the constructions placed thereon by the respective contracting parties differ upon matters of fundamental importance and interest to each."[1]

During the Senate debate on the Committee's new resolution, Elihu Root, Secretary of State under Roosevelt and now Senator from New York, spoke in support of abrogation. His arguments, designed to explain Taft's reasons for ending the Treaty, centered not on the passport dispute, which was the principal reason for the AJC's campaign, but on the

---

make no announcement on the subject. Knox to Guild, Dec. 15, 1911, in SDF 711.612/62a; Guild to Knox, Dec. 17, 1911, in SDF 711.612/64.

[1] U.S., Congressional Record, 62d Cong., 2d sess., 1911, XLVIII, Part 1, 453. The President had asked the Senate to ratify his actions but instead it used the joint resolution as its means of ratifying as well as giving Sulzer and the Congress credit for the victory. Laurence F. Schmeckebier and Roy B. Eastin, Government Publications and Their Uses (Washington, D.C., 1969), p. 475.

incompatibility of American and Russian emigration laws. According to Root, the United States was committed by law to the right of expatriation and could no longer live by the Treaty which obviated the principle. He urged the Senate to support the moderate reasoning and language of the Foreign Relations Committee's resolution and not Sulzer's wording which accused the Russians of violating the Treaty.[1]

The Senate followed Root's advice and defeated by a vote of 54 to 16 the move to substitute the Sulzer wording. On December 19, the Senate approved the President's action and the amended Sulzer resolution by a vote of 72 to 0. The following day, the House accepted the Senate version.

Following the House and Senate action, Knox informed Guild that the United States considered the abrogation controversy over--the "incident is closed." There would be no more discussion in St. Petersburg about abrogation because "the deliberations of the Congress are a domestic affair." Several weeks later, Knox wrote Guild that there would be no new treaty negotiations before Russia was ready to accept America's conditions relating to the "rights of access and sojourn of Jewish Americans or the status of naturalized

---

[1] The New York Times, Dec. 31, 1911, p. 2; U.S., Congressional Record, 62d Cong., 2d sess., 1911, XLVIII, Part 1, 482-83.

citizens of Russian origin."[1]

Naturally, Marshall, Schiff, and the AJC were elated by the abrogation victory and expected that negotiations would soon begin on a new treaty, which would affirm America's position on expatriation and free travel in Russia. Schiff called abrogation the greatest victory for the Jews since Napoleon granted them civil rights, because, as he would later explain, "we were unwilling to be differentiated against by our own government and treated as second-class citizens, and further because, as a humanitarian proposition, we hoped and believed that if the American government succeeded in removing the discrimination against foreign Jews at the Russian frontier, the pale of settlement against Russia's own Jews would, as a consequence, likewise have to go."[2]

---

[1] Knox to Guild, Dec. 22, 1911, in SDF 711.612/71; Knox to Guild, Feb. 6, 1912, in Knox Papers, Box 41. Guild suffered from an intense anti-American feeling that circulated in the Russian capital after abrogation. He wanted to appease the Russians by having the United States government admit that it had violated the Treaty too. Knox would not agree to that. Throughout 1912, Guild reported in detail on the anti-American and anti-Jewish sentiment which the Russian government encouraged in reaction to abrogation. Count Witte had a different view of the issue that he expressed in his Memoirs: "Our jingoists are naturally thundering against America. There is no doubt however, that we have driven the United States Government to this step." Sergei Witte, The Memoirs of Count Witte, trans. and ed. by Abraham Yarmolinsky (Garden City, N.Y., 1921), p. 385.

[2] Schiff to Charles P. Bloom, June 22, 1916, in Schiff Papers; Minutes, AJC, Dec. 25, 1911.

The leaders of the AJC thought that they had proved that they were a serious political force and had achieved the same rights that other Americans enjoyed. "Whatever Russia may eventually do is of little importance, compared to the fact that all civil disabilities have been removed from all holders of American citizenship," Marshall wrote. But in the euphoria of victory, Marshall and the others badly misunderstood the course of events and the reasons for their success. This attitude is evident as Marshall described the AJC's moment of glory: "the little snowball which began to roll from the mountain top, finally became a tremendous avalanche, which swept everything before it . . . the matter did not become one of partisan politics, but was disposed of on the ideal considerations of the integrity of American citizenship and of the equality of all of our citizens before the law."[1] Marshall seemed to have forgotten about Sulzer's ambitions, Taft's political vulnerability, the lure of the ethnic vote in the 1912 Presidential election., and the State Department's unwillingness to declare publicly its reasons, based upon immigration restriction, for opposing abrogation.

According to the AJC, its abrogation triumph

---

[1] Reznikoff, op. cit., p. 103.

indicated that American Jews had developed a powerful lobbying force in Washington. In fact, the victory actually meant that the AJC had employed skillful techniques and was extremely lucky in the timing of its abrogation campaign. For a little under $15,000, a "bargain," said Herbert Friedenwald, "for the results accomplished," the AJC made a public issue out of abrogation. The AJC itself spent $11,000 and its non-sectarian abrogation organization, the National Citizens Committee, spent another $3,380 for the propaganda effort which successfully appealed to American chauvinism and to an anti-business strain in Progressive America.[1] According to the AJC, the United States abrogated the Treaty because the government was committed to the goal of religious equality. In truth, however, victory came in Congress because it suited the needs of certain politicians and because, at the time, no one but Taft and the State Department cared about maintaining friendly relations with Russia.

The AJC also miscalculated the impact of abrogation on the Russian government. Despite the AJC's idealistic expectations, Russia and her European allies did not change their Jewish policies. Russia did not break the Pale or

---

[1] Friedenwald to Marshall, Dec. 22, 1911, in Marshall Papers, AJC.

improve the conditions of Russian Jewry; European countries refused to follow America's abrogation example; and the need for emigration on the part of Russian Jews remained as strong as ever. Abrogation did not bring the AJC any closer to resolving its primary source of concern--the Russian-Jewish immigration problem.

Soon after abrogation, in 1912 and 1913, the restrictionists waged another literacy test fight that presented a major threat to the interests of American Jewry. Ironically, the very success of the passport campaign made the AJC feel vulnerable before the American public. Therefore, the AJC refused to wage the same kind of public campaign against the literacy test that it had conducted in pursuit of abrogation. Although in 1910 and 1911 the AJC had expended an enormous effort, at Taft's expense, to terminate the Treaty, in 1912 the AJC suddenly needed his help. It quickly recognized that Taft was the only person capable of defeating the restrictionists in the second literacy test fight in the Progressive period.

CHAPTER IV

THE DEFIANT TAFT

In a climate of deep national concern about the social, economic, and political effects of the new immigrants, the AJC altered its lobbying techniques and objectives in the 1912-1913 literacy test fight. Afraid of appearing too prominent after its successful and highly publicized passport fight, the AJC sought to use other Jewish and non-Jewish anti-restrictionists as its spokesmen. Sensing even before the debates began in the House and Senate that it had little ability to prevent Congress from passing the test, the AJC now prepared for defeat by lobbying for a strongly worded exemption clause within the literacy test itself. Thus, the AJC narrowed its goals and concentrated on creating a loophole for its special constituency, the Russian-Jewish immigrants.

Both Congressional restrictionists and the AJC accepted the principle of an exemption clause, but they disagreed over its wording. Louis Marshall wanted the clause to exempt all illiterate Russian-Jewish immigrants, while the House and Senate restrictionists favored a token statement that would acknowledge America's tradition of accepting religious refugees, but would not nullify the purpose of the test--to reduce significantly the number of southern and eastern European immigrants.

In January, 1913, Congress actually passed a literacy test along with an exemption clause that greatly displeased the AJC. At that point, President Taft emerged as the only person who could prevent a complete restrictionist victory. Although Taft had refused to commit himself on the test throughout 1912, the AJC leaders pinned their hopes upon the President. Their hopes were in fact well placed because Taft decided, after great deliberation, to oppose the test and to defy Congress. Thus, the President took a position that relieved the AJC and infuriated the restrictionists; but this latest anti-restrictionist victory was one for which the Jewish lobbyists could claim no credit.

I.

"I thoroughly believe in legislation which will protect our country against immigration which would be injurious to it," Marshall wrote the arch-restrictionist Henry Cabot Lodge. However, Marshall added that he objected "to any general policy of restriction, because . . . it would be much more injurious to our country than the most liberal policy that could be imagined."[1] Unfortunately for Marshall, in 1912 and 1913, neither he nor the AJC as a whole could find a way to persuade Lodge and the majority of Congressmen to support the tradition of open immigration. The AJC could not prevent an upsurge of restrictionist sentiment that developed from the continuing high rate of immigration, national concern over labor unrest, the popular obsession with crime, and the conclusions reached in the Reports of the Immigration Commission.[2]

In 1912 and 1913, the supporters of the literacy test actively spread word of their concern over the number and character of the new immigration. Six million immigrants, mostly from eastern and southern Europe--of whom 667,528 were Jewish--poured into the United States from 1907 through 1913.[3] During the twelve-month period from June, 1912, through June, 1913 alone, 1,197,892 immigrants arrived in America. These people constituted the largest annual influx since 1906-1907--the year of the last literacy test fight.[4]

---

[1]Marshall to Henry Cabot Lodge, Jan. 26, 1912, in Marshall Papers, AJA.

[2]RIC, I-LXII.

[3]Anthony Caminetti, Annual Report of the Commissioner General of Immigration (Washington, D.C., 1914), p. 104.

[4]Ibid., p. 3.

The Jewish immigrants in 1912-1913 were similar to those who had arrived six years before, coming in large, poor, and frequently illiterate families. There were 101,330 Jewish immigrants of whom 57,148 were males and 44,182 females. Among the Jewish immigrants sixteen years and older, 16,662 were illiterate and 41,536 had $50 or less in their possession at the time of arrival. The southern Italians, for their part, accounted for 231,613 of the immigrants in 1912-1913; of them, 99,402 immigrants sixteen years and older were illiterate.[1]

These six million immigrants aggravated the anti-urban and nativist feelings that prevailed throughout the country. The accusations and complaints about the new immigrants often focused on specific problems, including that of industrial strife. As laborers struck for higher pay, better working conditions, and the acceptance of collective bargaining, the new immigrants played several roles and outraged many sides. When the immigrants acted as strike breakers they irritated native labor organizations. When the immigrants--predominately Slavs, Jews, and Italians--struck the textile industry in Lawrence, Massachusetts, in 1912 and the garment industry in New York City on several

---

[1] Ibid., p. 46.

occasions from 1909 through 1913, they alarmed the business community and the public.

The public and its politicians reacted fearfully to the frequent, intense, and disruptive labor disputes in this period. According to Philip Taft and Philip Ross, the labor historians, the years from 1911 to 1916 "rank among the most violent in American history, except for the Civil War," because of labor unrest. Furthermore, the strikes and disputes in those years "frequently attained a virulence seldom equaled in industrial warfare in any nation."[1]

Another specific evil that the public often attributed to the new immigrants was crime. The public feared that there was an increase in violent crimes, prostitution, and gambling in which the new immigrants were both the exploiters and the exploited. Although no historian or observer living in the Progressive period has proven that the number of crimes rose out of proportion to the increase in population, the public thought it had. Many social workers, journalists, and politicians posited a causal

---

[1] Philip Taft and Philip Ross, "American Labor Violence: Its Causes, Character and Outcome," in *Violence in America: Historical and Comparative Perspectives*, ed. by Hugh Davis Graham and Ted Robert Gurr (New York, 1969), p. 306.

connection between mental illness, poverty, and crime--and the new immigrants. The people concerned with these problems developed a new vocabulary to describe the criminals. According to Mark Haller, there was a "new type of social menace variously called the moral imbecile, psychopath, constitutional inferior, or (most commonly) defective delinquent."[1] Despite the lack of proof, the public believed that the mentally ill were subjecting society to a plague of violence and social and individual decay.[2]

Crime was an obsession of the period, both in urban and rural areas, with the latter regarding the cities as the major source of criminal behavior in the United States. The press, as usual, exploited the public's fascination with violence: national magazines included numerous articles tying immigrant Jews and Italians to the crime problem. In 1908, for example, the North American Review featured an article by New York City Police Commissioner Theodore Bingham

---

[1] Mark Haller, Eugenics: Hereditarian Attitudes in American Thought (New Brunswick, N.J., 1963), p. 104.

[2] Ibid., p. 80. The obsession with crime and inflammatory rhetoric are reminiscent of the 1960's and 1970's. Today, it is still not clear what the statistics and records indicate concerning a real increase in crime. What really matters is that the public is once again frightened and that it has attributed the cause of an intolerable crime wave to one identifiable group within the society.

in which he charged that the Jews committed 50 percent of all crimes in the city.[1]

In Congress itself the most important single justification for restriction derived from the recommendations of the Immigration Commission which issued its Reports in December, 1910. Authorized by the 1907 immigration law, the three-year study, which cost $1,000,000 to complete, provided Congress with a mandate for legislative action. The Reports consisted of forty-two volumes, the first two containing recommendations and conclusions based upon the vast body of factual information relating to the historic, economic, and social characteristics of the new immigrants. These two volumes received the most attention in Congress, but a limited coverage in the press. The forty background volumes, however, were ignored by everyone except a few immigration experts and politicians interested in the field.

The most important and publicized conclusion of the entire study appeared in the first summary volume where eight commissioners recommended adoption of the literary test. Actually, the nine commissioners--Senators Lodge,

---

[1] Theodore A. Bingham, "Foreign Criminals in New York," North American Review, CLXXXVII (Sept., 1908), 389-94. For a detailed discussion of the effect of the crime wave on the New York Jewish community, see Goren, op. cit., Chapters vii-viii.

Dillingham, and Le Roy Percy, Representatives Howell, Bennet, and John Burnett, and Presidential appointees Jeremiah Jenks, Charles P. Neill, and William Wheeler--concluded that the new immigrants presented an intolerable threat to the wages and working conditions of American labor. They maintained that the new immigrants flooded the market with cheap, unskilled labor that put the native labor force at a severe disadvantage. Concerned about America's "economic, moral, and social" development, eight commissioners--all except William Bennet--thought it advisable to adopt a literacy test and writing test as the "most feasible single method" of restricting immigration.[1]

Although the public and the press paid little attention to the Commission's research--as is the case with most Presidential and Congressional commissions--the Reports are a valuable key to the system of thought, attitudes, and prejudices of the restrictionist politicians and immigration experts. In the first place, the Reports divided the old and new immigrants into racial groups. The old immigrants from northern and western Europe had made up the overwhelming majority of immigrants before the 1880's: these were the Dutch, Flemish, English, German, Irish, Scandinavians, Scots,

---

[1] RIC, I, p. 48.

and Welsh. The new immigrants, predominantly from eastern and southern Europe, now greatly outnumbered those from northern and western Europe: these were the Armenians, Bohemians, Moravians, Bulgarians, Servians, Montenegrins, Croatians, Slovenians, Dalmatians, Bosnians, Herzegovianians, Finns, Greeks, Hebrews, northern Italians, southern Italians, Lithuanians, Poles, Portugese, Roumanians, Russians, Ruthenians, Slovaks, Spanish, Syrians, and Turks.[1]

Unfortunately, the commissioners analyzed the social and economic impact of the new immigrants in an unhistorical way: from the beginning of their study the commissioners assumed that the massive influx of new immigrants created "a widespread feeling of apprehension as to its effects on the economic and social welfare of the country."[2] The commissioners never looked back to note that the old immigrants had created the same feelings of "apprehension." Lacking comparisons between the economic and social characteristics of the new and old immigrants as well as America's reaction to each influx, the new immigrants appeared in a particularly unfavorable light. As a result, the difficulties that they faced in adjusting to American society appeared to stem from racial and historical characteristics that seemingly did not apply to the old immigrants.

---

[1]Ibid., p. 170.   [2]Ibid., p. 24.

Another major problem with the <u>Reports</u> was the discrepancy between the factual information, usually found in the background volumes, and the ambiguous conclusions based upon that information.[1] Two examples, concerning crime and illiteracy rates among the new immigrants indicate the nature of the problem. The <u>Reports</u> stated that native Americans committed more crimes than did the foreign-born population, but that children of immigrants (from ten to nineteen years old) committed relatively more crimes than the children of native Americans. The immigrants committed different kinds of crimes than those of native Americans: the Italians committed murder and rape, the Russians and French engaged in prostitution, and the Irish and Scots were often intoxicated. These facts were not necessarily damaging to the new immigrants, but the commissioners' conclusions, presumably based on these facts, were obviously unfavorable to the new immigrants: "While it does not appear from available statistics that criminality among the foreign born increases the volume of crime in proportion to the total population, nevertheless the coming of criminals and persons of criminal tendencies constitutes one of the serious social effects of the immigration movement."[2]

---

[1] Oscar Handlin, <u>Race and Nationality in American Life</u> (Boston, 1957), pp. 100-03.

[2] RIC, I, 27; <u>ibid</u>., II, 163-64.

The second example concerns the literacy test. In the background volume concerning Russian-Jewish conditions, the commissioners accounted for Jewish illiteracy on the basis of economic distress and religious bigotry.[1] But in the summary volume the commissioners discussed the literacy issue in racial terms--even though the specific recommendation for the test was justified by "economic, social, and moral" considerations: "Whether the high percentage of illiteracy among the newer immigrants is due chiefly to environment or to inherent racial tendencies cannot well be determined. The former would seem to be the more equitable explanation were it not for the fact that races living under practically the same material and political conditions show widely varying results."[2] (The commissioners were referring to the high rate of literacy among the German population in Austro-Hungary and Russia.)

The classification of new and old immigrants along racial lines as well as the attribution of characteristics--such as illiteracy--to inherent racial tendencies reinforced the racial assumptions of the period. The most conspicuous example of this thinking is contained in one of the forty-two

---

[1] Handlin, *Race and Nationality in American Life*, p. 121.
[2] RIC, I, 176.

volumes--the <u>Dictionary of Races</u>. Written as a reference work and index for the <u>Reports</u>, it classified and evaluated six hundred groupings of peoples. Sometimes the classifications were based upon language considerations, and sometimes upon historical, territorial, or physical characteristics. For example, the <u>Dictionary of Races</u> described the "Hebrew, Jewish, or Israelite" racial group by employing physical, historical, and sociological impressions with a smattering of statistical information. The definition of the Jews stated, in part: "the 'Jewish nose,' and to a less degree other facial characteristics, are found well-nigh everywhere throughout the race, although the form of the head seems to have become quite the reverse of the Semitic type."[1]

The Jews were defined as "more truly European than Asiatic or Semitic," although the Immigration Bureau treated them as part of the "Slavic grand division of the Aryan family." The digest of characteristics listed the fact that the Jews exhibited great "social solidarity." It also stated that the Jewish immigrants left Russia to escape religious persecution as well as to improve their economic condition.[2]

The commissioners used the racial classifications despite the objections of some American Jews such as Simon

---

[1]<u>Ibid</u>., V, 74.   [2]<u>Ibid</u>., pp. 73-75.

Wolf, who was a self-appointed spokesman in Washington for Jewish interests, and Julian Mack, now a judge on the United States Commerce Court, who was a highly respected and trusted member of the AJC.[1] Wolf had become concerned about the classification system in 1899 when the Immigration Bureau started identifying the racial and national identity of each immigrant. He maintained that Jews constituted a religious and not a racial group that should be classified only by nationality. Therefore, differentiating the Jews as a racial group was not only a mistake but a constitutional attack upon their religious liberty. In 1902 Wolf had asked ten leading members of the American Jewish community to express their opinion as to whether the Jews were a race or religion. Unfortunately, Wolf's correspondents were irreconcilably divided on the question.[2] Soon thereafter the State

---

[1] During the course of the immigration investigation the commissioners had invited recommendations from persons interested in the immigration problem. The AJC, B'nai B'rith and the Union of American Hebrew Congregations had presented a joint statement to the Commission in which they appealed for the continuation of open immigration and the liberalization of immigration laws and administrative practices. Ibid., XLI, 139-57.

[2] Nathan Goldberg, "Forty-five Years of Controversy: Should Jewish Immigrants be Classified as Jews?" in The Classification of Jewish Immigrants and its Implications, by Nathan Goldberg et al. (New York, 1945), pp. 91-96.

Department and Immigration Bureau learned of the division of opinion within the Jewish community and when objections were raised about classifying Jews according to race, the two departments frequently justified their system by pointing to the ambiguous responses to Wolf's inquiry.[1]

Because of their deep concern, Wolf and Mack arranged for a special hearing before the Commission to discuss the classification system. They urged the commissioners to avoid using racial categories in their study, and asked them to recommend that the government stop using them as well. During the hearing Senator Lodge pressed Wolf into admitting that he was afraid that distinguishing Jews from all other nationality groups would create prejudice against American Jews. "You do not think," Lodge asked Wolf, "that there is in this country any feeling of that sort to amount to anything?" To which Wolf retorted, "My dear Senator Lodge you, of all men, certainly do know that a great deal of it exists." Although Mack argued that the system would stir up "racial feelings," the commissioners were unswayed by

---

[1] Roosevelt made one such objection in a letter to William Williams, Commissioner General of Immigration at Ellis Island. Roosevelt to William Williams, July 7, 1911, in Roosevelt Papers, Series III, 23.

his arguments.[1] The outcome was that in the first summary volume the commissioners stated that some Jews objected to the classification system but the commissioners felt justified in using it nevertheless.[2]

In anticipation of the forthcoming literacy test fight, the AJC made two important decisions that established the strategy and tone of its 1912-1913 lobbying campaign. First of all, the AJC commissioned Isaac Hourwich, a Russian-born statistician who worked in the Census Bureau, to make an economic analysis of the Reports that anti-restrictionist Congressmen could use to refute the Commission's findings. When the AJC chose Hourwich, it deliberately decided to ignore the racial arguments against the new immigrants that permeated the Reports. At first, Cyrus Adler objected to an economic report, wanting instead to present a record of Jewish moral and religious contributions to American life and to the white race. Adler was eager to disprove the contentions of New England and southern restrictionists that the Jews were creating a racial problem, in addition to the one posed by the Negroes. But he quickly conceded that his type of argument would be difficult to construct, and

_____

[1] RIC, XLI, 272-74.   [2] Ibid., I, 19-20.

he recognized the necessity of using an economic approach.[1]

Hourwich's work ultimately appeared as *Immigration and Labor*. It keenly dissected the *Reports*, extricated the economic arguments, and refuted the anti-immigrant conclusions. He analyzed the statistics in the *Reports* drawn primarily from the recession years 1907-1908 and concluded that the new immigrants presented no economic threat to America. They did not lower the wage levels; nor did they produce unemployment. In fact, the presence of the new immigrants had the salutary effect of raising wages as native workers climbed the occupational scale into supervisory positions.

According to Hourwich, the new immigrants made America prosperous by providing unskilled, cheap labor for industrial expansion and by encouraging the expansion of the consumer market. He insisted that the new immigrants came in good times but rarely during recessions and depressions. They came at the urging of friends and relatives in the United States but not because of the solicitations of the steamship companies. Hourwich also denied that the new immigrants were different from the old: both groups of

---

[1] Adler to Friedenwald, Apr. 6, 1911, in Adler Papers.

immigrants had the same economic and social characteristics; and both groups had elicited the same fearful, antagonistic response from native Americans.[1]

The AJC's second important strategic decision established that the organization's most prominent men would stay in the background during the literacy test fight; instead, the AJC would use less well-known Jewish personages and non-Jewish organizations as its public spokesmen. At an executive committee meeting in December, 1911, Marshall, Schiff, Mayer Sulzberger, and Cyrus Adler agreed that they would turn to Max J. Kohler, a New York lawyer and representative of the Board of Delegates of the Union of American Hebrew Congregations, and Cyrus L. Sulzberger, an able but none-too prominent member of the AJC, to mount a public campaign against the test.[2] Therefore, during 1912, Kohler and Sulzberger made numerous anti-restrictionist speeches, appeared at Congressional hearings, and published their arguments against the test.[3]

---

[1] Isaac Hourwich, *Immigration and Labor: the Economic Aspects of European Immigration to the United States* (New York, 1912).

[2] Minutes, AJC, Dec. 25, 1911.

[3] Cyrus L. Sulzberger, *Is Immigration a Menace?* (New York, 1912).

Marshall, who would become President of the AJC in the fall of 1912 after Mayer Sulzberger retired, still directed the behind-the-scenes negotiations. His activities centered on discreetly pressing Congressmen to write liberal immigration legislation, arranging for other ethnic groups to lobby publicly against the test and making the AJC lobby in a non-conspicuous way. The last of these objectives was particularly important to Marshall as is illustrated by an incident involving Herbert Friedenwald. The AJC sent Friedenwald to Washington to negotiate with members of the Senate Immigration Committee about its immigration bill. When he returned to New York he reported back to the AJC and also gave an interview to a *New York Times* reporter as well. The following day, Marshall read an article in the *Times* about Friedenwald's Washington lobbying. "I had supposed that it had been understood," he complained to Friedenwald, "that we were to keep in the background and not indulge in any publicity at this time in connection with immigration matters. . . ." Marshall restated the position that the Jews were to take a "back seat" and concluded by questioning "whether the Senators would like any publication of this character, but would prefer to have it appear as though they were acting spontaneously."[1]

---

[1] Marshall to Friedenwald, Jan. 29, 1912, in Marshall Papers, AJA; *The New York Times*, Jan. 29, 1912, p. 4.

The AJC's cautious approach reflected several considerations, many of which were rooted in insecurity and ambivalence about the political role of Jewish lobbyists. Marshall, for one, feared that if the AJC continued its intense lobbying, evident during the passport campaign, the Jews would antagonize Congress and the public. The AJC would not assume the leadership of the 1912 literacy test campaign, Marshall wrote Edward Lauterbach, "in view of the fact that the passport contest has been so recent and we do not wish to have the suggestion made that we are trying to run the government." (Marshall also justified his low-keyed approach by stating, erroneously, that the literacy test would have an insignificant effect on Jewish immigrants as compared with other immigrants.)[1]

It is evident too that the AJC believed that a public fight against the test would be a wasted effort: the restrictionists were too powerful for the Jewish lobbyists to block. It appeared to them that there were no grounds for negotiations with the restrictionists, except, hopefully, on the exemption issue. Thus, Friedenwald wrote Adler in February, 1912, about the "hopeless" situation: "I fear . . .

---

[1] Marshall to Lauterbach, Apr. 29, 1912, in Marshall Papers, AJA.

that we are beaten in the Senate, as there does not seem to be any one Senator who is taking an active interest in opposition to the bill, at all comparable to Lodge's persistence in pushing it through."[1] Friedenwald's gloom deepened in March when he again wrote Adler that it was "very difficult to get any people except the Jews stirred up in this fight." He added dejectedly that he had also discovered that many Jews were not "as antagonistic towards restriction as they ought to be."[2] His pessimistic thoughts were well-timed because the restrictionists were indeed ready to force the issue of the test and to make no concessions to the AJC.

II.

The AJC suffered its first defeat when Senate restrictionists held several debates on the literacy test, which were low-keyed and sparsely attended. Nevertheless, they were important in two respects: the Senate modified the Senate Immigration Committee's bill in respect to the literacy test, and the restrictionist Senators who completely dominated the debates made many revealing arguments. These Senators hardly intended to change any minds; their purpose was rather to relieve popular anxieties about

---

[1] Friedenwald to Adler, Feb. 19, 1912, in Adler Papers.
[2] Friedenwald to Adler, Mar. 6, 1912, in Adler Papers.

the immigrants and to appeal to the voters back home.

The Senate Committee on Immigration presented a long, comprehensive, and complex bill which was mainly based upon a draft from Senator Dillingham, but which also incorporated many recommendations of the Immigration Commission as well as a few made by the AJC. Some of the salient revisions of the 1907 law were the following: "free white persons" and those of African birth or descent would be the only aliens eligible for entry into the United States, immigrants would be allowed to employ counsel in appearances before Boards of Special Inquiry, the administration of the Chinese immigration laws would be merged with that of the European immigration service, and all immigrants, not just Chinese immigrants, would be required to carry identification certificates.[1]

Although Dillingham wrote a literacy test into his original proposal, the Committee recommended that the Senate drop the test. That test provided for rejecting any male alien sixteen years of age or over "physically capable of reading and writing" who could not read a test prescribed by the Secretary of Commerce and Labor in "some language or dialect." A literate immigrant, however, could bring in or

---

[1] U.S., Congress, Senate, Committee on Immigration, Report: Regulation of Immigration, 62d Cong., 2d sess., Jan. 18, 1912, S. Rept. 208 to accompany S3175.

send for an illiterate father or grandfather over fifty-five years of age and an illiterate son who was not over eighteen. (Dillingham completely exempted women from the test.)[1]

As soon as the debate opened on March 18, Senator Simmons of North Carolina objected to the Committee's proposal to drop the Dillingham literacy test. Dillingham explained to Simmons that the Committee simply wanted to insure the passage of the other important parts of the bill. Nevertheless, Simmons proposed his own reading and writing test for all male and female immigrants over sixteen years of age. His test required that the immigrants read and write thirty to forty words from the United States Constitution. He also proposed that a literate immigrant be permitted to "bring in or send for his wife, his children under 18 years of age, and his parents or grandparents over 50 years of age," even if they did not meet the literacy requirements.[2]

According to Simmons, the major justifications for passing the test were the findings of the Immigration Commission and the thousands of literacy test petitions which restrictionists sent to Congress from 1906 to 1912. In his

---

[1] U.S., *Congressional Record*, 62d Cong., 2d sess., 1912, XLVIII, Part 3, 2081.

[2] *Ibid.*, Part 4, p. 3531.

speech he employed the full range of economic and political accusations popular among the restrictionists: the immigrants work for cheap wages; they create "foreign cities" such as Lawrence, Massachusetts; they are exploited by the steamship, mining, and textile companies; they are "birds of passage" who "gather up the fragments and crumbs that fall from the overflowing table of our prosperity" and then return to their native countries. Simmons asked his fellow Senators why America spent millions of dollars on educating its youth when it welcomed each year "two or three hundred thousand of as densely ignorant and illiterate people as live under God's sun."[1]

When the discussions over the bill continued in April they focused on the test as well as on the vast administrative changes proposed by the Committee. On April 17, Dillingham expounded upon the studies made by the Commission. He advised the Senate that the literacy test would exclude 50 percent of the immigrants who would inevitably settle in congested cities, accept pitifully low wages, hoard their money for their return to Europe, and never come into contact with American institutions.

---

[1] Ibid., pp. 3535-3543.

Relying upon unpublicized portions of the Reports, Dillingham tried to separate facts from erroneous charges made against the new immigrants. He commended them for being of good physical types—not infirm or mentally ill as was popularly thought. He defended the steamship companies from the accusation that they induced immigration. When Dillingham analyzed the relationship between crime and immigration, he concluded that the literacy test would not reduce the problem. Dillingham told the Senate that the only effective way to keep out criminals would be to use a certificate system requiring the disclosure of an immigrant's criminal record.[1]

Senator Elihu Root of New York declared in turn that he strongly favored the test because it would reduce the number of new immigrants who lacked the "acquired capacity for self-government." He insisted that the foreign illiterates were a danger to America because they held the power to strike and to paralyze America's basic industries. They were isolated from American institutions—"cut off from our ideas, from our thoughts, our sentiments, our feelings [and] our purposes by their own ignorance."[2]

---

[1] Ibid., Part 5, pp. 4906-4916.

[2] Ibid., pp. 4966-4968.

Senator William E. Borah of Idaho, another restrictionist, voiced a different set of fears. According to Borah, a high literacy rate was necessary because the American people were demanding political reforms and a greater voice in running the government. Borah asked what the reforms would be "worth in some of the congested centers of political degeneracy in our great cities." In his talk he hardly disguised his dislike for the new immigrants: "I am not favorable to the proposition of turning loose in this country an unfriendly and ignorant class of people who compete with American labor, degrade American manhood, and conspire against American institutions."[1]

On April 19, after the polemics were over, Lodge began to examine the specific wording of the Dillingham literacy test, the one that the Committee had asked the Senate to eliminate. Lodge raised and then withdrew the idea of citing Yiddish and Hebrew as acceptable languages for taking the test. In a conciliatory gesture for Jewish anti-restrictionists, he recommended instead adopting an exemption clause to benefit the Russian-Jewish immigrants and the Christians from Turkey. The exemption stated that the literacy test would not apply to persons who could prove

---

[1] Ibid., pp. 4970-4971.

to the immigration authorities that they were "seeking admission to the United States solely for the purpose of escaping from religious persecution."[1] In a quick succession of actions, the Senate added the Lodge exemption clause to the Dillingham literacy test and substituted the entire Simmons test--with Lodge's exemption clause in it--for the Dillingham provision. Finally and decisively, the Senate voted 9 to 56 against the Committee's proposal to drop the literacy test.[2]

Adopting the Simmons literacy test amendment and then voting against the Committee's recommendation might have seemed like a curious and awkward procedure, but the purpose was unmistakably clear. The Committee, which privately strongly favored the test, simply devised a way to prevent the AJC and other anti-restrictionists from lobbying

---

[1] Ibid., p. 5020.

[2] The Dillingham literacy test exempted Hawaii from the test because it needed southern and eastern European labor--even illiterate labor--to counterbalance the Asian population on the Islands. When the Simmons amendment did not include the Hawaiian exemption, Lodge failed to press the matter. Taft was interested in this exemption, writing to Representative James Mann, of Illinois: "I am not at all certain about the wisdom of the literacy test anywhere," but certainly it would be detrimental for Hawaii. Taft to James Mann, May 3, 1912, in Taft Papers, Series II, File 77.

with the Committee members and other Senators between January and April, after the Committee issued its report and before the Senate considered the test. The AJC could hardly attack the Committee after it had recommended dropping the literacy test. Therefore, when the Senate adopted the test the AJC suffered a major defeat and an embarrassing one as well. Fulton Brylawski, who replaced Adler as resident lobbyist for the AJC in Washington, described how Lodge handled the scheme:

> While I was talking with Senator Raynor Mr. Lodge came up and told him that the bill which was being considered was not objectionable to the American Jewish Committee as he had incorporated in it Mr. Marshall's suggestions and had expressly stricken out the literacy test. I told Senator Lodge that I understood it would come up in the Senate in connection with the present bill, to which he replied, "Certainly it will, I'm in favor of a literacy test and we are going to pass one. I had it stricken out of the Dillingham Bill but the Committee of the Whole refused to accept the Committee amendment and it is now up to the Senate to accept it or reject it."[1]

Once the Senate had passed the literacy test, it quickly considered other amendments. The Senate rejected proposals to increase the head tax to $24 or even $10; instead, it settled for increasing the tax to $5. It

---

[1]Fulton Brylawski to Friedenwald, Apr. 17, 1912, in Adler Papers. According to the AJC Annual Reports, Brylawski did not become a member of the AJC until 1914; therefore it is most probable that he was paid by the organization for his work on its behalf. American Jewish Committee, Annual Report, 1912-1914.

also adopted a highly controversial amendment suggested by Root to deport immigrants who used their "residence in the United States to conspire with others for the violent overthrow of a foreign government recognized by the United States."[1] Root intended to curtail the activities of Mexican revolutionaries in the United States, but the provision was broad enough to affect all foreign radicals.

The debate then shifted to other immigration problems. Mississippi Senator John Sharp Williams proposed that the bill exclude Negro immigrants from Africa and the West Indies along with others who were not "free white persons." Augustus Bacon of Georgia joined Williams in the appeal to western and New England restrictionists to reciprocate the support that the South had given to northern and western restrictionists. Root, however, contended that the proposal was no way to solve the southern racial problem and that it would also raise unpleasant diplomatic issues with Haiti and Brazil. But Bacon was hardly satisfied with Root's arguments: "Have we hesitated to break off friendly relations, if need be, with Japan or China? They are as important to us as Brazil. It is a question of whose ox is gored."[2]

---

[1] U.S., Congressional Record, 62d Cong., 2d sess., 1912, XLVIII, Part 5, 5027.

[2] Ibid., p. 5031.

Notwithstanding the consistent argument and the importance of the southern Democrats who comprised two-thirds of the Democrats in the Senate, the Senate defeated the Williams proposal. On April 19, the Senate passed the entire immigration bill on a voice vote and sent it to the House.

While the Senate was completing its debate over the Dillingham bill, on April 16 the House Committee on Immigration and Naturalization presented its literacy test which greatly displeased the AJC. John Burnett of Alabama, Chairman of the Committee, recommended that the House pass his bill that consisted of only one provision--a literacy test. The Burnett bill restricted all male and female immigrants over sixteen years of age "physically capable of reading, who cannot read the English language, or the language or dialect of some other country, including Hebrew and Yiddish." The test would consist of thirty to forty words chosen by the Secretary of Commerce and Labor. A literate immigrant would be able to bring in or send for his illiterate father or grandfather over fifty-five years old, his wife, mother, grandmother, unmarried or widowed daughters, and sons under sixteen years of age. Those immigrants "seeking admission . . . solely for the purpose of escaping religious persecution" would not have to take the test.[1] (This exemption was identical to the one sponsored by Lodge.)

In May, Burnett's Committee held hearings on two provisions of the Dillingham bill that the Senate had passed, the Root amendment and the one requiring immigrants to carry identification certificates.[2] Despite the hearings, the Committee decided to set aside the Dillingham bill and to report Burnett's literacy test bill--the one which it had first introduced in April.[3]

---

[1]U.S., Congress, House, Committee on Immigration and Naturalization, Report: Immigration of Aliens into the United States, 62d Cong., 2d sess., Apr. 16, 1912, H. Rept. 559.

[2]The Committee held hearings in January and February on the literacy test, then in May on the two amendments. The hearings were designed to allow individuals and organizations to express their views and gain publicity, but no one expected that the testimony would change the views of the Committee. The testimony contained little information and much foolishness. For example, Leon Sanders, president of HIAS, insisted that there were no Jewish immigrants who were illiterate and Samuel Gompers stated that the opening of the Panama Canal would allow European immigrants to inundate the West Coast. Gompers also stated that no Russian Jews were illiterate: "The Russian Jews--I know of none of them who cannot read." U.S., Congress, House, Committee on Immigration and Naturalization, Hearings, Relative to the Further Restriction of Immigration, 62d Cong., 2d sess., Part I, p. 62; Part 5, p. 10.

[3]U.S., Congress, House, Committee on Immigration and Naturalization, Report: Immigration of Aliens into the United States, 62d Cong., 2d sess., June 7, 1912, H. Rept. 851, to accompany S3175.

The Committee's reason for dropping the Dillingham bill and concentrating on the literacy test was based upon a simple strategy. The Committee included a number of outspoken anti-restrictionists such as Henry Goldfogle, J. Hampton Moore, George Konig, and Adolph Sabath--representing southern and eastern European constituents in New York, Philadelphia, Baltimore, and Chicago--who intended to dispute and dissect the intricate Senate bill. To avoid delay and dissension the restrictionist majority on the Committee set aside the Senate bill and reported the literacy test which already had been discussed thoroughly. The restrictionists knew that once the House passed the test--as it was sure to do--the Dillingham and Burnett bills would go to a House-Senate conference committee. Adolph Sabath, a Jewish immigrant himself, would be the only anti-restrictionist on that committee. Alone he would be unable to prevent the adoption of the Senate version, excluding the Root and certificate clauses which Burnett did not like. The conference committee would then report the Dillingham bill directly to the House and bypass the difficult House Committee.[1]

---

[1] Brylawski to Adler, June 6, 1912, in Adler Papers; David B. Truman has described this strategy in general terms: "Not infrequently, in fact, the dominant members of a standing committee and the interests having access to them design their strategy with an eye to the opportunities for last minute changes provided by the conference report." Truman, op. cit., p. 328.

The AJC, for its part, was resigned to the fact that both the House and Senate would pass a literacy test; therefore, it focused exclusively on Burnett's wording of the exemption clause--one that had an interesting history. Max J. Kohler traced the origin of the Lodge-Burnett clause to the English Aliens Act of 1905, in which an exemption applied to those immigrants likely to become public charges but not to illiterate immigrants. Although some members of Parliament were dissatisfied with the operation of the clause, the exemption was harmless in the British context because the architects of the legislation knew that the British Jewish community would care for the Russian-Jewish immigrants, thereby making an exemption clause superfluous. In June, 1906, the House of Representatives first adopted the English clause, after Lucius Littauer recommended that the exemption apply to the public charge issue. Under Cannon's influence the House passed the exemption clause for the public charge provision and for the literacy test as well. The House then dropped the literacy test and later the Senate-House conference committee also dropped the Littauer exemption relating to the public charge provision.[1]

---

[1] Max J. Kohler, "The Immigration Problem and the Right of Asylum for the Persecuted," *Jewish Comment* (Baltimore), Oct. 24, 31, 1913.

Because of the historical precedent there was no dispute between the AJC and the restrictionists about the desirability of an exemption clause. Even Jeremiah Jenks and W. Jett Lauck, the chief investigators for the Immigration Commission, recommended an exemption provision, stating: "In the judgment of the Commission, as well as of most other enlightened citizens, the United States should remain in the future as in the past, a haven of refuge for the oppressed, whether such oppression be political or religious. Any restrictive measure should contain a provision making an exemption of such cases."[1]

But Marshall and his coterie of lobbyists feared that despite Burnett's and Lodge's seemingly good intentions, Congress would adopt an ineffective exemption clause. Thus, throughout the winter and spring of 1912 Marshall repeatedly advised Burnett that his clause "solely to escape religious persecution" was too narrow and weak. Specifically, he objected to the fact that the phrase ignored political refugees and those who were leaving Russia because of the complex system of discrimination which involved economic, political,

---

[1] Jeremiah Jenks and W. Jett Lauck, The Immigration Problem: A Study of American Immigration Conditions and Needs (New York, 1926), pp. 411-12.

and social, as well as religious, factors. Therefore, he suggested to Burnett that the literacy test should not apply to any immigrant who "shall migrate from any country wherein persecution is directed against the religious domination to which he belongs by means of laws, customs, regulations, orders or otherwise, or to any person seeking to avoid persecution because of political beliefs or activities."[1]

In March, 1912, however, Burnett rejected the Marshall phraseology because it was "too inclusive."[2] Burnett felt no need or inclination to adopt the provision because he was certain that the House would be satisfied with the narrow exemption clause. But he did acknowledge the influence of the AJC lobbyists when he maintained in public and in his private dialogues with Marshall and Friedenwald that the literacy test was not directed at reducing the number of Jewish immigrants. Burnett not only insisted that there were few Jewish illiterates, but also that those few would be admitted because of his exemption provision.

Burnett, however, felt resentful when Marshall pressed him too hard on the exemption issue. In one

---

[1] Reznikoff, op. cit., I, 125.

[2] Friedenwald to Mayer Sulzberger, Mar. 8, 1912, in Adler Papers.

instance Burnett defended himself as a moderate restrictionist who was only promoting the literacy test and not some harsher provision. "The sooner some of you understand," Burnett wrote Marshall, "that unless conservative legislation is soon adopted that more radical legislation will be demanded, the better it will be for yourselves and for the country." Quite naturally, Burnett's words disturbed Marshall who was angered by the Congressman's implied threat as well as the trenchant use of "you" and "yourselves" which singled out the Jews and the AJC.[1]

In the spring of 1912, while the anti-restrictionists presented no obstacles to the passage of the test in the House, Burnett was unable to persuade Speaker Champ Clark and Oscar Underwood, the Democratic leaders in the House, to take up the literacy test bill. Both Clark and Underwood considered themselves serious candidates for the Democratic Presidential nomination; neither one wanted to identify himself or his party with an issue which was unpopular with several ethnic groups, especially after anti-restrictionists held rallies in New York, Boston, St. Louis, Baltimore, Philadelphia, and Cleveland. (The AJC split the cost of the rallies in New York and Philadelphia, but let other ethnic

---

[1]Reznikoff, op. cit., I, 119.

organizations receive the publicity and the credit.)[1] Clark and Underwood advised caution and therefore in late April or early May, the Democratic caucus in the House decided to defer to the ethnic vote and to postpone consideration of the literacy test until December, 1912.[2]

Monopolies, trusts, inflation, the income tax, tariff reduction, the rights of labor, the direct election of Senators, and the incalculable influence of strong personalities upon the electorate--these were the important issues in the exciting three-way 1912 Presidential election. Immigration restriction, however, mattered hardly at all except on the Lower East Side.[3] Despite this fact, the AJC tried to take advantage of the desire of all politicians to

---

[1] Friedenwald to Adler, May 3, 1912, in Adler Papers.

[2] Friedenwald to Adler, June 2, 1912, in Adler Papers.

[3] According to Arthur Goren, the literacy test was a key issue in the Lower East Side during the Congressional elections of 1908 and 1910. Goren studied the campaigns run by Morris Hillquist and Meyer London against Henry Goldfogle in the Ninth Congressional district. The votes indicated that the Jewish voters would not support Hillquist who had supported the restrictionist stand of his Socialist party. London, another Socialist, who had criticized the restrictionist platform, did much better and finally won in 1914. Arthur A. Goren, "A Portrait of Ethnic Politics: The Socialists and the 1908 and 1910 Congressional Elections on the East Side," *Publications of the American Jewish Historical Society*, L (Mar., 1961), 202-38.

please identifiable groups during an election campaign. Skillfully deploying its members who belonged to the Republican, Democratic, and Progressive parties, the AJC worked hard to prevent the three nominating conventions from writing restrictionist planks and also tried to get the three major Presidential candidates to declare their opposition to the test. (The leaders of the AJC never tried to get the conventions to write anti-restrictionist planks, realizing that it would not succeed and might possibly find the parties writing restrictionist planks instead.)

The Progressive party, reflecting the strong influence of social workers such as Jane Addams, emphasized programs designed to help the immigrants assimilate into American life. But the Progressives and Roosevelt himself remained completely neutral on the literacy test during the campaign. His major opponent, Woodrow Wilson, was much more sensitive to the pressure of the anti-restrictionists than was Roosevelt. To win the Presidency, Wilson desperately needed immigrant votes in the northern urban areas; yet he was the least attractive candidate to the ethnic groups, a fact which was made clear during the Democratic primaries when he lost numerous states with large numbers of foreign voters.

Wilson was plagued by views he had expressed during his pre-political, academic days and which his Democratic opponents such as William Randolph Hearst publicized during the primaries. By far the most damaging statement appeared in his History of the American People, published in 1902, in which Wilson wrote that the eastern and southern European immigrants were even less desirable and productive than the Chinese immigrants.[1] Therefore, in 1912, Wilson had to modify drastically his evaluation of the Chinese to please the West Coast, where Asian immigration was an anathema and for the East Coast, Wilson had to overhaul his low estimate of the new immigrants.

In an era of comparatively poor mass communications, Wilson was able to handle such a delicate maneuver. To win the California vote Wilson developed a firm restrictionist view against Asian immigration; therefore California Democrats compared Wilson's new stand with Roosevelt's impetuous call for the naturalization of Japanese immigrants made during the Japanese crisis in December, 1906. The strategy worked well; although Wilson lost California to Roosevelt by 174 votes, he received much credit and many votes because of his restrictionist stand.[2]

---

[1] Woodrow Wilson, A History of the American People (New York, 1931), V, 212.

[2] Daniels, op. cit., pp. 54-56.

In the East Wilson wooed the immigrant vote, especially the Jewish vote, by publicizing his early involvement in the abrogation movement, his membership in the NLIL, and his support from Jewish leaders such as Schiff and Henry Morgenthau.[1] But Wilson refused to oppose the literacy test despite negotiations on the issue among Schiff, Cyrus Sulzberger, Adler, and New York Senator O'Gorman, and three of Wilson's top campaign officials, Henry Morgenthau, William McAdoo and William McCombs. As a result of the talks Wilson agreed to write a public letter sympathetic to the new immigrants stating that "this country can afford to use . . . every man and woman of sound morals, sound mind, and sound body who comes in good faith to spend his and her energies in our life." Wilson then added in his official letter to Adler: "I should certainly be inclined, so far as I am concerned, to scrutinize very jealously any restrictions that would limit that principle in practice."[2]

The Republicans were even less responsive to the AJC than were the Democrats. The AJC designated Marshall,

---

[1] Although previously a Republican, Schiff switched to Wilson in 1912, causing an unusual but short-lived conflict between Marshall and Schiff. Marshall to Schiff, Aug. 13, 1912, in Marshall Papers, AJA.

[2] Woodrow Wilson to Adler, Oct. 21, 1912, in Adler Papers; Adler to Charles Jacobson, Oct. 17, 1912, in Adler Papers.

Julius Rosenwald, and Harry Cutler to promote the anti-restrictionist cause among the Republicans but they were far from successful at the convention. The party platform recited the restrictionist creed and for the first time since 1896 the party pledged itself to "give relief from the constantly growing evil of induced or undesirable immigration, which is inimical to the progress and welfare of the people of the United States."[1] Despite this position, Taft refused to commit himself on the literacy test. Marshall and Rosenwald, who actually served for a short period as the President of the Illinois Taft clubs, tried to pressure Taft to declare his opposition. But Taft, who strongly suspected that Wilson would defeat him, found no reason to play politics with the literacy test.[2]

For a short time in October, however, it seemed that Taft would give in to the anti-restrictionists. Charles Hilles, Taft's campaign manager, told the press that if Taft were re-elected he would definitely veto a literacy

---

[1] Kirk Porter, National Party Platforms (New York, 1924), p. 359.

[2] Taft told Gus Karger: "I will probably be defeated in November . . . but I am content. My victory came in June, when I was renominated in Chicago. And, no matter what happens, Roosevelt can't be elected." Sept. 7, 1912, in Karger Papers.

test.[1] In the same week Taft told an audience in Cambridge Springs, Pennsylvania, that he welcomed the new immigrants although they were uneducated and derived from backgrounds that were different from the old immigrants.[2] But the President said nothing about the literacy test. Then on October 31, Taft's executive clerk Rudolf Forster denied that Taft was "pledged to any course." Forster maintained that Taft would not declare his position unless Congress passed the test.[3] A few days later Taft lost the election; the Democrats now seized the opportunity to pass the literacy test and to force Taft to make up his mind on the issue of immigration restriction.

III.

A month after Woodrow Wilson won the Presidency, the House took up the literacy test bill. The debate which began on December 14, was short, repetitive, and uninteresting, for the outcome was never in doubt. The major participants were anti-restrictionists Joseph Cannon, James Curley of

---

[1] U.S., Congressional Record, 64th Cong., 1st sess., 1916, LIII, Part 5, 4772.

[2] Taft address at Cambridge Springs, Penn., Oct. 26, 1912, in Taft Papers, Series II, File 77.

[3] Rudolf Forster to Joseph Lee, Oct. 31, 1912, in Taft Papers, Series II, File 77.

Massachusetts, Richard Bartholdt of Missouri, and Albert Burleson of Texas, who opposed restrictionists Burnett, Gardner, and Martin Dies of Texas. The latter three argued that the literacy test would prevent unfair competition from foreign laborers, and reduce the amount of crime and moral decay. The anti-restrictionists argued that there was no economic and social need to require closing off the traditional refuge for the oppressed from Europe. The House decisively voted against Marshall's broad exemption clause which Martin B. Madden of Chicago had introduced. At the same time, the House refused to drop the Burnett exemption clause, because, according to Burnett, the provision was needed to protect Russian-Jewish immigrants. The debate ended on December 18 when the House passed the Burnett bill by a vote of 179 to 52, with the South, Far West, and Mid-West providing the great number of votes for the test against the anti-restrictionists who predominately represented northern and mid-western cities.[1]

The action of the House proved that neither the Representatives nor the public responded to an inconspicuous campaign on the part of the AJC. To create anti-restrictionist pressure on the House, the AJC had printed

---

[1] U.S., Congressional Record, 62d Cong., 3d sess., 1913, XLIX, Part 1, 864.

and distributed 25,000 copies of the first chapter of the Hourwich book as well as thousands of copies of a speech made by Cyrus Sulzberger.[1] To obtain the AJC's exemption clause, Adler, Mayer Sulzberger, and Julian Mack had discussed making a deal with Burnett: the AJC would support the literacy test if Burnett would agree to broaden the exemption clause to include political refugees. Burnett, however, had refused to make any concessions.[2] After the House passed the test, Adolph Sabath told Friedenwald, who had gone to Washington to be present during the vote, that "there was absolutely no chance to stop the passage of the bill, nor would there have been at any time."[3] Burleson, the single Texas Representative to vote against the test, said the restrictionists could never have been defeated and attributed their victory to labor lobbyists who "had terrorized the members of the House so that they did not dare to vote against Burnett's bill."[4]

---

[1] Sulzberger, op. cit.

[2] Minutes, AJC, Oct. 13, 1912; Adler to Julian Mack, Oct. 28, 1912, in Adler Papers.

[3] Friedenwald to Adler, Dec. 19, 1912, in Adler Papers.

[4] Minutes, AJC, Jan. 1, 1913.

The AJC expected that the House and Senate would now agree quickly to a compromise bill and, still wanting to remain in the background, it began searching for powerful allies who might convince Taft to veto the literacy test. A large group of non-Jews from the West would be organized along with recognized friends of Taft's, both Jewish and non-Jewish, to appear at a public hearing at the White House. The AJC also turned to other groups who specifically opposed the Root amendment: the Friends of Russian Freedom and non-Jewish Socialists, "New England, old American stock Socialists."[1]

Preparations were being made for Taft's public hearing on the literacy test when the conference committee report threw the AJC into a state of alarm. The conferees, Senator Ellison D. Smith, a Democrat from South Carolina, Lodge, Dillingham, Burnett, Sabath, and Gardner, followed the House scheme and converted the Burnett bill, that consisted of nothing more than the literacy test, into the comprehensive Dillingham bill. The conferees made several significant changes in the bill: they deleted the provision for reorganizing the Chinese immigration service; they dropped the

_____

[1] Ibid.; Adler thought the Socialists would be a "powerful ally." Adler to Friedenwald, Dec. 23, 1912, in Adler Papers.

Root amendment as well as the provision which would have required all immigrants to carry special identification cards; they dropped the Senate literacy test for the Burnett provision; and finally, the committee added a provision--previously not part of either the House or Senate bill--that required each immigrant arriving from a country that issued a certificate disclosing his criminal record to present the certificate to American immigration authorities.[1]

According to the AJC, Russia was among those countries which provided certificates of good character to those immigrants who wanted to emigrate legally. These Russian certificates contained the military and political records of all members of an emigrant's family. Therefore, the AJC was appalled by the possibility that in the future all Russian-Jewish immigrants would have to obtain certificates from the unfriendly Russian police and make their departures legal to satisfy America's immigration law.[2]

When the House considered the conference report on January 17, the debate was uneventful partially because many

---

[1] U.S., Congress, House, Conference Report: Immigration of Aliens, 62d Cong., 3d sess., Jan. 16, 1913, H. Rept. 1340 to accompany S3175.

[2] Marshall to Lodge, Jan. 20, 1913, in Marshall Papers, AJA.

Representatives had not had time to read the conference bill; but mainly because the restrictionists commanded such a great majority. The debate pitted Gardner and Burnett against Sabath and Bartholdt over the possible effects the certificate system could have on the Russian-Jewish immigrants. Repeatedly, the House voted against sending the report back to the conference committee and after a day-long discussion the House accepted the report on a voice vote.

By the time that the House had finished its debate, Marshall and the AJC had moved from the background and the "back seat." On January 21, Marshall went to Washington to speak to the President and to lobby with Congressmen about both the certificate system and the literacy test.[1] On January 24, Friedenwald sent an urgent letter to all AJC members asking them to assemble petitions and pressure their Congressmen to oppose the immigration bill.

It was Friedenwald who actually did the most effective lobbying for the AJC when he reached Robert La Follette

---

[1] Marshall was also lobbying against Sulzer's bill to create a Department of Labor which would include the Bureau of Immigration. Marshall was afraid that anti-restrictionist labor men would run the Bureau. Taft, however, refused to veto the Sulzer bill. Reznikoff, op. cit., I, 123.

of Wisconsin and Miles Poindexter, two Progressive Senators who supported the literacy test. For once, the AJC was able to go beyond the small pool of habitual anti-restrictionist Senators--Isidor Raynor, James Martine of New Jersey, William J. Stone of Missouri, and James O'Gorman of New York --who by themselves were unable to defeat the restrictionists. Friedenwald recounted to Adler the course of events: "I telegraphed W. J. Stone to get La Follette stirred up and he spent several hours with him on Sunday with the results as you know." Friedenwald continued: "I also spent over an hour going over the bill with Senator Stone who was thus well primed. . . . Senators Poindexter and Martine were also primed to start up if there had been any occasion for it."[1]

As a result of these activities the AJC created strong opposition in the Senate to the certificate clause and thereby made questionable the quick passage of the literacy test. Consequently, the debate over the clause was "short, sharp and decisive."[2] Lodge was on the defensive as soon as the debate opened on January 20, declaring that the State Department had assured him the certificate system

---

[1] Friedenwald to Adler, Jan. 21, 1913, in Adler Papers.
[2] Ibid.

would apply only to the Italian immigrants--not to the Russian Jews.[1] Lodge maintained that the conferees had never considered the Russian system applicable; the United States did not ask immigrants for passports and therefore the government would not require the Russian certificates which were used to get the Russian passports.

Lodge, however, could not convince Stone, La Follette, and Arthur Gronna that the Russian Jews would be safe from the operation of the certificate system. La Follette, in particular, delivered blows that were factual and well articulated. He argued that the certificate provision would prevent the immigration of German, French, and Russian men who failed to complete their military service. After describing the oppressive residential and occupational laws which Russia directed against the Jews, La Follette informed the Senate that the Jews who violated those laws would be unable to obtain the required certificates. Adopt the certificate system, La Follette told his fellow Senators,

---

[1] Secretary of State Knox became interested in the certificate idea in 1910, suggesting that several of his European Ambassadors present the idea. By 1912 it was clear that England, Russia, and Germany would not accept the system, therefore, the State Department advised requiring certificates from only those countries which already issued them. Charles Nagel to Charles Norton, Nov. 28, 1910; Knox to Taft, Apr. 21, 1911, Huntington Wilson to Nagel, May 14, 1912 in Taft Papers, Series II, File 77.

if you want to "exclude . . . people who are opposed to the Russian system but who do believe in the system of government we have in the United States, and who would like to see that system of government adopted in Russia. . . ."[1]

La Follette also used the momentum that was building up against the conference report to criticize the Burnett literacy test. He objected to the fact that the Burnett provision was tougher than the Simmons version adopted by the Senate. The House version allowed a literate person to bring in his illiterate father over fifty-five years of age while barring illiterate sons over sixteen years old. The Senate version provided for admitting fathers over fifty years old and sons under eighteen years of age. La Follette objected to these specifications because they would serve to break up families.

Lodge informed La Follette that the conference committee could revise the literacy test to meet his objections. This, in fact, was the first of the concessions that Lodge made to the opposition in a debate which was going badly for the restrictionists. La Follette and William J. Stone were now scrutinizing many provisions of the complex bill which

---

[1] U.S., Congressional Record, 62d Cong., 3d sess., 1913, XLIX, Part 2, 1772.

the Senate had accepted without question in April, 1912. Therefore, Root and Simmons advised Lodge to send the report back to the conference committee in order to expunge the certificate system, since by practice a conference report could not be amended in the Senate but only in the conference committee. Lodge agreed to retreat and to withdraw the conference bill because he and the other Senate restrictionists were not willing to sacrifice the literacy test, that is, risk defeat of the entire bill, for the criminal certificate provision.

Three days later the second conference committee issued its second report. The conferees dropped the certificate provision but maintained the Burnett literacy test.[1] The debate in the House then went smoothly for the restrictionists; after listening to several speeches the House passed the report by a vote of 167 to 72.

The second report had to go back to the conference committee due to ambiguous language, despite the House vote; and on January 28, the committee issued its third and final report.[2] While the House considered the third report, its

---

[1] U.S., Congress, House, Conference Report: Immigration of Aliens, 62d Cong., 3d sess., Jan. 23, 1913, H. Rept. 1378 to accompany S3175.

[2] U.S., Congress, House, Conference Report: Immigration of Aliens, 62d Cong., 3d sess., Jan. 28, 1913, H. Rept. 1410, to accompany S3175.

members filled the Congressional Record with page after page of restrictionist and anti-restrictionist speeches, editorials, organization resolutions, and petitions. Burnett strongly defended the literacy test as a necessary measure to protect American labor from illiterate male competition. He tried to discredit the campaign of the Jewish anti-restrictionists who proclaimed that the literacy test was, as he put it, "an attack on all foreigners, and yet they--everyone--know that the Jews and the people from northwestern Europe will not be affected by it."[1] Once again the House supported Burnett's cause and accepted the conference report. On February 1, without any debate or division vote, the Senate also passed the immigration bill. Thus the 62nd Congress sent President Taft a literacy test--the first one passed since 1897.

IV.

Nobody knew what Taft would do about the immigration bill--not even Taft himself who was preparing to relinquish the terrible burdens of the Presidency at the time that Congress sent the test to him. His term in office had been a painful experience. He had fought with Roosevelt and the

---

[1] U.S., Congressional Record, 62d Cong., 3d sess., 1913, XLIX, Part 3, 2295.

insurgents in his own party and had suffered an amazing series of election defeats in 1912, first in the primaries against Roosevelt and La Follette and then in November when he carried only two states. But at the time when he considered the test he was happier and more serene than he had been in years; he had defeated Roosevelt at the convention and Wilson had kept Roosevelt from becoming President again.

Until February, 1913, Taft had had little reason to clarify his own thinking on the literacy test and immigration problem. As a politician from Ohio, as a state and federal circuit judge, and then as Secretary of War Taft had made little contact with the new immigrants and had had no inclination or reason to enter the controversy over immigration restriction. Of course during the 1908 election, Taft became concerned with ethnic politics and immigration problems; therefore he courted the ethnic vote by making speeches extolling the immigrants. Once during the campaign he made a speech to a large labor gathering in New York City and visited the Lower East Side. Along with several New York Republican politicians, Otto Bannard, William Bennet, Herbert Parsons, and Samuel Koenig, Taft visited Bergers Restaurant. There Taft met some leaders of the Jewish immigrant community and, according to Bennet, was favorably impressed by the immigrants; he "got an entirely new view of the immigrant question."[1]

Throughout his term in office various restrictionists such as Prescott Hall, A. Lawrence Lowell, Henry Holt, and Madison Grant asked Taft to support restriction, but Taft refused to commit himself personally. Customarily, when he received letters about the literacy test he referred them to his Secretary of Commerce and Labor Charles Nagel. Nagel, a second generation American, was the son of a doctor who fled Germany in the 1840's. He had practiced law in St. Louis and had been active in state politics as well as in Taft's 1908 campaign. As a reward for his help, Taft had appointed Nagel to the Cabinet.

The leaders of the AJC had ambivalent feelings about Nagel: they often criticized his decisions and administrative procedures which involved immigration. They cited the obstruction of the Galveston project and the policy of rejecting immigrants who had, at the time of arrival, less than $25 in their possession. Yet on the literacy test issue, Nagel was a persistent and outspoken critic of the test; the AJC could not have asked for a more resolute ally.

---

[1]Bennet, op. cit., p. 92.

In 1910, Taft asked Nagel to comment upon the literacy test in a letter to restrictionist A. Lawrence Lowell, President of Harvard University. Illiteracy, Nagel wrote, "weighs against the applicant" and is "always considered as one of the factors in determining the question of admission or rejection." But Nagel added that the question of literacy "standing alone . . . has not been accepted as conclusive; nor do I think that it should be unless the whole theory . . . undergoes a radical change."[1]

In January, 1911, Nagel made a highly publicized address to the representatives of the Union of American Hebrew Congregations, one day before Marshall made his abrogation speech and attack on the Taft Administration. Nagel told his sympathetic audience that he was unequivocally opposed to the literacy test.

If Nagel had had his way, Taft would have taken a strong stand against the test during the 1912 campaign. At Taft's request Nagel had written a speech on immigration restriction, but Taft had not used the draft nor had he made his position clear. In his memorandum to the President, Nagel admonished against the use of the test which was

---

[1] Nagel to Taft, Dec. 7, 1910; A. Lawrence Lowell to Taft, Nov. 4, 1910, in Taft Papers, Series II, File 77.

"based more upon a desire to exclude generally than upon justice to the immigrants or real wisdom for our country."[1]

As for the President himself, none of his speeches or correspondence indicates that he attributed crime, violence, and other social problems to the new immigrants as did the restrictionists. According to Stanley Solvick, a Taft biographer, there existed "an optimism and sunniness in both Taft's thought and his character which led him to a view of man more hopeful than that ordinarily held by conservatives."[2] In contrast to the restrictionists, Taft expressed his faith in the worth of the new immigrants, in the continuation of America's economic expansion, and in the beneficial effects of American institutions on the new immigrants. He articulated these beliefs in October, 1912, to a gathering of immigrants:

> I do not share in the fear that our citizenship is ultimately likely to suffer by the coming from other continental countries for the purpose of permanent settlement of any people who are now coming. We have a right to have, and ought to have, immigration laws that shall prevent our having thrown upon us undesirable members of other communities, like criminals, the imbeciles, the insane and the permanently disabled, but we have a vast

---

[1] Nagel to Taft, Sept. 19, 1912, in Taft Papers, Series II, File 77.

[2] Stanley Donald Solvick, "William Howard Taft and the Progressive Movement: A Study in Conservative Thought and Politics," (unpublished Ph.D. dissertation, University of Michigan, 1963), p. 303.

territory here not yet filled, in the development of
which we need manual labor of a constant and persistent
kind and I think we have shown in the past, as we shall
show in the future, that our system of education is sufficiently thorough and sufficiently attractive to those
who come here that they of all others avail themselves
of it with promptness and success.[1]

Interest in the immigration bill mounted while it lay on Taft's desk in January, 1913. The State Department wanted to inform him of the objections to the bill raised by various foreign governments. Letters, resolutions, and telegrams inundated the President. On February 7, two hundred people appeared at the White House for a three-hour public hearing on the immigration bill. Anti-restrictionist Italian, German, Irish, Scandinavian, and Jewish groups, and restrictionist labor and patriotic organizations all sought to influence the President.

Taft told the gathering that the burden of proof was on the anti-restrictionists since Congress so strongly favored the test. Marshall, who was making his first public appearance in the 1912-1913 fight, appealed to Taft for a sympathetic understanding of the victims of religious and political persecution. He also emphasized that the illiterate immigrants presented no threat to American life because they made great educational strides once they settled in

---

[1] Taft address at Cambridge Springs, Penn., Oct. 26, 1912, in Taft Papers, Series II, File 77.

America. From Marshall's point of view, the hearing went extremely well, reporting to Schiff that "there was a very large attendance, and, fortunately, other nationalities were represented to so great an extent, that it was demonstrated that the opposition to the bill is not confined to the Jews."[1]

On February 10, Taft discreetly indicated a forthcoming veto to Senator Theodore E. Burton, a Republican from Ohio, who had requested a private meeting if Taft intended to oppose the test. Therefore, the President asked Burton to come to his office, noting that he was "rather inclined to veto it."[2] Three days later, however, Taft responded to the intense bi-partisan support for the test and seemed to be unsure about what he wanted to do. On the 13th, he consulted privately with Nagel, then with his Cabinet. Finally, he called Samuel Gompers, William Williams (the Commissioner-General of Immigration), Representatives Richard Bartholdt and William Bennet to the White House to argue the pros and

---

[1] Marshall to Schiff, Feb. 7, 1913, in Marshall Papers, AJA. The Jewish immigration issue might have been of some importance to Taft as was indicated in a note from Hilles to Taft. Hilles informed Taft that Lodge believed that only 2 percent of the Jewish immigrants were illiterate. Charles Hilles to Taft, Feb. 9, 1913, in Taft Papers, Series II, File 77.

[2] Taft to Burton, Feb. 10, 1913; Theodore E. Burton to Taft, Feb. 7, 1913, in Taft Papers, Series II, File 77.

cons of the literacy test.[1] Still undecided on the 15th, the very last day that he could veto the bill, Taft consulted again with his Cabinet which was divided on the merits of the test.[2]

With but a few hours left to act, Taft accepted Nagel's view. In a one-page handwritten letter he informed Congress of his veto, explaining that he could not approve the immigration bill because of his dissatisfaction with the literacy test. As part of his message he included Nagel's brief against the test--which Taft had himself requested. Nagel criticized both the basic objectives and the specific details of the test, characterizing the test as an "uncompromising" measure aimed at a "danger which does not exist." He insisted that the country still needed unskilled, cheap labor because the immigrants held jobs native laborers would not accept.

Nagel also provided census statistics to demonstrate that the new immigrants, like the old, were settling on farms and also taking advantage of America's educational

---

[1] Bennet, op. cit., p. 93.

[2] Franklin MacVeagh to Woodrow Wilson, Jan. 11, 1915, in Woodrow Wilson Papers (Library of Congress, Washington, D.C.), Series IV, Folder 92. Cited hereafter as Wilson Papers.

opportunities in their effort to become literate and productive American citizens. He rejected the contention that illiteracy was the result of racial or social inferiority; instead, illiteracy resulted from "a denial of the opportunity to acquire reading and writing." The new immigrants, Nagel wrote, "are really striving to free themselves from the conditions under which they have been compelled to live."[1]

Why did Taft veto the test? Most probably a combination of factors shaped his decision: his current political situation, his ideological disposition, and his personal experiences. In February, 1913, Taft was ready to leave public office and to free himself of the need to please an unfriendly Congress and electorate. Therefore, he was willing to resort to the veto to thwart the will of Congress.[2] Secondly, Taft's deeply held ideological views reflected a great

---

[1] U.S., Congressional Record, 62d Cong., 3d sess., 1913, XLIX, Part 4, 3269-3270. Nagel was highly appreciative of Taft's action: "I need not say to you," he wrote Hilles, "that I am much relieved at this outcome. Without discussing the question again, I want to say how deeply I appreciate the recognition which the President has shown me in a matter in which I was so profoundly interested." Nagel to Hilles, Feb. 13, 1913, in Taft Papers, Series II, File 77.

[2] William Howard Taft, The Presidency: Its Duties, Its Powers, Its Opportunities and Its Limitations (New York, 1916), pp. 112-14.

respect for traditions such as open immigration and for institutions such as the American educational system. Finally, Taft's personal experience, based upon his visit to the Lower East Side in 1908, loomed large in his mind. William Bennet recalled that after the veto Taft said "that that one evening on the East Side had given him an entirely different view of the immigration question and had been largely influential in causing him to veto the bill."[1] Two years after the veto Taft spoke in New York once again and told of his visit to the city in 1908 as well as of his veto of the literacy test: "It was a visit through the east side that led me to veto the Immigration Bill containing the literacy test when it finally came to me. I saw among the young men and girls of the east side a spirit of appreciation, a gratitude, a patriotism that wouldn't hurt some of those whose fathers and great-grandfathers were born in this country."[2]

After the veto, the Senate on February 18 again took up the immigration bill. The debate was short and similar to all previous discussions of the literacy test. Lodge, for his part, attacked the steamship companies for stirring

---

[1] Bennet, op. cit., p. 93.

[2] The New York Times, Jan. 17, 1915, p. 2.

up opposition to the test. He also stated that the test was needed to maintain the quality of American citizenship and American educational standards. The "belief in education in this country is one of our great beliefs," Lodge told the Senate, ". . . why should we, in the case of foreigners alone, set a premium on ignorance?"[1] Lodge prevailed when the Senate agreed to override the veto by a vote of 72 to 18.

The House considered the veto the following day but the result was significantly different from that in the Senate. The restrictionists failed to obtain the necessary two-thirds vote on the immigration bill, losing by the margin of five votes when 213 Representatives voted to override the veto while 114 voted to uphold Taft. Representatives from the South and Far West provided the main strength for the restrictionist cause, but they were not strong enough to overcome the opponents of the test from northern and midwestern states.[2]

After the House vote the AJC breathed a deep but troubled sigh of relief, although nobody but the Congressmen involved in the fight knew which men had provided the margin

---

[1] U.S., Congressional Record, 62d Cong., 3d sess., 1913, XLIX, Part 4, 3317.

[2] Ibid., p. 3429.

of defeat and for what reasons.[1] The AJC had called upon its members to pressure Taft and Congress, but there is no reason to believe that it had influenced the President or affected the final vote in the House.[2] For reasons of their own, Taft, the son of a native American, and Nagel, the son of an immigrant, saved the AJC and the Russian-Jewish immigrants from the literacy test and the country from a breach in the tradition of open immigration.

With the veto Taft triumphantly ended his involvement with the restriction issue. Taft had defied the restrictionist Congress--this was the most important point --but the vote on the veto was so close that the anti-restrictionists could not feel comfortable. The AJC rightly anticipated that the lobbying and fighting over the test

---

[1] Prescott Hall, a leader of the Immigration Restriction League, commented upon the anti-restrictionist defeat: "to hell with Jews, Jesuits, and Steamships." Soloman, op. cit., p. 180. Marshall wrote Cannon to thank him for defeating the literacy test in 1913 as well as in 1906. Marshall to Cannon, Feb. 22, 1913, in Marshall Papers, AJA.

[2] The AJC's lobbying was so restrained that Louis Lipsky, chairman of the American Federation of Zionists, asked Marshall to state the AJC's position on the test. Marshall, somewhat irritated, wrote Lipsky that "it has been largely through its [AJC's] efforts that during the past six years, the law has been unchanged, in spite of the propaganda of the restrictionists." Marshall to Louis Lipsky, Dec. 17, 1912, in Marshall Papers, AJA.

would resume when the Democrats took control of Congress and the White House. A new President, who refused to commit himself on the test, and a new Congress, which southern Democrats would dominate, would now face the unresolved issue of immigration restriction. Yet, despite the apparent strength of the restrictionists, as the AJC waited for the next fight to begin it again changed its lobbying style and techniques. The AJC's lobbyists now developed an enthusiastic and combative spirit, quite different from the motivating force in the 1912-1913 fight.

CHAPTER V

WILSON TRIUMPHS

In a manner characterized by increasing vigor and sophistication the leaders of the AJC fought another literacy test battle between January, 1914, and February, 1915. By fully utilizing a broad range of nation-wide contacts, both Jewish and non-Jewish, the AJC sought to persuade President Wilson and Congress to resist the demands of the restrictionists and, in particular, to protect the Russian-Jewish immigrants. Louis Marshall set the tone of the AJC's campaign, when he wrote in December, 1913, "that it is the part of prudence for us to see what we can do for ourselves, rather than to act as the champions of all the world. . . ."[1] Fighting for "ourselves" meant blocking the literacy test while preparing, at the same time, for passage of the test by obtaining a strong exemption clause.

The AJC clearly recognized that the 63rd Congress regarded the test as an important piece of unfinished

---

[1] Marshall to Adler, Dec. 9, 1913, in Marshall Papers, AJA.

business from the past. To justify the need for the test, the restrictionists continued to associate the new immigrants with the problems of crime, political corruption, labor unrest, and racial antipathies. In addition, the depression and accompanying unemployment in 1914 strengthened Congress' desire to adopt an effective test as part of a general rewriting of the immigration law of 1907.

So strong was the desire for restriction that the Democratic Congress, which worked closely and constructively with Wilson on tariff, banking, and labor legislation, was willing to defy him on the literacy test. Therefore, Wilson became, as Taft had been, the decisive figure in the 1914-1915 fight. And as was the case with Taft, Wilson's idealism led him to veto the test and stymie the restrictionist Congress. As for the AJC, the political pressure that it applied on behalf of its dual aims, to defeat the test and to gain its exemption clause, made little impression on the chief executive and Congress. The AJC's campaign, although intense and carefully worked out, was a peripheral matter since the basic conflict over the test pitted Wilson against the Democrats in Congress.

I.

"We are practically the only ones who are fighting" the literacy test while a "great proportion" of the world is "indifferent to what is done," lamented Marshall in 1913.[1] Not only was there indifference to contend with but between 1913 and 1915 the AJC watched many people adopt an increasingly unfriendly attitude toward minority and ethnic groups, as a climate of nativist and racist opinion engulfed the nation. Anti-Semitism erupted with the tragic Leo Frank case.[2] Tom Watson and Wilbur Franklin Phelps spread anti-Catholic and anti-Semitic sentiment throughout the South and Middle West.[3] The California legislature, reflecting the deep hostility towards Japanese immigrants, passed the racially discriminatory Alien Land Act in 1913. And in Washington, D.C., President Wilson allowed southern Democrats (temporarily) to reinstate segregated facilities in several federal departments and to implement a patronage policy that kept Negroes out of his Administration.[4]

---

[1] Ibid.

[2] Leonard Dinnerstein, The Leo Frank Case (New York, 1968).

[3] Higham, Strangers in the Land, pp. 179-81, 185-86.

[4] C. Vann Woodward, The Strange Career of Jim Crow (New York, 1966); Kathleen Long Wolgemuth, "Woodrow Wilson's Appointment Policy and the Negro," Journal of Southern History, XXIV (Nov., 1958), 457-71.

Although deeply troubled by this nativist-racist trend of events, particularly as evidenced in the Frank case, the leaders of the AJC nevertheless felt secure enough in 1914 to regard the position of the Jews as distinctly different and superior to that of the Japanese, Chinese, and Negroes in the United States. In fact, in the restriction fight as well as in various battles against anti-Semitism, the AJC was not ready to gather support from these maligned groups, although it welcomed help in the literacy test fight from Italian and German organizations. During these years, the AJC had only one constituency, a Jewish one; therefore, the organization focused exclusively on Jewish problems and not on the general issue of racism that involved other ethnic groups as well. This concentration on Jewish issues may be attributed to the inexperience of a young organization as well as the unstated fear that American Jews might jeopardize their political and social position if they identified with Asians and Negroes--two groups that American society refused to accept and assimilate.[1]

---

[1] Two examples of this narrow attitude will suffice. In 1913, Leo Friedman of Boston wanted the annual meeting of the AJC to pass a resolution condemning the reimposition of segregated facilities in several federal departments. Marshall and the executive committee refused the request. Minutes, AJC, Nov. 8, 1913. (Schiff, however, wrote Wilson

The AJC decided to wage a strong lobbying campaign against the literacy test in 1914 and 1915 despite the upsurge in racism and the obvious strength of the restrictionists both within Congress and without.[1] There are two plausible reasons why the Jewish lobbyists abandoned the cautious approach that characterized the 1912-1913 fight. In the first place, AJC leaders gained confidence from their expectation, but not certain knowledge, that Woodrow Wilson, a strong President and party leader, would be an ally in the forthcoming fight. Secondly, the abrogation campaign of 1911, in which the AJC displayed its most forceful lobbying

---

to protest this policy. Schiff, op. cit., I, 315.) Secondly, in 1916 during a House hearing Representatives John E. Raker and John Burnett asked Marshall his opinion of Japanese and Chinese exclusion. Marshall replied that he had given no thought to the problem, maintaining that while he knew very little about Asian immigration matters he was certain that they should be kept separate from European immigration matters. Finally, Raker pressed Marshall to concede that on humanitarian grounds he opposed the restriction of Japanese immigration. U.S., Congress, House, Committee on Immigration and Naturalization, Hearings, Restriction of Immigration, 64th Cong., 1st sess., 1916, p. 20. In the 1920's, however, Marshall personally identified with the problems of the Negroes and the Japanese when he became a director of the NAACP and appealed the Alien Land Act before the Supreme Court in 1923.

[1] The AJC was still afraid of making the immigration issue a Jewish issue, therefore, the AJC decided not to publish an English translation of D. L. Hersch's Le Juif Errant d'Aujourd'hui for fear that it would make the Jewish immigrants too conspicuous. Minutes, AJC, Nov. 8, 1913.

tactics, was nothing more than a dim memory to Congress and the public. Since in 1914, there was no visible progress toward a new passport agreement, the AJC felt free to devote its full energies to the literacy test fight.

Marshall, again the major force behind the AJC campaign, realized that his organization could not hope to defeat the test in Congress--only Wilson could rally enough anti-restrictionist votes. But Marshall and the AJC expected that they could obtain Congressional acceptance of his exemption clause in lieu of the one favored by John Burnett and Ellison D. Smith, the Chairmen respectively of the House and Senate Immigration Committees. This latter clause, that the AJC regarded as narrow and ineffective, applied to immigrants seeking admission to the United States "solely" to escape religious persecution. Instead, Marshall wanted the exemption to apply to those who "are seeking admission to the United States to avoid religious or political persecution, whether such persecution be evidenced by overt acts, or by discriminatory laws or regulations."[1]

Despite Marshall's efforts, in December, 1913, the House Committee presented its immigration bill that contained Burnett's exemption provision. Notwithstanding this initial

---

[1] Reznikoff, op. cit., I, 128.

setback, Marshall optimistically, but mistakenly, believed that the AJC could persuade the House to drop Burnett's clause for his own. The AJC would continue to fight the literacy test on the "broad ground," Marshall wrote Herbert Friedenwald. "But I do not think," he added, "that we would be justified in staking our welfare on a single card. There is every reason to believe that we have a strong chance of winning on the exemption clause."[1] To this end, in December the AJC issued a four-page letter to all general members describing in detail the objections to the test and Burnett exemption clause. A month later, the AJC sent anti-literacy test press releases to many newspapers and to its membership in an effort to gain mass support for the anti-restrictionists.

Not content with trying to win over the public through the press and the efforts of the national network of AJC members, Marshall also sought to enlist the aid of President Wilson. Thus Marshall obtained an appointment with Wilson on January 29, to enlighten the President about the test and exemption clause and, in Marshall's words, "to urge him to induce Congress to accept the exemption clause as I have framed it."[2] Anticipating significant results from

---

[1] Marshall to Friedenwald, Dec. 23, 1913, in Marshall Papers, AJA.

[2] Ibid. Adler, Simon Wolf, Abram Elkus, and Judge Samuel Kalish of Newark, New Jersey, were also invited to attend.

his prospective meeting with the President, Marshall requested that Representative Henry M. Goldfogle postpone a House vote on the exemption issue until after the meeting with Wilson at which Marshall would "drive home" the value of the AJC's exemption clause. If Wilson "indicates a desire that the bill shall be amended," Marshall wrote Goldfogle, "there can be no doubt but that his suggestion would be adopted."[1]

Focusing on Congress as well, Marshall tried to arrange for an influential non-Jewish Wilson Democrat to sponsor the AJC's exemption clause during the House debate over the literacy test. He chose A. Mitchell Palmer, a prominent Democratic Representative from Pennsylvania, who was thought to be close to Wilson. Marshall had received word from Ephraim Lederer, an AJC member in Philadelphia, that Palmer favored the AJC's clause and even thought that the House would pass it.[2] Therefore, one day after discussing the AJC's position with Wilson, Marshall wrote confidently to Palmer that "I am quite satisfied that the President does not look with favor upon the illiteracy test. I am also of the opinion," Marshall added, "that he would welcome

---

[1] Marshall to Henry M. Goldfogle, Jan. 24, 1914, in Marshall Papers, AJA.

[2] Ephraim Lederer to Adler, Jan. 6, 1914, in Adler Papers.

the amendment which you have so kindly consented to favor, although he did not say so in so many words."[1]

Thus, despite the cautious afterthought, Marshall assumed that both Wilson and Palmer would advocate the AJC's exemption clause. But unfortunately for Marshall, his assumption was wrong. On January 30, the House began considering the comprehensive sixty-page immigration bill presented by the Committee on Immigration and Naturalization. This bill, similar to the one Taft had vetoed the previous year, regulated the steamship companies, described the responsibilities of the Immigration Bureau, and defined the physical, economic, political, and moral requirements for entry into the United States. There were, however, some significant changes affecting anarchists and other radical political activists. One provision called for the rejection of all immigrants "who advocate or teach the unlawful destruction of property." Another provision required the deportation of "any alien who within five years after entry shall be found advocating or teaching the unlawful destruction of property, or advocating or teaching anarchy, or the overthrow by force

---

[1] Marshall to A. Mitchell Palmer, Jan. 30, 1914, in Marshall Papers, AJHS.

or violence of the Government of the United States or the assassination of public officials."[1]

The Burnett literacy test remained exactly the same as in the 1913 bill. All aliens over sixteen years of age were required to take a literacy test in any language of their choice, including Hebrew and Yiddish. A literate alien could bring in or send for his father or grandfather over fifty-five years of age, his sons under sixteen years of age, and his wife, mother, grandmother, and widowed or unmarried daughters. The exemption pertained to "aliens who shall prove to the satisfaction of the proper immigration officer or to the Secretary of Labor that they are seeking admission to the United States solely for the purpose of escaping religious persecution."[2]

---

[1] U.S., Congress, House, Committee on Immigration and Naturalization, Report, Immigration of Aliens into the United States, 63d Cong., 2d sess., Dec. 16, 1913, H. Rept. 149, to accompany H6060. The first provision excluded "anarchists, or persons who believe in or advocate the overthrow by force or violence of the Government of the United States or of all forms of law, or who disbelieve in or are opposed to organized government, or who advocate or teach the unlawful destruction of property; persons who are members of or affiliated with any organization entertaining and teaching disbelief in or opposition to organized government. . . ." The immunity provision stated: "That nothing in this act shall exclude, if otherwise admissible, persons convicted of an offense purely political, not involving moral turpitude." Ibid.

[2] U.S., Congressional Record, 63d Cong., 2d sess., 1914, LI, Part 3, 2497.

Once again the House was considering a literacy test during a period of heavy immigration of poor, unskilled, and illiterate immigrants from eastern and southern Europe. From June, 1913, through June, 1914, 1,218,480 immigrants arrived in the United States, of whom 138,051 were Jewish.[1] And once again, in tedious debates that hardly differed from those in 1906 and 1912-1913, the restrictionists pointed to crime, urban congestion, labor competition, racial differences, and the heavy rate of immigration as the key issues.

Representatives on both sides of the dispute used caustic and inflammatory arguments--of greater interest and benefit to the constituents at home than to the members of the House. The restrictionists led by Burnett and Gardner accused the new immigrants of not being able to assimilate into the American way of life. The anti-restrictionists, led by Republican Richard Bartholdt of St. Louis, Missouri, accused the restrictionists of using the literacy test as an indirect attack against certain racial and national groups. Burnett in effect concurred with Bartholdt's accusation as the Committee Chairman enthusiastically projected that the test would prevent the entry of 30 percent of the Polish

---

[1] Anthony Caminetti, *Annual Report of the Commissioner General of Immigration* (Washington, D.C., 1918), p. 141.

immigrants, 40 percent of the Greeks, 60-70 percent of the Turks, but not more than 1 percent of the Jews. "This bill is not aimed at the Jews," Burnett said in a conciliatory gesture to American Jews, ". . . because we allow them if they can read their Yiddish and Hebrew, or if they are fleeing from religious persecution. . . ."[1] The anti-restrictionists, for their part, sarcastically wondered why southern restrictionists like Burnett were so concerned about European illiteracy when a high proportion of white and Negro southerners were illiterate too.

Because Burnett and his followers completely controlled the House during the debate, Marshall's efforts, centering on his meeting with the President, his letter to Palmer, and his circulars to AJC members were of no apparent value. In fact, Marshall failed to understand the normal workings of the House, underestimating the power of the committee system whereby a committee usually shapes the essential features of a bill.[2] Particularly disappointing was Palmer's performance since he deserted the AJC's exemption

---

[1] U.S., Congressional Record, 63d Cong., 2d sess., 1914, LI, Part 3, 3597-3598.

[2] According to David B. Truman, "few bills are passed in a form substantially different from that given them at the committee stage." Truman, op. cit., p. 331.

cause and actually left Washington before the debate on the clause began. Despite Palmer's sudden disappearance, Marshall remained hopeful, telegraphing Brylawski "there is still the possibility of winning though unexpected absence of Palmer is most disconcerting."[1] Instead of Palmer, Democrat William H. Murray of Oklahoma, an advocate of the literacy test, introduced the exemption clause, although he deleted the word "political" from the provision.

The restrictionists were fortified with strong arguments, solid votes, and a sure path to victory over the anti-restrictionists. Both Gardner and Burnett assailed Marshall's provision now introduced by Murray, for giving the Jews special treatment. Furthermore, Burnett decried the fact that the exemption would apply to the Mexicans and Syrians, thus allowing large numbers of them to enter the United States. The House defeated the Murray amendment by a vote of 65 to 77, as well as an identical measure introduced by Alexander W. Gregg of Texas. Next the House rejected Henry Goldfogle's proposal to drop the literacy test entirely, by a vote of 140 to 239. Moreover, unwilling to make any conciliatory moves towards the anti-restrictionists, the House repeatedly

---

[1] Marshall to Brylawski, Feb. 1, 1914, Fulton Brylawski to Marshall, Jan. 31, 1914, in Marshall Papers, AJHS.

refused to drop the word "solely" from the exemption clause.

The debate on the immigration bill extended for several days as Representatives dwelled upon several other controversial aspects of the bill relating to Asian immigration, contract labor, and the steamship companies. Finally, on February 4, the House easily passed the Burnett bill by a vote of 253 to 126, and sent it to the Senate.

The Senate referred the bill to its Immigration Committee headed by "Cotton Ed" Smith, a staunch conservative from South Carolina. The Committee strongly supported the Burnett bill although Smith had learned directly from the President that he opposed the literacy test. Wilson also conveyed his objections in a letter to Smith in which the President asked that the Senate Committee concentrate on the problem of the distribution of immigrants, "one of the keys to this difficult subject," and ignore the issue of restriction.[1]

At the suggestion of Senator Boies Penrose, a Republican from Pennsylvania, Smith also got in touch with Mayer Sulzberger to ascertain the AJC's opinion of the Burnett bill. After expressing strong opposition to the test in

---

[1] Wilson to Ellison D. Smith, Mar. 5, 1914, in Wilson Papers, Series IV, Folder 292.

response to the inquiry, Sulzberger wrote Marshall that it was important for Smith's Committee to recognize the "weight of the arguments" set forth by the AJC, "but also the fact that they represent the convictions of a large mass of Jewish citizens of the United States."[1]

Despite the position of the AJC and, even more important, that of President Wilson, on March 19 the Committee presented the Burnett bill, in a slightly amended version, to the Senate. For example, the Committee increased the head tax from $5 to $6, but reduced it to $4 in the case when an alien entered with his wife and children. The Committee also recognized the popular fear of criminal mental defectives by barring immigrants who suffered from "constitutional psychopathic inferiority." Most important, Burnett's literacy test and exemption clause remained intact.[2] Wilson, however, was able to persuade the Senate Democratic leaders to postpone consideration of the bill until after the November Congressional elections. The party again deferred to the ethnic voters--although only for a few months.

[1] Mayer Sulzberger to Marshall, Feb. 18, 1914, in Marshall Papers, AJHS.

[2] U.S., Congress, Senate, Committee on Immigration, Report: Regulation and Restriction of Immigration, 63d Cong., 2d sess., Mar. 19, 1914, S. Rept. 355 to accompany H6060.

II.

On December 2, one day after the opening of the second session of the 63rd Congress, the Senate took up the immigration bill. In the ensuing debate a relatively small number of Senators spent many hours debating the literacy test, the exemption clause, and many other aspects of the long, intricate bill. It was clear from the beginning of the debate, however, that the restrictionists never felt threatened by the small group of informed and aggressive anti-restrictionist Senators or by the far-reaching lobbying efforts of the AJC.

In preparing for the Senate debate, Marshall fully utilized the AJC's network of contacts throughout the country, in Congress, and in the White House. Hardly satisfied with issuing general calls and impersonal invitations to action, Marshall pleaded with his contacts to work hard to protect the hundreds of thousands of illiterate Jews who would want to emigrate from Russia. For the first time, in fact, Marshall acknowledged that the literacy test would seriously hurt Russian-Jewish immigrants of whom 26 percent were illiterate, and he made a serious effort to inform the AJC members and Congressmen of this fact.

Among others, Marshall successfully appealed to Victor Rosewater, a newspaper publisher in Omaha, Nebraska;

to Julius Rosenwald, president of Sears, Roebuck in Chicago; to Louis Horkheimer, a merchant in Wheeling, West Virginia; to A. Leo Weil, a lawyer in Pittsburgh; to Simon Fleishmann, a lawyer in Buffalo, New York and president of the Erie Country Bar Association; and to Rabbi Eugene Mannheimer in Des Moines, Iowa.[1] In response to the AJC's appeals, Mannheimer, for one, replied to Marshall that he had discussed the literacy test "with several of our local bankers and businessmen of influence with the Senators from Iowa and they agreed to write the desired letters on the same day."[2]

Marshall also asked Adolph Lewisohn, a copper magnate who was president of the United Metals Selling Company and Adolph Lewisohn & Sons, to discuss the literacy test and exemption clause with President Wilson. Consequently, Lewisohn spoke with Wilson and reported that the President felt he was under great pressure from the restrictionists. According to Lewisohn, Wilson was sympathetic to the idea

---

[1] Victor Rosewater to Marshall, Dec. 18, 1914; Louis Horkheimer to Marshall, Dec. 18, 1914; William C. Graves (secretary to Rosenwald) to Marshall, Dec. 18, 1914; A. Leo Weil to Marshall, Dec. 18, 1914; Simon Fleischmann to Marshall, Dec. 18, 1914, in Marshall Papers, AJHS.

[2] Eugene Mannheimer to Marshall, Dec. 21, 1914, in Marshall Papers, AJHS.

of an exemption clause that would aid the immigrants fleeing from religious persecution, but Wilson also added that he was not certain that an exemption would work well. With Lewisohn, Wilson discussed the difficulty of defining "religious persecution" and questioned the practicality of an exemption clause "as it would force the United States Government to decide whether this condition exists or not and might be held to be interference."[1]

Once again Marshall was eager to arrange for a non-Jewish Democrat to introduce the AJC exemption clause in the Senate. This time, however, he had much better luck than he had had with A. Mitchell Palmer. Marshall approached Charles Thomas of Colorado in the spring of 1914, although he already knew that Thomas favored the literacy test. In December, Thomas agreed to introduce the exemption clause in the Senate despite his reservations about it—reservations that he expressed to Marshall.

> I have given, and very largely on your account, considerable thought to the subject matter of your argument, and while I have reached the point of voting for it as it came from your hands and as I introduced it, I do not believe that the last clause is a wise one. Its general phraseology will admit of the broadest construction, and will go a long way toward, if not entirely obliterating the purpose of the literacy test. I have not withdrawn

---

[1]Adolph Lewisohn to Marshall, Dec. 14 and Dec. 18, 1914, in Marshall Papers, AJHS.

> it nor shall I withdraw it. Since my colloquy with
> Senator Reed, I have been requested not to do so. I
> shall vote therefore, for it.[1]

It is possible that Thomas felt some obligation to help Marshall because Marshall's law partner Samuel Untermyer had helped Thomas during his last Senatorial campaign. "Please remember me kindly and gratefully to Mr. Untermyer," Thomas wrote Marshall, "whose speech in my behalf during the campaign was far more potent in its effect than the size of the audience would appear to indicate."[2]

When Thomas introduced the exemption amendment he set off a sharp debate between restrictionists Ellison D. Smith and John Sharp Williams, on the one hand, and anti-restrictionists William J. Stone from Missouri, James O'Gorman from New York, and James Reed, a Democrat from Missouri. The latter three not only supported the Thomas amendment but broadened it to include immigrants who sought admission to avoid "religious, political, and racial persecution whether such persecution be evidenced by overt acts or discriminatory laws or regulations."[3] The restrictionists

---

[1] Charles Thomas to Marshall, Dec. 30, 1914, in Marshall Papers, AJHS.

[2] Thomas to Marshall, Dec. 14, 1914, in Marshall Papers, AJHS.

[3] U.S., *Congressional Record*, 63d Cong., 3d sess., 1914, LII, Part 1, 786.

argued on the broad ground that high educational standards were necessary for enlightened political behavior. They fiercely contended that the liberal exemption clause would negate the literacy test. Reed counterattacked by insisting that the opposition to the Thomas amendment stemmed from a desire to stop all Jewish immigration. But "Cotton Ed" Smith denied this accusation by stating that the Jews would not be affected by the literacy test. He added, however, that the Thomas amendment was too radical under any circumstances: "I appreciate fully the object sought to be attained--the opening of our doors as far as may be to the Jews alone. We might not be adverse to that as a general proposition were we assured that it could not be used for other purposes . . . , I am quite sure that the effect would be to nullify the literacy test."[1]

John Sharp Williams then defended the restrictionist position with a sharper, more eloquent argument than Smith had provided. He directed the debate away from the narrow issue of Jewish immigration and the Thomas amendment to the bigger one of restricting all undesirable immigrants. Williams supported the test because it "happens accidentally to admit a very large proportion of the best races of the

---

[1] Ibid., p. 350.

world and to exclude a very large proportion of the worst."[1] As far as Williams was concerned the eastern and southern Europeans were the worst and the Belgians, who were suffering from the recent German invasion, were among the best--even illiterate Belgians. In line with this thinking, Williams introduced an amendment to exempt illiterate Belgians from the literacy test.

When the voting took place on December 31, the restrictionists held their firm majority. The Senate defeated the Thomas amendment by a vote of 26 to 34. Senator Martine of New Jersey then proposed dropping the literacy test entirely but the Senate defeated his proposal by a vote of 12 to 47. Finally, the Senate gave in to the anti-restrictionists on one point by agreeing to Senator O'Gorman's proposal to delete the word "solely"--"solely to escape religious persecution"--from the Burnett exemption clause.

After the anti-restrictionists suffered these major defeats, the skillful and pugnacious James A. Reed started to make trouble for the restrictionists. He added new restrictive clauses to the bill by which he intended to make it offensive to Mormons as well as certain Republicans, especially Missouri Republicans, who had Negro constituents.

---

[1]Ibid., p. 397.

First Reed proposed to exclude arbitrarily all non-Caucasian immigrants. Ironically, Smith, who was hardly a friend of the Negroes, argued that the Reed amendment would lead to diplomatic complications for the United States. Reed shot back that treaties and diplomacy were hardly the issue since the Senate was ready to discriminate against certain nationalities by means of the literacy test. The Senate defeated Reed on his first proposal but not on two of his next amendments. The Senate agreed to exclude all Negro and African immigrants as well as to make more difficult the entry of immigrants who practiced polygamy. The Senate also adopted Williams' Belgian amendment. Finally, on January 2, the Senate passed the Burnett bill by the overwhelming vote of 50 to 7.

As was expected, when the bill went back to the House, a majority of Representatives objected to Reed's amendment relating to the exclusion of Negroes and Williams' exemption for the Belgians. The House found other points of disagreement with the Senate's modifications of the Burnett bill and therefore appointed Augustus Gardner, John Burnett, and Adolph Sabath to confer with Senators Henry Cabot Lodge, Ellison D. Smith, and Democrat Joseph T. Robinson of Arkansas. Without any protracted discussion the conferees dropped the highly controversial Reed and

Williams amendments and settled their other differences. The conferees also tightened up the Burnett exemption clause by reinserting the word "solely."[1] On January 14, the Senate agreed to the conference report by a voice vote. One day later the House followed suit by passing the Burnett bill by a vote of 227 to 94. The pattern of voting was the same as in the past: the South, Far West, and non-urban areas of the Middle West provided the overwhelming number of restrictionist votes, while the anti-restrictionists drew upon support from Chicago, Philadelphia, New York, Massachusetts, and Wisconsin.

Despite President Wilson's discouraging letter to Senator Smith in March, 1914, Samuel Gompers, Secretary of Labor William B. Wilson, and John Sharp Williams, men who had access to the President, worked hard to prevent another Wilson veto. William Wilson, whose department now included the Immigration Bureau, was a confirmed restrictionist. Not only had he voted for the literacy test when he was a Representative from Pennsylvania in 1913, but after he became Secretary of Labor, he proposed the radical idea that all immigrants pass an army physical to qualify for admission

---

[1] U.S., Congress, Senate, Conference Report: Regulation of Immigration, 63d Cong., 3d sess., Jan. 11, 1915, S. Doc. 712, to accompany S6060.

into the United States.[1] Senator Williams, for his part, continued the aggressive campaign on behalf of the test which he had begun in the Senate debates. In a letter to President Wilson, he recommended that Wilson sign the immigration bill and thereby disregard any "entangling promises" made during the campaign at "headquarters."[2] (Williams was referring to a discussion among William McAdoo, Schiff, Morgenthau and others in 1912 concerning Wilson's position on the test. As a result of the talk Wilson had written a letter to Cyrus Adler in which he expressed sympathy--in general terms--for the new immigrants.)[3]

Wilson, however, was not willing to follow the advice given by Gompers, Labor Secretary Wilson, and Williams. "Nothing is more distasteful to me than to set my judgment against so many of my friends and associates in public life," Wilson wrote to Williams on January 7. Nevertheless, Wilson took a firm stand against the test:

---

[1] The New York Times, Jan. 24, 1914, p. 3. Organized labor had great success with the Wilson Democrats. Marc Karson estimates that between 1913 and 1915 Congress passed twenty-six bills which the A.F.L. wanted. Karson, op. cit., p. 81.

[2] John Sharp Williams to Wilson, Jan. 4, 1915, in Wilson Papers, Series IV, Folder 292.

[3] Adler to Charles Jacobson, Oct. 17, 1912, in Adler Papers.

I myself made the most explicit statements at the time
of the Presidential election about this subject to
groups of our fellow-citizens of foreign extraction
whom I wished to treat with perfect frankness and for
whom I had entire respect. In view of what I said to
them, I do not see how it will be possible for me to
give my assent to the bill. I know that you will
appreciate the scrupe [sic] upon which I act.[1]

For the public, however, Wilson maintained a facade of uncertainty and suspense. The President received hundreds of letters on the literacy test from prominent anti-restrictionists such as Schiff, Jane Addams, Andrew Carnegie, and Oswald Garrison Villard, and from restrictionists such as William Dillingham, John Burnett, and Franklin MacVeagh, Taft's Secretary of the Treasury. To MacVeagh, Wilson wrote: "My present judgment is that the test proposed is a mistaken one, but I never close my mind until the moment for action has come and the decision must be made."[2] Nine days later Wilson wrote Charles Eliot, the ex-President of Harvard University and an outspoken anti-restrictionist: "I must keep my mind open to both sides, but my present judgment is with yours."[3]

---

[1] Wilson to Williams, Jan. 7, 1915, Wilson Papers, Series IV, Folder 292.

[2] Wilson to Franklin MacVeagh, Jan. 13, 1915, in *ibid*.

[3] Wilson to Charles Eliot, Jan. 22, 1915, in *ibid*.

On January 22, the President held a public hearing for five hundred representatives of labor, ethnic, and patriotic groups who were interested in the immigration bill. The hearing lasted three and one-half hours with the time equally divided between the restrictionists and the anti-restrictionists. Marshall harshly criticized the literacy test for discriminating against eastern European immigrants; he did not, however, discuss the exemption clause.

Like Marshall, most of the participants focused on the literacy test but there were strong objections to other aspects of the bill as well. For example, Oswald Garrison Villard, on behalf of the Friends of Russian Freedom, argued that many provisions in the bill would destroy the right of political asylum. He specifically objected to the prohibition against the entry of persons affiliated with groups advocating or teaching the destruction of property and the overthrow of organized governments. (The Friends of Russian Freedom also objected to the literacy test, but they were not primarily concerned with it because most Russian radicals were literate.)[1]

---

[1] Paul Kennady to Editor, The New York Times, Jan. 18, 1915, p. 10.

It is evident from President Wilson's letters to Senator Williams, Franklin MacVeagh, and Charles Eliot that he was never affected by indecision, as President Taft had been, or by the restrictionists around him. Wilson never seriously consulted with his Cabinet about the test, as Taft had done, because he was sure of his position and because he feared a leak to the press.[1] He never even read a memorandum on the merits of the bill that Secretary of Labor Wilson had prepared for him.[2] He did, however, speak with House and Senate conferees on January 25 after they requested a meeting with him.

Consequently, six days after his public hearing Wilson used the veto for the first time in his Administration to reject the immigration bill. In his message to Congress Wilson expressed two separate reasons for his dissatisfaction with the bill. In the first place, Wilson did not approve of the sections relating to radical political activists which he maintained would effectively end the traditional "right of political asylum." Wilson declared that the bill "seeks to all but close entirely the gates of asylum, which

---

[1] Arthur S. Link, "A Portrait of Wilson," *Virginia Quarterly Review,* XXXII (Autumn, 1956), 353.

[2] David F. Houston, *Eight Years with the Wilson Cabinet: 1913-1920* (Garden City, N.Y., 1926), I, 127.

have always been open to those who could find nowhere else the right and opportunity of constitutional agitation for what they conceived to be the natural and inalienable rights of men."[1]

Secondly, Wilson did not support the literacy test which he viewed as "an even more radical change in the policy of the nation." The literacy test, Wilson wrote, "excludes those to whom the opportunities of elementary education have been denied without regard to their character, their purposes, or their natural capacity." Wilson disapproved of the basic purpose of the test: to restrict arbitrarily. He also wrote that there was no compelling popular mandate for restriction since none of the major parties in 1912 had appealed to the voters on a restriction plank.[2]

Wilson publicly justified his veto on only these two grounds, therefore it is important to note that he ignored the exemption issue that the AJC was so concerned with. He did not object to or even discuss the Burnett exemption clause, nor did he raise the issue of political persecution

---

[1] U.S., Congressional Record, 63d Cong., 3d sess., 1914, LII, Part 3, 2481-2482.

[2] Ibid.

in connection with the literacy test. Some historians have maintained that Wilson objected to the literacy test because it did not contain an exemption for political refugees. For example, John Higham has written that Wilson "was especially struck by the failure of the bill to exempt from the literacy test refugees from political persecution."[1] But this interpretation is not borne out by a close reading of the veto message, subsequent Congressional action, and Wilson's veto in 1917.

It is not clear whether Wilson used his 1912 election commitment, described in his January 7 letter to Senator Williams, as an excuse for having to displease his southern followers, or whether he believed that the commitment was firmer than it really was. It is evident that during the campaign Wilson had spoken sympathetically about Jewish, Polish, and Italian immigrants and had lauded the tradition of open immigration. A letter from Wilson to Illinois Representative Adolph Sabath is a good example of this attitude: "The Democratic Party could not without forgetting its very origin advocate an illiberal policy in the matter of immigration." Wilson then went on to state: "There must be regulation of immigration. Criminals must not be admitted.

---

[1] Higham, Strangers in the Land, p. 192.

Those who are diseased or defective must be excluded in order to safeguard the physical integrity of our people. . . . The necessary limits have been recognized again and again in such legislation."[1] Wilson, however, never put himself on record as opposing the literacy test, despite his generous campaign rhetoric in regard to the new immigrants. The leaders of the AJC had tried to get Wilson to commit himself on the test, but time and again during the election he had refused to take a definite position.

If Wilson's political commitments might have greatly influenced his decision to veto the literacy test, he kept this reason from the public. Instead, he maintained that his idealism--which burned strongly during the First World War-- turned him against the immigration bill. According to the veto message, the tradition of open immigration was an essential part of America's greatness; it differentiated her from other countries. Wilson maintained that he was using the veto to protect the "long-established policy of this country, a policy in which our people have conceived the very

---

[1] U.S., *Congressional Record*, 63d Cong., 3d sess., 1914, LII, Part 2, 1387. Sabath, a Clark supporter in 1912, refused to endorse Wilson because of his attitude towards the new immigrants. Only after a meeting was held between the two men, did Sabath become friendly to Wilson. *Current Biography: 1946* (New York, 1947), p. 530.

character of their Government to be expressed, the very mission and spirit of the nation in respect of its relations to the peoples of the world outside their borders."[1]

After the veto, restrictionists and anti-restrictionists worked feverishly to influence the vote in the House. "I have been moving heaven and earth to get the necessary votes," Marshall wrote Cyrus Adler on February 1, "and have been much encouraged by the response which I have met in certain directions."[2] Marshall, however, would not resort to mass meetings since he feared that an anti-restrictionist rally would stimulate labor to stage an even larger and louder demonstration in favor of the test.

Marshall and other AJC leaders used many different arguments touching upon idealistic, humanitarian, and religious matters to gain new allies, although Marshall's 1915 "speciality" was that the literacy test was a southern measure. He employed this argument when he asked Edgar T. Bruckett to influence his Congressman to vote for Wilson or not to vote at all. Tell him, Marshall wrote Bruckett, that voting for the literacy test would be "playing into the hands

---

[1] U.S., Congressional Record, 63d Cong., 3d sess., 1914, LII, Part 3, 2481-2482.

[2] Marshall to Adler, Feb. 1, 1915, in Marshall Papers, AJA.

of the southern democracy which fathers this brutal legislation. Kindly telegraph at my expense and bring all possible influence to bear on the Congressman."[1]

Marshall appealed to Isaac Adler in Rochester, New York, to influence Republican Representatives Henry G. Danforth and Thomas Dunn who had previously voted for the literacy test. To William Barnes, Jr., Chairman of the Republican State Committee, Marshall wrote that the literacy test was "purely a Southern Democratic measure" and asked Barnes to telegraph all Republican members of the New York Congressional delegation to oppose the test. To New York's Democratic Governor Martin Glynn, Marshall wrote that the literacy test was both anti-Jewish and anti-Catholic. Marshall requested Glynn to telegraph, at Marshall's expense, all Democratic members of the New York delegation.[2]

On February 4, the House debated Wilson's veto and the familiar impassioned arguments were heard on both sides. When the House finally voted, the restrictionists lost once again by a vote of 261 to 136, this time the margin of

---

[1] Marshall to Edgar T. Bruckett, Feb. 1, 1915, in Marshall Papers, AJHS.

[2] Marshall to Isaac Adler, Feb. 1, 1915; Marshall to William Barnes, Jr., Feb. 1, 1915; Marshall to Martin Glynn, Feb. 1, 1915, in Marshall Papers, AJHS.

defeat being only five votes. Thus a small but decisive number of Representatives, possibly under pressure from the White House, were responsible for perpetuating the tradition of open immigration for at least another few years.[1] The AJC openly and aggressively lobbied against the test and for its exemption clause, but it is not apparent that it deserves much credit for this third restrictionist defeat. Once again, the President, for reasons of his own and independently of Jewish pressure, was the decisive influence.

All parties to the dispute--the restrictionists, Wilson, and the AJC--sensed that the battle would start again in the near future. But none of them could know how different their world would soon be. At the time of Wilson's veto, just six months after the outbreak of the First World War, ominous forces were at work that would finally defeat the anti-restrictionists. This last literacy test battle in the Progressive era was fought against the background of America's precarious neutrality in respect to the European war.

---

[1] Higham, Strangers in the Land, p. 193.

CHAPTER VI

VICTORIES AMID DEFEATS

From 1915 to 1917 the First World War affected American Jewry in several important ways. Among its many effects, the war gave rise to a divisive and precarious American neutrality program, a siege of eastern European Jewry, the overthrow of the Czarist regime, and a split between the AJC and the American Jewish congress movement. The war also thwarted the main objectives of the AJC's anti-Russian policies: a rapprochement between the United States and Russia shattered the dream and expectation that the AJC could aid Russian Jewry. No longer could Jewish leaders hope to solve the American-Jewish immigration problem by the formulation of a hostile United States policy towards Russia.

Moreover, the war decisively affected the outcome of the second and final Wilsonian battle over the literacy test in 1916 and 1917. The restrictionists used the war to convert the southern and eastern European immigration problem into a frightening symbol of turmoil in Europe. They argued, convincingly, that the war would let loose a deluge of refugees who would inundate the United States and exacerbate the problems of crime, labor competition, political corruption, and racial accommodation.

Faced by this overwhelming restrictionist sentiment, the AJC persisted in trying to gain Congressional acceptance of a strong exemption clause. Its efforts finally proved successful when both the House and Senate accepted a clause satisfactory to the AJC. For the AJC, however, there was a price to pay for this major lobbying victory: by gaining the exemption measure, both the AJC and American Jewry became vulnerable to the charge of promoting preferential treatment and special interest legislation. Unhappily, the AJC faced complaints, expressed in the Senate and press, about the deplorable effects of Jewish immigration and Jewish lobbying.

When the test issue shifted to the White House, Wilson once again vetoed the restrictive immigration bill; this time, however, he could not prevail over Congress. And once again the war left its unmistakable mark: not only did the European conflict provide the restrictionists with the necessary justification--and fears--for finally repassing the test over Wilson's veto, but ironically, the war caused the President to oppose the AJC's exemption clause as an irritant to good Russian-American relations.

I

For many months after President Wilson took office the AJC leaders had reason to be pleased with the way that he responded to their foreign policy requests. The President was accessible to Jewish leaders such as Jacob H. Schiff, Henry Morgenthau, Louis Marshall, Rabbi Stephen Wise, and of course Louis Brandeis. Soon after Wilson entered the White House he proved his good faith to the American Jews by promising American diplomatic aid to help obtain civil and religious rights for the Jews in the Balkan countries.

During the Balkan War in 1912, Bulgaria, Greece, and Serbia defeated Turkey and occupied areas in which 250,000 Jews lived. Those Jews had enjoyed civil and political rights when they were part of the Ottoman Empire. Fearing strong anti-Semitism in the Balkan countries--especially Bulgaria--the AJC asked President Taft and later President Wilson to intervene in the peace negotiations on behalf of the Balkan Jews. Taft refused the request but Wilson was willing to allow the United States government to intervene in the London negotiations because of American Jewry's concern for the Balkan Jews.[1]

---

[1] Marshall to Wilson, July 30, 1913, in Marshall Papers, AJA.

Now, in 1914, the AJC's requests concerning Russian-American relations became increasingly difficult for Wilson to meet and he was no longer fully responsive to the organization's foreign policy demands. The leaders of the AJC had three major objectives: to maintain their own financial boycott of Russia, established after the turn of the century, and to prevent American businessmen from investing in Russian trade and loans; to keep the American public from becoming sympathetic to the Russian war effort; and to stop the United States government from writing a new treaty with Russia that would ignore American-Jewish rights in the passport matter.

Unhappily for the AJC, the war made Russian-American relations vastly more important than they had been during the Roosevelt and Taft years: by 1915, the Wilson Administration deemed it essential for the United States to maintain good relations with Russia. Secretary of State Robert Lansing expressed this view in 1915 to Colonel Edward M. House, Wilson's close friend and adviser: "In no event should we take a course that would seriously endanger our friendly relations with Great Britain, France, or Russia . . . for our friendship with Germany is a thing of the past."[1]

---

[1] Charles Seymour, *The Intimate Papers of Colonel House* (Boston, 1926), II, 70.

Within the framework of a controversial and shifting neutrality program, "friendly relations" meant carrying on a flourishing trade with the Allies. This trade in raw materials, ammunitions, and food stuffs made the United States prosper and grow dependent on its European customers. As for the Russians, in the first months of 1915, American bankers and businessmen began to invest heavily in Russian trade: they extended credits to Russia for her purchases and looked forward to the time when they could float loans in the American market for all the Allied countries. They did not have to wait long because President Wilson, Secretary of State Lansing, and Treasury Secretary William McAdoo, fearful of causing a second depression during their administration, rescinded their earlier prohibition against loans to belligerent countries.[1] In September, 1915, Wilson and the State Department privately gave their approval for the floating of loans to the Allied governments and soon thereafter American bankers raised hundreds of millions of dollars for the Allied powers. In June, 1916, for example, the National City Bank sponsored a three-year loan to Russia of $50 million.

The leaders of the AJC strongly disapproved of

---

[1] Paul Birdsall, "Neutrality and Economic Pressure, 1914-1917," *Science and Society*, III (Spring, 1939), 222.

Wilson's policy that allowed the United States financial community to invest money in the Russian government. Their objections, however, had no effect. First, in January, 1915, Schiff and Marshall objected to William McAdoo about the news that banks within the Federal Reserve System would be able to extend $25 million in credits to the Russian government.[1] Then later in the year, Schiff refused to participate in any of the loans to the Allies, although several of the partners at Kuhn, Loeb, & Co., including his son, were eager for the company's involvement.[2] In June, 1916, when the Boston investment banking firm of Lee, Higginson, & Co. asked Marshall to participate in a Russian loan, he not only refused the offer but castigated its partners for caring more for their profits than for the honor of American citizens. (With Marshall's consent, the New York Evening Journal published his reply.)[3]

Schiff tried hard to use his leverage as one of America's most powerful bankers to pressure the Russians: he expressly maintained that as soon as Russia granted civil

---

[1] Marshall to William McAdoo, Jan. 15, 1915, in Marshall Papers, AJA.

[2] Schiff, op. cit., II, 251.

[3] Marshall to Messr. Lee, Higginson, & Co., June 19, 1916, in Marshall Papers, AJA.

rights to the Jews, he would raise $200 million for it.[1] Until that time, however, Schiff refused, and would continue to refuse, to aid all the Allies since Great Britain and France insisted on sharing their loans with Russia. Schiff's lucrative offer, however, failed either to affect relations among the Allies or to entice Russia into changing her policy toward the Jews. Thus, the leaders of the AJC were totally unsuccessful in applying financial pressure, a fact which Schiff lamented in 1916: "With the present active and profitable relations with Russia it will be difficult if at all possible to get our Government to undertake something positive to give effect to the situation which should have been brought about by the abrogation of the Commercial Treaty some four or five years ago."[2]

Furthermore, heavy American investments in Russia as well as friendship for her as a member of the Allied cause prompted the Wilson Administration to open discussions about a new Russian-American commercial treaty in 1915. Wilson's first Ambassador to Russia was George T. Marye of California, an active and wealthy contributor to the Democratic party,

---

[1] Zosa Szajkowski, "Jewish Diplomacy," *Jewish Social Studies*, XXII (July, 1960), 135.

[2] Schiff to Dr. Blank, June 6, 1916, in Schiff Papers.

who previously had not held any diplomatic posts. No important events in American-Russian relations marked his stay in St. Petersburg until July, 1915, when Wilson, Lansing, and Marye agreed that the time was right to begin negotiations for a new treaty.[1] Wilson and Lansing, however, doubted that Marye would be able to handle the delicate negotiations and therefore in 1916, Wilson appointed David R. Francis, a former Governor of Missouri, to replace Marye, who resigned for reasons of ill health.[2]

Wilson and Lansing were eager to write a new treaty before the Presidential election of November, 1916: such an agreement would indicate to Congress and the American voters the skillfulness of Wilson's diplomatic efforts. "If a treaty such as the one proposed can be negotiated before Congress meets, I think it would be a distinct triumph for the Administration," Lansing wrote Wilson in July, 1915.[3] But both the President and his Secretary of State predicted that a majority of Senators would oppose a new treaty unless

---

[1] George T. Marye to Robert Lansing, June 23, 1915, in SDF 711.612/242.

[2] Wilson to Lansing, July 29, 1915, in SDF 711.612/242 1/2.

[3] Lansing to Wilson, July 26, 1915, in SDF 711.612/242.

it resolved the passport matters in a way pleasing to their Jewish supporters. "Of course the passport question must be included," Lansing supposed, "otherwise there would be no hope of securing Senatorial consent."[1] Wilson had earlier recognized this requirement in a letter to Schiff: "I am very anxious to enter into and conclude such a treaty but you may be sure that it will not be done without a satisfactory adjustment of the great question to which you allude."[2]

While Wilson's *sine qua non* of the negotiations satisfied the AJC, it displeased Francis. Despite the fact that he had conferred in New York with several AJC leaders, who tried to win him to their cause, Francis was not willing to allow the passport matter to impede the treaty negotiations. He advised President Wilson in April, 1916 that "our Jewish friends must not expect too much. They are but 3% of the population of Russia." In the same letter to Wilson, Francis minimized the importance and validity of the Russian-Jewish problem as conceived by American Jews: "many cultured and well-meaning Russians have no desire to oppress the Jews; in fact they consider the Jewish question almost immaterial

---

[1] *Ibid*.

[2] Wilson to Schiff, Apr. 11, 1915, in Wilson Papers, Series III.

compared with other problems in their hands and have no conception of the proportion the issue has assumed in the United States."[1] On his own Francis tried to work out various solutions to the passport matter, proposing that America allow Russia to distinguish between American-born Jews and naturalized American-Jewish citizens who wanted to travel in Russia.

Despite his efforts and the Wilson Administration's desire to write a new treaty, Francis learned in May, 1916 that Russia would not enter into serious negotiations. Francis reported that Russia was preoccupied with the war and questions affecting her economic ties to her Allies. At the same time Francis learned that Russia would not discuss the Jewish question in future negotiations with the American Ambassador, nor did she intend to terminate the Pale before the end of the war.[2] Consequently, in the late summer of 1916 the State Department adopted a wait-and-see attitude towards American-Russian affairs. Frank L. Polk, counselor to the State Department, instructed Francis "to show no

---

[1] David R. Francis to Wilson, Apr. 8, 1916, in SDF 711.612/247 1/2.

[2] Francis to Lansing, May 2, 1916, in SDF 711.612/248 1/2; Francis to Lansing, May 7, 1916, in SDF 711.612/249 1/2.

interest whatever in a new treaty or in closer commercial relations." Polk concluded that "a treaty is not necessary at the present time."[1]

Francis was deeply disappointed by the failure to complete an agreement, a failure he attributed in large measure to the AJC's insistence that a treaty permit all United States citizens to travel freely throughout Russia. "It would not only be impossible to negotiate such a treaty at this time but very impolitic to attempt to do so," Francis wrote Polk in July, 1916.[2] Furthermore, his opinion of the Russian Jews was most unfavorable although he said that he admired Jews like Oscar S. Straus, had some Jews as "personal friends," and felt "no prejudice against the Jews as a class nor as a race." In Russia, however, things were different: if Russia emancipated the Jews "the peasants would stand no show whatsoever with the designing, usurious, and pitiless Jews," wrote Francis. "It seems that while all of the Jews are not spies, a decided majority of the spies are Jews."[3]

---

[1] Frank L. Polk to Francis, Aug. 18, 1916, in Frank L. Polk Papers (Yale University, New Haven, Conn.). Cited hereafter as Polk Papers.

[2] Francis to Lansing, July 12, 1916, in SDF 711.612/248.

[3] Francis to Polk, Aug. 30, 1916, in Polk Papers.

The war not only created foreign policy imperatives which were too powerful for the AJC to resist, but it also provided the opportunity and justification for a fight for leadership within the American-Jewish community. The "opportunity" developed when Louis Brandeis headed the American Zionist movement in 1914; the "justification" concerned controversies over the organization of relief for eastern European Jews, the rights of Jews in Palestine and eastern Europe in the post-war world--minority rights versus nationality rights and Jewish autonomy--and the distribution of power within the American-Jewish community.[1] But the AJC's fight against restriction and the literacy test, it is important to note, was never an issue between the opposing factions within American Jewry.

"The Committee, being the representative Jewish body in America," Schiff declared in August, 1914, "ought to lead the movement for the amelioration of the condition of the Jews throughout the world, and not the Zionists."[2] Power was the essence of the struggle between the two opposing

---

[1] For a discussion of the highly complicated minority rights question see Oscar I. Janowsky, The Jews and Minority Rights: 1899-1919 (New York, 1933).

[2] Minutes, AJC, Aug. 31, 1914.

factions. Since 1906 the AJC had been the undisputed spokesman on political and foreign matters for the German-Jewish and Russian-Jewish communities in the United States. The leaders of the AJC felt secure with a tight organizational structure in which Marshall and Schiff established policy for the entire AJC and for American Jewry as well. The AJC believed in the necessity and propriety of making policy in private as well as carrying on discreet negotiations with Congress and the executive branch--except, of course, in the passport campaign.[1] Marshall and Schiff prided themselves on their roles as leaders and patently did not want to share their power with new people and ideological enemies. Those enemies were the Zionists and the congress movement that the Zionists spawned, which seemed to threaten Jewish assimilation into American life. If American Jews want to wipe out

---

[1] The AJC's approach to the Mendel Beiliss ritual murder case in Russia clearly illustrates its self-defeating style. Marshall gave information about the case to newspapers and Protestant organizations. But he wrote Schiff: "It has been our idea that in a case of this sort, it is highly dangerous and imprudent for the Jews to be too much in evidence. . . . It would be folly, however, for us to make these facts known, because it would deprive the apparently spontaneous outburst of indignation to which the press has given voice, of much of its force." Marshall to Schiff, Oct. 30, 1913, in Marshall Papers, AJA. (When Beiliss was acquitted the AJC feared that he might capitalize on his fame and join a vaudeville act in the United States. The AJC was willing to pay him up to $5,000 to stay in Europe. Minutes, AJC, Jan. 18, 1914.)

anti-Semitism, warned Jacob Schiff, they can continue to be "Jews in faith" but there must be no "strings" to their citizenship. "We need feel that politically no one has any claim upon us but the country of which, of our own free will, we have become citizens. . . . "[1]

Schiff's arguments notwithstanding, the Zionists became a group capable of challenging the AJC after Brandeis became President of the Provisional Executive Committee for Zionist Affairs in August, 1914. From time to time, men close to Marshall and Schiff, such as Judah Magnes, Julian Mack, and Mayer Sulzberger, involved themselves in the Zionist movement. But Brandeis, with his great prestige, access to the President, and talent for attracting large numbers of supporters to his cause, made the Zionists a serious ideological and political threat to the AJC. Backed by the Yiddish press and the great body of Russian-Jewish immigrants, Brandeis, Rabbi Stephen Wise, Felix Frankfurter, Horace Kallen, and Richard Gottheil rebelled against the AJC's exclusive representation of American Jewry. The schism drew strength from historic, cultural, religious, and class differences between the German Jews and the Russian Jews in America. "Intellectuals and idealists were aligned with the

---

[1] Schiff, op. cit., II, 165.

masses" in the fight against "the capitalistic paternalism of the AJC," according to one explanation advanced by Horace Kallen.[1]

The great body of American Jews regarded the brilliant and prominent Brandeis as a charismatic leader and they welcomed his concern for the cultural heritage of eastern European Jewry. Despite the fact that many American Jews rejected Zionism as too controversial and radical, they nevertheless hailed Brandeis' program for deposing the AJC and giving power to a democratically elected Jewish congress. To have "self-respect," Felix Frankfurter wrote, "the Jews in America must think their own thoughts, make their collective personal sacrifices, express their own will, [and] choose their own leaders. . . ."[2]

To the leaders of the AJC, however, the idea of a democratically elected, permanent Jewish congress was abhorrent, not only because they disliked losing power, but also because they feared exposing and isolating themselves as a

---

[1] Horace Kallen to Louis Brandeis, June 3, 1916, in Brandeis Papers (American Zionist Archives, New York). For a full discussion of Brandeis' involvement with the Zionists see Yonathan Shapiro, "Leaderships of the American Zionist Organization: 1897-1930" (unpublished Ph.D. dissertation, Columbia University, 1964).

[2] Felix Frankfurter to Marshall, June 29, 1916, in Dr. Harry Friedenwald Papers (American Zionist Archives, New York).

separate group. At a time when the United States was tense over neutrality, the hyphenate issue, and the preparedness movement, Schiff and Marshall ruefully predicted that a Jewish congress would express anti-Allied sentiments, antagonize the American public, and raise questions about the loyalty of American Jews. We "will become a people by ourselves," Schiff declared at a meeting of the AJC's executive committee, and will bring on the "darkest day for Jewry." A congress will create a "nation within a nation" and make "Jewish Americans" not "American Jews"; it will mean "the establishment of a new government, a government for the Jews by which the Jews are to be bound."[1]

Ironically, at the time that Schiff was making an issue of the loyalty of the Zionists and congress advocates, Theodore Roosevelt accused pro-German sympathizers--of whom Schiff was thought to be one--of being "professional German

_____

[1] Minutes, AJC, May 9, 1915. "To my mind the problems with which we have to deal are of so delicate a nature, that the mob cannot grapple with them," Marshall wrote Israel Zangwill in August, 1915. Reznikoff, op. cit., II, 519. To Lord Reading, Chief Justice of England, Marshall wrote: "Those with pro-German proclivities have sought to bring about the convening of what they are pleased to call a Jewish Congress, at which it is expected that the Jewish question shall be publicly discussed, with the inevitable result of attempting to create public opinion in favor of Germany and Austria, and against the Allies." Ibid., II, 511.

Americans" who instead should be "Americans of German origin."[1] For like Schiff, great numbers of American-Jewish immigrants were pro-German largely because of their antipathy for Russia; only after the Russian Revolution did they adopt the pro-Allied position of most Americans.[2]

The conflict within the Jewish community over leadership, organization, and ideals was tense and enervating. From 1914 through 1916 the leaders of the congress movement and the AJC disseminated propaganda, waged organizational warfare, and held a series of unpleasant and unfruitful negotiations aimed at resolving their differences. Finally, in the fall of 1916 the leaders of the two groups made peace by agreeing to call a Jewish congress as soon as the war ended.[3]

The fighting had touched upon many different Jewish issues, but it is important to restate that the dispute never involved the AJC's fight against the literacy test.

---

[1] Higham, *Strangers in the Land*, p. 198. Marshall also characterized Schiff as having "pro-German proclivities." Marshall to Adler, Sept. 22, 1915, in Marshall Papers, AJA.

[2] See Joseph Rappaport, "The American Yiddish Press and the European Conflict in 1914," *Jewish Social Studies*, XIX (July-October, 1957), 113-28.

[3] For a full discussion of the complicated and important schism see Janowsky, op. cit.; Shapiro, op. cit.; Goren, *New York Jews and the Quest for Community*.

The congress people never entered the anti-restriction territory of the AJC. They deferred to the AJC in this matter because they recognized that it was best equipped to lobby with Congress during the fourth and final battle over the test in the Progressive period.

II

In 1916, although no one concerned with the immigration controversy really could know what the end of the war would bring, Marshall and other AJC leaders argued that Congress should adopt a wait-and-see attitude before writing new legislation. Congress, however, was in no mood to delay since the restrictionists grimly predicted that the end of the war would release a flood of refugees from Europe. Clearly, the crux of the matter was not the current rate of immigration but that of the future. In 1915 and 1916 immigration dropped to unprecedented low levels: in 1915, there were 326,700 immigrants; in 1916, there were 298,826 as compared with 1,218,480 in 1913-1914. The Russian Jews, in particular, had no escape routes from Russia and across the Atlantic; therefore, only 26,497 Jews arrived in the United States in 1915 and 15,108 in 1916.[1]

---

[1] Caminetti, Annual Report (1918), p. 141.

Despite the very low immigration levels in 1916 and 1917, both restrictionists and anti-restrictionists sensed that the literacy test would become law in the near future. This expectation led some of the important participants in the restriction battle to propose concessions: Marshall was willing to make concessions to gain Congressional acceptance of his exemption clause; Representative John Burnett, Chairman of the House Immigration and Naturalization Committee, was willing to make concessions to Marshall which he hoped would weaken the ardor of the anti-restrictionists and insure enough support in Congress to override another veto.

In the spring of 1915 Burnett suggested that he might include an exemption clause acceptable to the AJC if the AJC would end its opposition to the literacy test. No understanding, however, was reached at the time. Then in January, 1916, when the House Committee was working on its new literacy test bill, Marshall revived the compromise idea when he instructed Fulton Brylawski, the AJC's resident lobbyist in Washington, to discuss Burnett's idea--but not to agree to it. Marshall directed Brylawski to see what Burnett's "attitude" would be "with regard to inserting such an exemption clause, if as a result of its insertion we would refrain from active opposition." Marshall was well aware that he was on delicate ground. "This of course must be done very discreetly," he added, "because I do not wish it to be understood that we are taking the initiative in this regard or that we are prepared to agree to withdraw active opposition."[1]

Burnett and the AJC never worked out any firm deal along the lines that Marshall had indicated. For the very first time, however, in January, 1916, the House Committee made a major concession to the Jewish lobbyists on the exemption clause when the Committee proposed an exemption for the following immigrants:

> all aliens who shall prove to the satisfaction of the proper immigration officer or to the Secretary of Labor that they are seeking admission to the United States to avoid religious persecution in the country of their last permanent residence, whether such persecution is evidenced by acts or by laws or government regulations that discriminate against the alien or the race to which he belongs because of his religious faith.[2]

Despite Marshall's persistence the Committee still refused to cite "political persecution" along with "religious persecution" as he had proposed because it feared an influx of Mexican revolutionaries.[3]

---

[1] Marshall to Brylawski, Jan. 8, 1916, in Marshall Papers, AJA.

[2] U.S., Congress, House, Committee on Immigration and Naturalization, Report, Immigration of Aliens into the United States, 64th Cong., 1st sess., Jan. 31, 1916, H. Rept. 95, to accompany H10384.

[3] Reznikoff, op. cit., I, 156.

Marshall was satisfied with the exemption clause although the wording was slightly different from his own proposal, applying to immigrants who were seeking admission to the United States "to avoid religious or political persecution, whether such persecution be evidenced by overt acts, or by discriminatory laws or regulations."[1] It is not clear whether Marshall wanted to withdraw the AJC from the anti-restriction fight once Burnett had accepted the new exemption clause. If this is what Marshall had in mind, Schiff clearly indicated that he was against such a change in policy. "I am not so very certain," Schiff wrote Marshall, "that a literacy test in any form should be approved by us, for there is a principle at stake in this which we should not surrender."[2] Therefore the AJC policy on the test fight was set: oppose the test, fight for an even more liberal exemption clause that would pertain to political persecution too, and mobilize the AJC network as in the past.[3]

On March 24, 1916, the House began debating the Burnett bill, in many respects a tougher one than any presented in the past. Except for the new exemption clause,

---

[1] Ibid., p. 150.

[2] Schiff to Marshall, Feb. 2, 1916, in Schiff Papers.

[3] Minutes, AJC, Mar. 12, 1916.

the literacy test remained exactly the same as the 1915 provision. The Committee raised the head tax from $4 to $8 for each immigrant except children under sixteen years of age. (The old head tax applied to all members of a family.) Immigrants suffering from "constitutional psychopathic inferiority" would be barred from entry. And Hindus and all individuals not eligible for citizenship would be automatically rejected, along with those already excluded by treaties and agreements.

The bill also provided for the deportation of immigrants who taught or advocated the unlawful destruction of property, within five years after entry into the United States. The Committee retained the restriction written in the 1915 bill against those who advocated, taught, or were affiliated with organizations that advised the destruction of property and the overthrow of organized governments. But the Committee took Wilson's 1915 veto message into account in respect to the political asylum provisions by adopting a new immunity clause: "That nothing in this Act shall exclude, if otherwise admissible, persons convicted, or who teach or advocate the commission, of an offense purely political."[1]

---

[1] U.S., Congress, House, Committee on Immigration and Naturalization, H. Rept. 95.

It was evident from the beginning of the debate that the House was deeply committed to passing Burnett's tough restrictive bill. The restrictionists even felt strong enough to use some scare tactics as Burnett threatened to propose a really severe restrictionist measure, if the literacy test failed again. Augustus Gardner, ever active in the restrictionist cause, said that he favored the termination of all immigration for ten years because of the threat of millions of Europeans arriving from the war-torn continent.

In addition to these threats, the restrictionists spoke repeatedly about the racial differences between the new and the old immigrants. John C. McKenzie, a Republican from Illinois, stressed the racial aspect when he associated the new immigrants with those from Asia, whom he regarded as the most unacceptable of all. McKenzie told the House that "the congenial assimilation of races so different in temperament and tradition as those of southern Europe and Oriental countries with the races of northern and western Europe is a practical impossibility even in this land of freedom." The southern Europeans, he added, "lacking in comprehension of the true spirit of our institutions," would only lower the "true standard of American citizenship."[1]

---

[1] U.S., *Congressional Record*, 64th Cong., 1st sess., 1916, LIII, Part 5, 4777.

Albert Johnson of Washington, riding high upon the crest of an anti-radical and anti-immigrant campaign in his home state, used different arguments. He informed the House that there was no more room in the cities or on public lands to accommodate the new immigrants. The war, Johnson said, would cause millions of undesirable immigrants to flood the United States, particularly the West Coast, as was evident from the fact that Russian-Jewish immigrants were already arriving at West Coast ports via Japan and the Pacific Ocean.[1] Then Jacob E. Meeker of Missouri raised some political objections to the new immigrants by arguing that the American democratic system could not survive the presence of a large illiterate population that was the tool of the bosses and trusts.

The anti-restrictionists fought back as hard as they could. Joseph Cannon, Isaac Siegel, Adolph Sabath, Julius Kahn, a Republican from San Francisco, and Meyer London, a Socialist from New York City, dwelled upon the inequities of the literacy test. They decried the religious and racial prejudices against the new immigrants, they mocked the high illiteracy rates prevalent in southern states, and they extolled the wisdom of three Presidential vetoes of the literacy test.

_____

[1] Ibid., p. 4785.

As was expected, however, the anti-restrictionists were unable to support their arguments with sufficient votes. On March 27, when Sabath asked the House to vote down the literacy test, he was defeated by a teller vote of 82 to 225. Sabath then tried to insert the word "political" into the exemption clause. The House said no again by a vote of 43 to 140 on an unrecorded vote. Siegel asked the House to drop the term "constitutional psychopathic inferiority." Again the restrictionists won. Finally, on March 30, the House voted by the overwhelming margin of 307 to 87 to pass the immigration bill and send it to the Senate.

The AJC was inactive during the House debate over the test because the Jewish lobbyists had gotten much of what they wanted from the Immigration Committee. Lobbying against the test would have been futile and might even have been counter-productive, possibly jeopardizing the exemption compromise.[1] But while Marshall and the AJC were resigned to defeat on the literacy test in the House, they were infuriated by a public attack against their involvement in the literacy test legislative fight. In April, 1916, Harper's

---

[1] Marshall did keep a close eye on other aspects of the bill concerning the transportation of illiterate relatives of literate immigrants and the Humphrey amendment. Marshall to Isaac Siegel, Mar. 5, 1916, in Marshall Papers, AJA.

Weekly published an editorial, "The Jews and the Immigration Bill," which severely criticized the "political Jews" and the lobbying of the AJC. Norman Hapgood, editor of Harper's Weekly, attacked the "unwise political campaign" of the Jews who required the inclusion of Hebrew and Yiddish as acceptable languages for the literacy test. Hapgood assailed the Jews not only for demanding special favors in the immigration bill but also for requiring exceptional consideration in the proposed Russian-American commercial treaty. According to Hapgood, the "political Jews" would insist that a new treaty specifically state that it pertained to all United States citizens "including Jews," or else they would oppose the treaty. "Words wholly redundant and needlessly critical of Russia have no place either in the immigration bill or in the hoped-for treaty."[1]

It is not exactly clear why Hapgood, a prominent journalist and outspoken Wilson supporter, made his attack on the AJC. He was displeased with the anti-Russian attitude of the AJC since he strongly favored a new Russian treaty. To this end, he had published a series of articles in 1915 and 1916 about the liberalization of the Czar's

---

[1] Norman Hapgood, "Jews and the Immigration Bill," Harper's Weekly, LXII (Apr. 15, 1916), 391.

regime and the value of close Russian-American ties. Of equal importance was Hapgood's friendship with Brandeis, his sympathy for Zionism, and his awareness of the conflict between the congress advocates and the AJC. Whatever his motives were, the attack against the AJC was ill-informed, for the editorial completely overlooked the AJC-sponsored exemption clause in the test, that actually contained the anti-Russian implications, and was the overriding concern of the AJC.

Greatly angered, Marshall wrote a long letter of rebuttal which Hapgood published in May. In it, Marshall disclaimed any responsibility for the insertion of Hebrew and Yiddish. Instead, he discussed the exemption clause which constituted the only significant result of Jewish pressure politics: "this provision merely recognizes the right of asylum which it has been the proud privilege of the American people to maintain. It is quite possible that this provision may operate in favor of the Russian and Roumanian Jews. I can scarcely deem it conceivable, however, that you would favor the closing of the doors of opportunity to them, if they come here to avoid religious persecution."[1] Cyrus Adler was so infuriated that he wrote a heated letter to

---

[1] Marshall to Editor of Harper's Weekly, Apr. 15, 1916, in Marshall Papers, AJA.

Henry Morgenthau, declaring that Hapgood, who would soon be working full-time for Wilson's re-election, would have to avoid internal Jewish matters and purge himself of his pro-Russian sympathies if he "is to be useful to Mr. Wilson during the coming campaign."[1]

Meanwhile, the Senate, as firmly committed to the test as the House was, yielded to the demands of election-time politics. Although the Senate Committee on Immigration presented a modified version of the Burnett bill on April 17, the President and the Senate Democratic leaders decided to defer action until after the Presidential election in November. Wilson greatly appreciated the delay despite the fact that many Senate Democrats were openly displeased with having to postpone passing the test. In fact, in August a combination of Democrats and Republicans made a strong bid to take up the bill. They discussed many aspects of the bill, excluding the literacy test, but they could not get sufficient votes to force consideration of the test.[2]

The 1916 Presidential candidates, Wilson and Charles Evans Hughes, focused on the issues of peace, preparedness,

---

[1] Adler to Henry Morgenthau, Apr. 30, 1916, in Adler Papers.

[2] Memorandum for President Wilson, Aug. 22, 1916, in Wilson Papers, Series IV, Folder 292.

and progressive legislative reforms, but not on the issue of immigration restriction. Wilson stood on his record of the veto, stressed primarily to immigrant voters, but Hughes, his Republican opponent, did not publicize his position on the literacy test or exemption clause, as Marshall urged him to do.[1]

On December 7, the second session of the 64th Congress took up the House bill which the Immigration Committee had modified. The Committee made one important change in the House bill by dropping the provision excluding Hindus and those ineligible for citizenship. Instead, the Committee proposed the use of geographical demarcations to designate the areas from which America would and would not accept immigrants. The State Department advocated the use of geographical lines to exclude Asian immigrants in such a way as to avoid insulting the Japanese government. According to Henry Cabot Lodge, the Senate version would work as effectively as the House version: the lines would exclude "all Asiatic immigration not now excluded by gentlemen's agreement or by treaty."[2]

---

[1] Reznikoff, op. cit., I, 155-56. Schiff contributed $10,000 to Wilson's re-election campaign. Schiff to Morgenthau, Sept. 22, 1916; Norman Hapgood to Schiff, Sept. 25, 1916, in Schiff Papers.

[2] U.S., Congressional Record, 64th Cong., 2d sess., 1916, LIV, Part 1, 155; U.S., Congress, Senate, Committee on

The Senate debate was caustic and unpleasant for the few who participated in it, as well as for the AJC that watched it closely. (The attendance was so low at one point that one amendment was defeated by a vote of 5 to 6.) Republican Senator Jacob H. Gallinger from New Hampshire and Democrat James A. Reed from Missouri argued sharply about the new exemption clause and the geographic restriction. Gallinger assailed the literacy test exemption for giving preference to the Jews, as he questioned whether Russian Jews made good citizens. He compared the Jews and the Negroes by stating in a derogatory way that he did not think that the Russian Jews sent their children to school in any greater numbers than did Negro parents--when allowed to do so.[1]

Reed came to the defense of the Jews not only in regard to the exemption clause but also concerning the geographic restriction, which happened to cover Siberia:

> Now it seems to me there is a very large-sized bug under this chip and that this amendment ought to be entitled "an amendment to exclude Jews from the United States" because they are Jews. There is no other reason that can be assigned for including nearly one-half of Russia

---

Immigration, Report, Regulation and Restriction of Immigration, 64th Cong., 1st sess., Apr. 17, May 18, Dec. 7, 1916, S. Rept. 352 to accompany H10384.

[1] U.S., Congressional Record, 64th Cong., 2d sess., 1916, LIV, Part 1, 157-58.

save that which is implied in the remark of the Senator from New Hampshire who inquired whether I thought that a Jew was as desirable a citizen as a colored man from Africa.[1]

Reed once again proposed that the bill exclude all black immigrants, as he had done during the 1914 debate. This time, however, the Senate immediately defeated his proposal. Reed then successfully pressured the Senate into exempting all white persons from the geographic restriction.

Porter J. McCumber of North Dakota joined Gallinger in attacking the exemption favoring the Jews. "If you come from a country where the laws discriminate against the Jews, he can come in," McCumber indignantly told his fellow Senators, "but you, a Christian gentleman cannot come to the United States because you are illiterate." McCumber asked whether the Jews wanted special treatment and "class legislation." Was the clause "a bait" to American Jews, he wondered?[2] In answer to the question, William Dillingham responded that the House included the exemption because of political pressure. Although he did not say so directly, he clearly implied that special legislation was exactly what the Jews wanted.[3]

Although Robert LaFollette defended the exemption

---

[1] Ibid., p. 159.   [2] Ibid., p. 266.   [3] Ibid.

because of the Russian system of discrimination against the Jews, McCumber persisted. He asked Ellison D. Smith, the Chairman of the Senate Immigration Committee, how the literacy test could improve the quality of American citizenship if illiterate Russian Jews were free to enter. Finally, Thomas Sterling of South Dakota came to McCumber's aid by proposing a new exemption clause. The Sterling amendment pertained to immigrants avoiding "religious persecution in the country of their last permanent residence and which persecution involves a restriction or denial to any class or sect of such aliens of the means or opportunities of obtaining an education sufficient to comply with the literacy test."[1] The Senate agreed to the substitution on a voice vote. On December 13, the Senate passed the immigration bill by a vote of 64 to 7.

Marshall was greatly upset by the Senate debate. In the first place, he strongly opposed the geographic restriction since it covered vast portions of Russia. He feared that if the proposed amendment passed, Russia would be justified in continuing to discriminate against American-Jewish travelers to Russia. Therefore Marshall asked Senator Smith

---

[1] Ibid., p. 270.

to revise the amendment to affect India and Indochina but not Russia or Persia.[1]

In the second place, Marshall was highly critical of the Sterling amendment because "it overlooks the most insidious form of persecution, namely that created by discriminatory laws and government regulations."[2] Marshall wanted the exemption to be as strong as possible as well as to accuse indirectly the Russian government of fostering the oppressive system against the Jews. He personally urged Burnett to stand firmly behind his exemption passed by the House, maintaining that the Sterling amendment would present "insuperable" problems for immigration authorities in determining if "persecution shall involve a restriction or denial to any class or sect of such aliens of the means or opportunities of obtaining an education sufficient to comply with the literacy test."[3]

Not content with appeals to Burnett, Marshall wrote Henry Morgenthau, formerly America's Ambassador to Turkey, to ask him to persuade Smith to withdraw the Sterling amendment:

---

[1] Marshall to Smith, Dec. 26, 1916, in Marshall Papers, AJA.

[2] Marshall to Bennet, Dec. 16, 1916, in Marshall Papers, AJA.

[3] Reznikoff, op. cit., I, 157-58.

"I hope . . . that you will at once put yourself in communication with Senator Smith and such other members of the Conference Committee as you may be able to reach. . . ."[1] This was Marshall's second letter within a week to Morgenthau, who was regarded by the AJC as close to Wilson and a very influential Democrat. In the first letter, Marshall had asked Morgenthau to pressure Senate leaders to postpone their consideration of the literacy test because it would not be smart politics for the Democrats. "I know," wrote Marshall, "of course, that the South is very strongly in favor of restrictive immigration, but there must be some Democratic leaders of the South who could open the eyes of the Southern Senators to the serious objections to this bill."[2]

Finally, in response to the Senate debate, Marshall was deeply disturbed by the accusations that the Jews were gaining special favors through the exemption clause. Clearly the AJC's victory on the exemption issue had produced a backlash among many Senators such as Gallinger, McCumber, and Sterling. Marshall counterattacked by pleading with

---

[1] Marshall to Morgenthau, Dec. 16, 1916, in Marshall Papers, AJA.

[2] Marshall to Morgenthau, Dec. 9, 1916, in Marshall Papers, AJA.

Burnett to ignore the argument that the exemption was for the Jews: "the fact that they would come within the beneficent scope of the exemption clause which you have adopted, is no reason for destroying it." The exemption was important, Marshall advised Burnett, because it applied to the Jews, Finns and Letts of Russia, and Armenians in Turkey.[1]

Marshall was especially troubled and "disgusted" by Gallinger's remarks which compared the educational motivation of Russian Jews with that of Negroes. He wrote long, indignant letters to several Congressmen including Isaac Siegel and Senator Reed Smoot of Utah. To Siegel, Marshall wrote that the Republican party would lose its Jewish voters if Gallinger continued to make invidious comparisons between Negroes and Jews.[2] With Smoot, Marshall pointedly recalled that New York, New Jersey, Pennsylvania, Illinois, and Connecticut--all states with large numbers of Jewish voters-- had gone Republican in 1916: "It is however rather disconcerting to one who has devoted so much time and thought and money to our party cause, to find that one of its leaders, immediately after the election, is grievously insulting the

---

[1] Reznikoff, op. cit., I, 157-58.

[2] Marshall to Isaac Siegel, Dec. 4, 1916, in Marshall Papers, AJA.

men for whose suffrages we were but a few months ago so very anxious."[1] Marshall then described what he regarded as the impressive record of assimilation of Russian-Jewish immigrants; at the same time he vigorously denied that the Jew was an "inferior being" or on the "same footing as the native of Africa," two accusations that had unpleasant racial connotations.[2]

Smoot presented Marshall's letter to Gallinger, who then wrote Marshall a five-page apology, admitting that he had committed "a serious blunder" by not reading the bill before the debate and erroneously assuming that Russian-Jewish immigrants were exempted "by name." The New Hampshire Republican then referred to his statement in the <u>Congressional Record</u> asking if the Jew were a desirable citizen. "What I meant to say, and what I supposed I did say, was 'Is he an especially desirable citizen,' meaning thereby to ask if he was more desirable than the people of certain other nationalities who are coming to our shores from countries where they are oppressed."[3] Finally, he wrote Marshall that it was not

---

[1] Marshall to Reed Smoot, Dec. 20, 1916, in Marshall Papers, AJA.

[2] Ibid.

[3] Jacob Gallinger to Marshall, Jan. 3, 1917, in Marshall Papers, AJHS.

"just or fair" to believe that he placed the Jews and Negroes on the "same footing." After receiving this apology Marshall calmed down and informed Gallinger that he was fully satisfied with the explanation. He assured the Senator that he would try to "correct the impression" that Gallinger disliked the Jews. "I can readily see how it happened," Marshall wrote, "that you made the remarks to which exception has been taken."[1]

The conference committee consisting of Representatives Burnett, Sabath, and California Republican Everis A. Hayes and Senators Smith, Lodge, and Georgia Democrat Thomas W. Hardwick issued their report on January 8. They agreed to drop the Sterling amendment and to redraw the geographic lines to exclude Siberia from the restricted area. The conferees also decided to drop the provision that had exempted all whites within the restricted areas. As was expected, the Burnett literacy test was left intact.[2]

The Senate accepted the report on the 8th by a vote of 56 to 10. The House considered the report on the 16th

___

[1] Marshall to Gallinger, Jan. 4, 1917, in Marshall Papers, AJHS.

[2] U.S., Congress, House, Conference Report: Regulation of Immigration, 64th Cong., 2d sess., Jan. 8, 1917, H. Rept. 1266 to accompany H10384.

with the debate centering on the issue of Asian exclusion, but not the literacy test. On the same day, the House passed the immigration bill without a division vote and for the second time within two years, Congress presented President Wilson with a literacy test measure.

As far as Wilson was concerned, "no material new points" were "in question" in regard to the test in 1917.[1] Therefore, either because he expected to gain little from a debate in the White House, similar to the one in 1915, or possibly because he had very little interest in Congressional and domestic matters in early January, Wilson decided against holding a public hearing.[2] Still, the restrictionists made great efforts to persuade the President to accept the new bill. Burnett, for one, was eager for the President to realize that Congress had removed one of his two objections to the 1915 bill: "In your veto of the Immigration bill two years ago you laid stress on an objection which you had to the provision for excluding those who advocate or teach the

---

[1] Wilson Memorandum, January, 1917, in Wilson Papers, Series IV, Folder 292.

[2] William McAdoo, Wilson's son-in-law and Secretary of the Treasury, complained to Col. House that the President took no interest in domestic matters in early January. The Diaries of Edward M. House, Jan. 12, 1917, in Edward M. House Papers (Yale University, New Haven, Conn.). Cited hereafter as House Papers.

unlawful destruction of property. I think that we have fully met that objection."[1] Secretary of Labor Wilson presented a memorandum to the President which recommended approval of the new bill, pointing to the provisions affecting political asylum and to the broadened exemption clause in the test which is "almost, if not quite, acceptable to those who had opposed it before."[2]

Once again, however, the restrictionists failed to convert the President to their cause, when on January 29, he vetoed the immigration bill containing the literacy test. Again, Wilson had two major objections. The first one was expected as he stated that he could not favor the literacy test because he regarded it as an unfair test of character and because it hurt aliens who had been denied educational opportunities in their native countries. Wilson described the test as "a penalty for the lack of opportunity in the country from which the alien . . . came." Illiterate immigrants, the President wrote, were not necessarily undesirable immigrants.

Wilson's second objection was completely unexpected as he disapproved of the Burnett-Marshall exemption clause

---

[1] Burnett to Wilson, Jan. 20, 1917, in Wilson Papers, Series IV, Folder 292.

[2] Memorandum from William B. Wilson to Woodrow Wilson, Jan. 24, 1917, in Wilson Papers, Series IV, Folder 292.

which he concluded "might lead to very delicate and hazardous diplomatic situations." The President maintained that "very serious questions of international justice and comity" might arise if American immigration authorities decided that certain foreign laws and practices constituted religious discrimination.[1] Wilson had expressed his concern over the exemption clause in his interview with Adolph Lewisohn in December, 1914. At that time, Lewisohn had reported to Marshall that the President questioned whether an exemption was "practicable, as it would force the United States Government to decide whether this condition exists or not and might be held to be interference." The discussion with Lewisohn, however, seems to have been the only instance when Wilson expressed reservations about the exemption clause before January, 1917.[2]

---

[1] U.S., Congressional Record, 64th Cong., 2d sess., 1917, LIV, Part 3, 2212-13.

[2] Lewisohn to Marshall, Dec. 14, 1914, in Marshall Papers, AJHS. Arthur S. Link wrote that the exemption "had, ironically, been inserted to meet objections that Wilson had raised in his veto of the first Burnett bill." Arthur S. Link, Wilson: Campaigns for Progressivism and Peace, 1916-1917 (Princeton, N.J., 1965), V, 328. The New York Times reported in a similar vein about the exemption clause: "Singularly this feature of the bill was inserted to meet the objections raised by President Wilson in his first veto." The New York Times, Jan. 30, 1917, p. 1. These two interpretations are inaccurate: in his first veto Wilson did not

What factors then account for Wilson's strong interest in the exemption question? The answer centers on Wilson's overriding involvement in diplomatic affairs and the shifting and precarious relationship between the United States and Germany and the United States and Russia. In the beginning of January, Wilson held the optimistic belief that his neutral government could instigate a settlement of the European conflict. Therefore, on January 17, he made a major and controversial foreign policy address in which he called for peace without victory and outlined his plans for a post-war league of nations. A few days later, however, Wilson prepared for an ominous change in German-American relations, writing apprehensively to his close friend Colonel Edward M. House: "with the preparations they are apparently making with regard to unrestricted attacks on merchantmen . . . there is a terrible likelihood that the relations between the United States and Germany may come to a breaking point and everything assume a different aspect."[1] Ultimately, on January 31, Germany officially informed Washington that her navy would once again attack neutral ships, shattering Wilson's

---

discuss the Burnett religious exemption clause but he objected to the literacy test and the political asylum provisions.

[1] Link, Wilson: Campaigns for Professivism, p. 278.

hope that the United States could effect a settlement of the war as a neutral party between the two blocs. "This means war," the President told his secretary Joseph Tumulty when he received the official pronouncement. "The break that we have tried to prevent seems inevitable."[1]

Although the United States' declaration of war was still a few weeks away, it was clear to Wilson that a German enemy meant a Russian ally. But Russia, a crucial part of the Allied cause, was an enormous problem at the moment. Great Britain, France, and now the United States wondered whether she would be strong enough to hold up the eastern front. The British, in particular, were terribly worried about the possibility of Russia's defection and of a separate peace between Russia and Germany; Colonel House and French Ambassador Jean Jules Jusserand agreed that Russia was the "danger point for the allies."[2]

In the last week of January, 1917 Wilson regarded Russian goodwill as an extremely important matter for the United States. The President could not condone a bill which would have the effect of indirectly criticizing Russia's

---

[1] Hofstadter, *The American Political Tradition*, p. 269.

[2] House Diaries, Jan. 12, 1917, in House Papers.

Jewish policy and which might damage the delicate relations between the United States and Russia. Gratuitous expressions of anti-Russian sentiment, voiced on behalf of American and Russian Jews, were an anachronism that Wilson could hardly afford to approve of. With the United States close to war, Wilson did not want additional "delicate and hazardous diplomatic situations" that might possibly stem from the Marshall-Burnett exemption clause.

Despite Wilson's position and the importance of good American-Russian relations, the House and Senate remained obsessed with the need for restriction and determined to pass the test over the veto. The AJC, nevertheless, tried to ward off final defeat. Marshall, who had expected the veto, had begun to gather support for the President's position, even before Wilson's message was written. He asked Adolph Ochs to write an editorial in the New York Times supporting the President's probable action; he requested Dr. Harry Friedenwald to enlist the aid of Cardinal Gibbons of Baltimore; from Representative William Bennet, Marshall sought the names of doubtful Representatives so that the AJC network could apply pressure in the most sensitive areas. Finally, Marshall sent an urgent letter to all AJC members asking them to contact their Congressmen.[1]

"If the bill becomes a law," Marshall wrote anticipating defeat, ". . . it is as harmless so far as we are concerned as it can possible [sic] be made."[2] On this point, both the anti-restrictionists and restrictionists were in agreement. In fact, Burnett and Gardner now strongly supported the AJC's exemption when the House debated the veto for forty minutes on February 1. Gardner reversed his earlier position and defended the exemption clause, rejecting Wilson's argument on the grounds that the United States government had judged the laws and regulations of other countries when it accepted immigrants who had committed political offenses abroad. "Neither the Jews nor the northwestern Europeans" would be "excluded scarcely at all," Burnett stated, trying to nullify the impact of Jewish opposition to the test.[3] He attacked the anti-restrictionists, and Adolph Sabath in particular, for supporting the veto and thereby campaigning against the AJC's exemption clause. Abandoning

---

[1] Marshall to Adolph Ochs, Jan. 19, 1917; Marshall to Dr. Harry Friedenwald, Jan. 20, 1917; Marshall to Bennet, Jan. 20, 1917, in Marshall Papers, AJA.

[2] Marshall to Adler, Jan. 20, 1917, in Marshall Papers, AJA.

[3] U.S., Congressional Record, 64th Cong., 2d sess., 1917, LIV, Part 3, 2456.

his own child was what Sabath was doing, according to Burnett.[1] His final argument appealed to the House on the issues of crime and labor radicalism, as he asked his fellow Representatives to adopt the test to fight the International Workers of the World and the Black Hand, the Italian mafia of the Progressive period.

The House voted 287 to 106 to override President Wilson's veto, with a great applause greeting the final vote.[2] The following day the Senate listened to a plea for passage by Henry Cabot Lodge, who had first introduced the test in the House in 1891. With no fanfare or difficulty the Senate agreed to override the veto by a vote of 62 to 19 and the literacy test finally became a law.

The battle was over and the AJC had lost the war against restriction. Although it appears that Marshall did not make a deal with Burnett in 1916, the AJC's spirit of opposition was hardly as vigorous as in 1914 and 1915. Regarding the literacy test as "inherently vicious" Marshall went through the motions of contacting important men and alerting the AJC's general membership to the need to pressure Congressmen. But once having obtained the AJC-sponsored exemption

---

[1] Ibid., p. 2454.

[2] The New York Times, Feb. 2, 1917, p. 16.

clause, Marshall sensed that it was the very best that he and the AJC could hope for. He was "very much pleased" with the conference report. "The bill," he wrote Congressman Sabath, "is now in such form as to do the least possible injury to those whose interests we have sought to safeguard."[1] Thus, for the Jewish lobbyists, the exemption constituted a small victory within a great defeat.

Although Marshall and Schiff did not remark upon Wilson's criticism of the exemption clause, his position must have been upsetting to them. The veto not only singled out the one solid achievement gained by the AJC in its literacy test battles, but it also reaffirmed how important friendly Russian-American relations had become. Although the United States had failed to write a new Russian-American commercial treaty in 1916, the rapprochement between the two countries, evident in American investments in Russia and the President's veto message, was a defeat for the interests of the AJC.

Wilson's failure to stymie the restrictionists in Congress deeply disappointed the AJC, but in 1917 the restrictionist fever was too high for the President to control.

---

[1] Marshall to Adolph Sabath, Jan. 9, 1917, in Marshall Papers, AJHS.

In this last fight the restrictionists continued to accuse the new immigrants of ruining America's cities, causing crime, contributing large numbers of mental defectives, instigating labor's difficulties, and promoting labor radicalism. The restrictionists also maintained that Anglo-Saxon America could not withstand the pressure of new unassimilable groups. All of these issues were important--but the war inevitably caused the restrictionist victory. In passing the literacy test Congress expressed its apprehensions about the chaotic conditions in Europe and an unmanageable flood of post-war refugees. In the final analysis, the restrictionists won because they exploited America's fears about the post-war world.

CONCLUSION

From 1906 through 1917 the leaders of the AJC developed political sophistication and expertness in their practice of ethnic pressure politics. The intellectually astute, energetic, and perservering AJC leaders made an impressive record of lobbying efforts on behalf of Jews in Russia and Russian-Jewish immigrants in the United States. The AJC's lobbying campaigns varied from year to year: at times its leaders fought vigorously against America's Russian policy and against the literacy test; at other times, they felt the need to pressure Congress and the President in an inconspicuous way. But whatever the techniques and whatever the instances of success and failure, the AJC's objectives remained the same: to pressure the Russian government through the force of United States foreign policy, to defeat the literacy test, and to convince Congress to accept a broad exemption clause to keep open the routes of escape for Jews out of Russia to the United States.

Today, some sixty years later, it appears that Schiff, Marshall, and their coterie of "establishment Jews" engaged in their spirited lobbying efforts because of a combination of idealistic and practical considerations. They were motivated, in large part, by their optimism concerning the existing status and future development of American Jewry. But while they rejoiced over their existence in America's tolerant and prosperous society, they were appalled by the outbursts of pogroms and the generally depressed conditions of Russian Jewry. Refusing to accept Russian-Jewish hardships as inevitable or unchangeable, the AJC leaders felt morally bound to try to improve the lives of Russian Jews. Furthermore, in a practical vein, the AJC leadership perceived the political need, if it was to survive as the prominent spokesman for American Jewry, to concern itself with problems that were of burning interest to the majority of the American-Jewish community.

Nevertheless, neither this sense of responsibility nor the desire to maintain their leadership positions in any way brought the uptown Jews to a close or satisfactory relationship with the Russian-Jewish immigrants. The established, elite group of German Jews insisted on keeping their distance from the new and culturally different Jewish immigrants, as well as preventing them from sharing power in the representation of American Jewry. Obviously, there is a striking and unexplained contradiction between fighting the restriction movement on behalf of the Russian-Jewish immigrants and discriminating against them in social areas and denying them a voice in the most prominent Jewish organizations.

However important these social, political, and cultural discords were to Jews in the Progressive period--and even today--they have blurred and distorted the AJC's record as an active lobbying organization. From 1906 through 1917 the AJC leaders used their organization to reinforce their access to government, an access based upon their impressive financial resources, their understanding of intricate legislative and diplomatic issues, and their ability to create the impression that the AJC could deliver the Jewish vote and reward its friends with respect to Russian-American relations and the literacy test.

The AJC used many different devices in its lobbying efforts. It published books and articles critical of the literacy test and Russia's treatment of her Jews, and in favor of the AJC's exemption clause. The organization provided information on the complex aspects of the Russian issue and the literacy test to numerous Congressmen, and it rewarded certain of them by reprinting and distributing speeches favorable to the AJC's positions. (The AJC relied upon Jewish Congressmen to gather information on the progress of bills and resolutions, but for its most crucial work, the sponsorship of the abrogation resolution and the exemption clause, it turned to influential non-Jews who seemingly had no parochial interest in the issues.) As an organization, the AJC never endorsed candidates for office, but the individuals who ran the AJC often gave endorsements and financial aid to politicians such as William Sulzer and Woodrow Wilson, who aided Jewish interests. Finally, the organization depended heavily upon its national network of contacts, not for the purpose of flooding Congressmen with anti-Russian and anti-literacy test letters but to exploit personal connections between Congressmen and their influential Jewish and non-Jewish constituents.

Thus it is clear that the leaders of the AJC were deeply committed to changing the course of the United States' relations with Russia as well as to defeating the literacy test. But how should we evaluate and judge the results of these intense efforts and what salient factors account for the AJC's strengths and weaknesses? In the first area of consideration, American-Russian relations, the AJC's activities were a mixture of successes and failures. The leaders of the Jewish community could not pressure President Roosevelt to create an international controversy over the pogroms in 1905 and 1906. In contrast, the AJC engineered the abrogation of the Treaty of 1832 in a skillful, high-pressured, and well-timed campaign that was aided in crucial ways by ambitious, aggressive Democrats in search of Jewish votes and by the ineptitude of President Taft and Secretary of

State Knox, who failed to impress upon Congress the importance of friendly American-Russian relations. Finally, although the AJC effectively blocked the writing of a new commercial treaty with Russia in 1916, it could not stop the rapprochement between Russia and the United States based upon economic, diplomatic, and ultimately military needs resulting from the First World War.

In the second area of consideration, it is apparent that the AJC's campaigns against the literacy test were never conducted with the same degree of assurance as were the foreign policy campaigns. This factor, however, did not prevent the organization from exaggerating the importance of the role that it played. At the "insistence" of American Jews, Marshall proclaimed in February, 1915, the "restrictive immigration laws have been defeated." "It was the Jews...who kept open the doors of opportunity for their brethren"; urging Wilson to veto the test and succeeded "in inducing the House of Representatives to sustain the Presidential veto."[1] But, in truth, bi-partisan domestic opposition from the restrictionists caused the AJC to fight often in a defensive and uncertain manner. From 1906 through 1917, Marshall, with Friedenwald and Brylawski as his agents, had

---

[1] Reznikoff, op. cit., II, 801.

access to influential Congressmen in making recommendations to shape immigration legislation. But only in 1916 did their access prove fruitful and effective in negotiating a change in the exemption clause for which they had been working since 1912. Despite their oft-repeated claims of success in defeating the literacy test, the AJC leaders realized that only the President or Speaker could defy the restrictionists who represented a widespread concern about the lifestyles, economic threats, and racial derivations of the new immigrants. It was Cannon, Taft, and Wilson, not the AJC, who frustrated and over-powered the restrictionists for eleven years.

The most obvious reason for the AJC's strength was the high quality of its leadership. Schiff, a man of great wealth and moral dedication, and Marshall, a brilliant and persevering strategist, created and ran a stable, cohesive, and extremely well-funded organization. The AJC changed little during its first eleven years of existence: in 1917, ten of the fifteen men on the executive committee had served in 1906 as well. And although during the same period, the general membership nearly doubled from fifty-seven to one hundred and five, Marshall and Schiff continued to set the goals and practices of the entire organization. The hundred general members, drawn from numerous towns and cities in all sections of the country, gave the impression that the AJC was a broadly-based organization, but it was an oligarchy to which all of its members deferred.

Thus, successful lobbying derived from a combination of factors: strong leadership, internal cohesion, well-funded programs, sophisticated lobbying techniques, well-chosen non-Jewish allies, and good timing (especially at the time of the 1912 elections). Furthermore, the AJC's successes should also be attributed to its interest in matters that aroused little popular interest in the Progressive period: the public was not yet clamoring for the imposition of severe immigration quotas, although immigration restriction was a much-debated question; friendly American-Russian relations hardly concerned the general public or the Senate.

In retrospect, it was relatively easy for Jewish leaders to lobby against immigration restriction from 1906 to 1917, especially when compared to the immigration conflicts of the twenties and thirties when the desperate needs of German and eastern European Jewish refugees were blocked by a seemingly impenetrable quota system. And yet, even in this earlier period, one of relative stability and confidence, AJC leaders occasionally moved in a cautious and timid way. Their behavior was sometimes similar to that of Jewish leaders during the thirties who felt resigned to and fearful

of attacking the harsh restrictive system. For in the
Progressive period, the AJC worked hard to avoid converting
the immigration issue into a Jewish question, and thereby
stimulating anti-Semitism. Therefore, at times, Schiff and
Marshall were reluctant to press the restrictionists too
hard and to give the public the impression that they wielded
great political power.

Undoubtedly, the history of the AJC as a lobbying
organization was shaped by its leaders' fears of provoking
anti-Semitism because of Jewish political activity. Furthermore, the AJC leaders deceived themselves about the relation
of the Jewish vote to American politics because of their
ambivalence concerning the propriety of Jewish lobbying, as
well as their part-time involvement in politics. Marshall
and Schiff, for example, were deeply interested in local,
state, and national politics, but they viewed these matters
from some distance. Usually, the AJC leaders came to politics only after and as a consequence of their success in
other fields, such as law and banking. Unlike many Irish
immigrants, who entered politics as a way of making a living
and as a means of achieving upward mobility, these "uptown
Jews" made money and achieved status elsewhere. Then they
came to politics because of specific Jewish-oriented issues.
For the German Jews, both philanthropic activity and political

involvement developed, in large part, from a sense of _noblesse oblige_ and a responsibility for the less fortunate Jewish immigrants.

The "uptown Jews" formed their elite lobbying group in the early part of the twentieth century when the Jewish immigrants became a stable source of some political power. Unlike many other immigrant groups, the overwhelming number of Jewish immigrants remained in the United States, providing a reservoir of votes and a series of issues that were of singular interest to this ethnic group. Thus, the ability of the Jewish community and the AJC to make its demands felt on Jewish-related issues depended on the potential mobilization of Jewish votes.

But what was the most effective and safest way of using these votes? The AJC position was not clear on this significant point. Both Marshall and Schiff opposed the formation of Jewish Democratic or Republican clubs, as well as separate Jewish army units and liberty bond groups during the First World War. Jews were either Republicans or Democrats, Marshall declared in 1912, but "there is no such thing as a Jewish Republican or a Jewish Democrat." Jews should not "segregate" themselves "for political purposes" because they have "no political interests which are different from those of our fellow citizens."[1]

Four years later Marshall again objected to the identification of Jewish Democrats and Republicans, this time criticizing an appeal from Henry Morgenthau to American Jews on behalf of Wilson's re-election. Yet, at the same time Marshall confirmed that "Jews as such, or any part of our population as such," could be "justified in voting for or against a public official because of personal considerations." Marshall was referring to the possibility that the Wilson Administration might accept a new treaty with Russia, unsatisfactory to American Jews, and then the "Jews would be justified in voting as a man against the party which would be guilty of such an attack upon their citizenship."[2] One must assume that Marshall's curious distinctions were governed by pragmatism as well as by some need to disguise the activities of Jewish lobbyists. According to the AJC, the Jewish vote did not exist--unless, of course, politicians failed to support the organization on such issues as abrogation and Russian-American treaty relations.

When Marshall and the AJC threatened to retaliate through votes, they were open to a number of idealistic

---

[1] Ibid., II, 809.

[2] Ibid., II, 810.

criticisms concerning the divisive, even subversive nature of lobbying organizations. E. Pendelton Herring, for example, has objected to lobbyists who limit a Congressman's freedom of action, make him a "mere spokesman" for the interests of a specific group, place the organization's interests before the welfare of the people and thereby threaten "the very roots of a democratic government."[1]

Yet, when the AJC sought to convert Presidents, Congressmen, and other politicians to its cause through idealistic arguments and the subtle use of votes of the Jewish population, it was operating within the democratic tradition and playing within the rules of the lobbying game in the Progressive period. In fact, the AJC's lobbying techniques were low-keyed: it never tried to galvanize the Jewish vote; it never made Congressmen its "mere spokesmen"; it never employed high-powered, prominent lobbyists or resorted to bribery; nor did it use inside information to gain an advantage over its opponents.

In truth, the AJC was reaffirming the democratic tradition in its fight against the literacy test: American democracy in its ideal form is not only based upon promoting the welfare of the people but also upon a respect and toler-

---

[1] Herring, op. cit., p. 242.

ance for all groups. The organization was fighting for a democratic goal when it opposed the bigotry of the restrictionists and denied that the new immigrants were racially, politically, socially, and economically inferior to the old. Unquestionably, the AJC entered the restriction fight to protect its own narrow constituency, the Russian-Jewish immigrants, but the leaders of the AJC also fervently believed in the idealistic expectation that the United States should continue to provide a haven for the oppressed from the old world.

Despite their hatred of bigotry and their fears of growing anti-Semitism in the United States, the AJC leaders nevertheless remained confident about their place in American society. Although they were concerned, and sometimes distressed by unflattering stereotypes and overt acts of anti-Semitism, the AJC leaders did not want to jump at every anti-Semitic challenge and, through publicity and open arguments, add fuel to the campaigns of their enemies. Despite signs of hostility in the restriction movement and evidence of social discrimination, these uptown Jews had deep trust in America's institutions and in her seemingly effective legal system. Morris Waldman, a Jewish social worker, has described this strain of optimism during the "Schiff era": "We in America truly believed that the brotherhood of man was just around the corner; that although here and there age-old prejudices manifested themselves, they were of the harmless exclusive country-club variety...that the prejudices would before long disappear in the gloriously free and tolerant atmosphere of America...."[1]

With this optimistic spirit, from 1906 to 1917 Marshall, Schiff, and the AJC felt confident and proud of their record as leaders of the American-Jewish community and as active proponents of the politics of ethnic pressure. For the signs of open intolerance in the twenties--the outbreak of the Red Scare with its emphasis on eastern and southern European radicals, the fame of the Protocols of the Elders of Zion, the growth of the Ku Klux Klan, and the writing of quota systems that reduced Russian-Jewish immigration to a few thousand a year--had not yet surfaced.

---

[1] Morris D. Waldman, *Nor By Power* (New York, 1953), p. 324.

BIBLIOGRAPHY

Archival Sources

American Jewish Archives. Cincinnati, Ohio.

    Gus Karger Papers.
    Louis Marshall Papers.
    Jacob H. Schiff Papers.

American Jewish Committee. New York, New York.

    Cyrus Adler Papers.
    Louis Marshall Papers.
    Minutes of the Executive Committee.
    Mayer Sulzberger Papers.

American Jewish Historical Society. Brandeis University.
    Waltham, Massachusetts.

    Max J. Kohler Papers.
    Louis Marshall Papers.
    Simon Wolf Papers.

American Zionist Archives. New York, New York.

    Louis Brandeis Papers.
    Dr. Harry Friedenwald Papers.

Columbia University. New York, New York.

    Columbia University Oral History Project. William Bennet.

Library of Congress. Washington, D.C.

    Philander C. Knox Papers.
    Theodore Roosevelt Papers.
    Oscar S. Straus Papers.
    William Howard Taft Papers.
    Woodrow Wilson Papers.

Massachusetts Historical Society. Boston, Massachusetts.

    Henry Cabot Lodge Papers.

National Archives. Washington, D.C.

    General Records of the State Department: Russia, Political Relations with the United States.

Yale University. New Haven, Connecticut.

    Edward M. House Papers.
    Frank L. Polk Papers.

Yivo Institute for Jewish Research. New York, New York.

    Hebrew Sheltering and Immigrant Aid Society of America Papers.
    National Liberal Immigration League Papers.

Public Documents

Caminetti, Anthony. *Annual Report of the Commissioner General of Immigration: For the Fiscal Year Ended June 30, 1913.* Washington, D.C.: Government Printing Office, 1914.

_____. *Annual Report of the Commissioner General of Immigration: For the Fiscal Year Ended June 30, 1918.* Washington, D.C.: Government Printing Office, 1918.

Hull, Harry E. *Annual Report of the Commissioner General of Immigration: For the Fiscal Year Ended June 30, 1925.* Washington, D.C.: Government Printing Office, 1925.

Sargent, Frank P. *Annual Report of the Commissioner General of Immigration: For the Fiscal Year Ended June 30, 1906.* Washington, D.C.: Government Printing Office, 1906.

U.S. *Congressional Record.* Vols. XL, XLI, XLVIII, XLIX, LI, LII, LIII, LIV.

U.S. Congress. House.

    Conference Report: Immigration of Aliens, etc. Report No. 1340. 62nd Cong., 3d sess., Jan. 18, 1913.

Conference Report: Immigration of Aliens, etc. Report No. 1378. 62nd Cong., 3d sess., Jan. 23, 1913.

Conference Report: Immigration of Aliens, etc. Report No. 1410. 62nd Cong., 3d sess., Jan. 28, 1913.

Conference Report: Regulating the Immigration of Aliens into the United States. Report No. 7607. 59th Cong., 2d sess., Feb. 13, 1907.

Conference Report: Regulation of Immigration. Report No. 1266. 64th Cong., 2d sess., Jan. 8, 1917.

Committee on Immigration and Naturalization. Hearings, Relative to the Further Restriction of Immigration. 62nd Cong., 2d sess., 1912.

_____. Hearings, Restriction of Immigration. 64th Cong., 1st sess., 1916.

_____. Report: Immigration of Aliens into the United States. Report No. 4912. 59th Cong., 1st sess., June 11, 1906.

_____. Report: Immigration of Aliens into the United States. Report No. 559. 62nd Cong., 2d sess., Apr. 16, 1912.

_____. Report: Immigration of Aliens into the United States. Report No. 851. 62nd Cong., 2d sess., June 7, 1912.

_____. Report: Immigration of Aliens into the United States. Report No. 149. 63rd Cong., 2d sess., Dec. 16, 1913.

_____. Report: Immigration of Aliens into the United States. Report No. 95. 64th Cong., 1st sess., Jan. 31, 1916.

U.S. Congress. Senate.

Conference Report: Regulation of Immigration. Doc. No. 712. 63rd Cong., 3d sess., Jan. 11, 1915.

Jewish Immigration: Report of a Special Committee of the National Jewish Immigration Council Appointed to Examine into the Question of Illiteracy Among Jewish Immigrants and Its Causes. Doc. No. 611. 63rd Cong., 2d sess., 1914.

Reports of the Immigration Commission. Doc. No. 747, 748, 662, 764. 61st Cong., 3d sess., Dec. 5, 1910. Vols. I, II, IV, V, XLI.

Committee on Immigration. Report: Immigration of Aliens into the United States. Report No. 2186. 59th Cong., 1st sess., Mar. 29, 1906.

_____. Report: Regulation of Immigration. Report No. 208, 62nd Cong., 2d sess., Jan. 18, 1912.

_____. Report: Regulation and Restriction of Immigration. Report No. 355. 63rd Cong., 2d sess., Mar. 19, 1914.

_____. Report: Regulation and Restriction of Immigration. Report No. 352. 64th Cong., 1st sess., Apr. 17, May 18, and Dec. 7, 1916.

Books and Unpublished Studies

Adler, Cyrus. Louis Marshall: A Biographical Sketch. New York: American Jewish Committee, 1931.

_____, and Margalith, Aaron. With Firmness in the Right. New York: American Jewish Committee, 1946.

Bailey, Thomas A. Theodore Roosevelt and the Japanese-American Crisis. Stanford, Cal.: Stanford University Press, 1934.

Baron, Salo. The Russian Jews Under Czars and Soviets. New York: Macmillan Co., 1964.

Birmingham, Stephen. "Our Crowd": The Great Jewish Families of New York. New York: Harper & Row, 1967.

Blum, John Morton. *The Republican Roosevelt*. New York: Atheneum, 1965.

Bolles, Blair. *Tyrant from Illinois: Uncle Joe Cannon's Experiment with Personal Power*. New York: W. W. Norton & Co., 1951.

Carey, John Joseph Jr. "Progressives and the Immigrants," Unpublished Ph.D. dissertation, Department of History, University of Connecticut, 1968.

Cohen, Naomi Wiener. *A Dual Heritage: The Public Career of Oscar S. Straus*. Philadelphia: The Jewish Publication Society of America, 1969.

Cremin, Lawrence A. *The Transformation of the School: Progressivism in American Education, 1876-1957*. New York: Vintage Books, 1961.

Current Biography: 1946. New York: H. W. Wilson Company, 1947.

Daniels, Josephus. *The Wilson Era: Years of Peace, 1910-1917*. Chapel Hill, N.C.: The University of North Carolina Press, 1944.

Daniels, Roger. *The Politics of Prejudice: The Anti-Japanese Movement in California and the Struggle for Japanese Exclusion*. University of California Publications in History, LXXI. Berkeley, Cal.: University of California Press, 1962.

Dinnerstein, Leonard. *The Leo Frank Case*. New York: Columbia University Press, 1968.

Dubnow, Semen M. *History of the Jews in Russia and Poland: From the Earliest Times to the Present Day*. 3 vols. Translated by I. Friedlander. Philadelphia: The Jewish Publication Society of America, 1916-1920.

Florinsky, Michael T. *McGraw-Hill Encyclopedia of Russia and the Soviet Union*. New York: McGraw-Hill Book Co., 1961.

Flournoy, Richard W. Jr., and Hudson, Manley O., eds. <u>A Collection of Nationality Laws of Various Countries as Contained in Constitutions, Statutes and Treaties</u>. New York: Oxford University Press, 1929.

Friedman, Jacob Alexis. <u>The Impeachment of Governor William Sulzer</u>. New York: Columbia University Press, 1939.

Garis, Roy Lawrence. <u>Immigration Restriction: A Study of the Opposition to and Regulation of Immigration into the United States</u>. New York: Macmillan Co., 1927.

Gerson, Louis L. <u>Woodrow Wilson and the Rebirth of Poland, 1914-1920: A Study in the Influence on American Policy of Minority Groups of Foreign Origin</u>. New Haven, Conn.: Yale University Press, 1953.

Goldberg, Nathan, et al. <u>The Classification of Jewish Immigrants and Its Implications</u>. New York: Yiddish Scientific Institute--Yivo, 1945.

Gompers, Samuel. <u>Seventy Years of Life and Labor</u>. Vol. II. New York: E. P. Dutton and Co., 1925.

Goren, Arthur A. <u>New York Jews and the Quest for Community: The Kehillah Experiment, 1908-1922</u>. New York: Columbia University Press, 1970.

Gossett, Thomas F. <u>Race: The History of an Idea in America</u>. Dallas: Southern Methodist University Press, 1963.

Gwinn, William Rea. <u>Uncle Joe Cannon, Archfoe of Insurgency: A History of the Rise and Fall of Cannonism</u>. U.S.A.: Bookman Associates, 1957.

Haller, Mark H. <u>Eugenics: Hereditarian Attitudes in American Thought</u>. New Brunswick, N.J.: Rutgers University Press, 1963.

Handlin, Oscar. <u>Race and Nationality in American Life</u>. Boston: Little, Brown, & Co., 1957.

_____. <u>The Uprooted: The Epic Story of the Great Migrations that Made the American People</u>. Boston: Little, Brown, & Co., 1950.

Herring, E. Pendelton. <u>Group Representation Before Congress</u>.
Baltimore: The Johns Hopkins Press, 1929.

Hersch, L. "Jewish Migrations During the Last Hundred Years."
<u>The Jewish People Past and Present</u>. Vol. I. New York:
Jewish Encyclopedia Handbooks, Inc., 1946.

Higham, John. "American Anti-Semitism Historically Reconsidered." <u>Jews in the Mind of America</u>. Edited by
Charles Herbert Stember, <u>et al</u>. New York: Basic Books,
1966.

_____. <u>Strangers in the Land: Patterns in American
Nativism, 1860-1925</u>. New York: Atheneum, 1966.

Hofstadter, Richard. <u>The Age of Reform: From Bryan to F.D.R.</u>
New York: Vintage Books, 1960.

_____. <u>The American Political Tradition: And the Men
Who Made It</u>. New York: Alfred A. Knopf, 1951.

Holt, James. <u>Congressional Insurgents and the Party System,
1909-1916</u>. Cambridge: Harvard University Press, 1967.

Hourwich, Isaac. <u>Immigration and Labor: The Economic Aspects of European Immigration to the United States</u>.
New York: G. P. Putnam's Sons, 1912.

Houston, David F. <u>Eight Years with the Wilson Cabinet:
1913-1920</u>. Vol. I. Garden City, N.Y.: Doubleday,
Page, & Co., 1926.

Howe, Mark Anthony DeWolfe. <u>George von Lengerke Meyer:
His Life and Public Service</u>. New York: Dodd, Mead,
& Co., 1920.

Janowsky, Oscar I. <u>The Jews and Minority Rights (1898-1919)</u>.
New York: Columbia University Press, 1933.

Jenks, Jeremiah W., and Lauck, W. Jett. <u>The Immigration
Problem: A Study of American Immigration Conditions and
Needs</u>. New York: Funk & Wagnalls Co., 1933.

<u>Jewish Encyclopedia</u>. Vol. X. New York: Funk & Wagnalls,
1925.

Jones, Maldwyn Allen. *American Immigration*. Chicago: University of Chicago Press, 1961.

Joseph, Samuel. *Jewish Immigration to the United States: From 1881-1910*. New York: Columbia University Press, 1914.

Karson, Marc. *American Labor Unions and Politics: 1900-1918*. Carbondale, Ill.: Southern Illinois University Press, 1958.

Key, V. O., Jr. *Politics, Parties, and Pressure Groups*. New York: Thomas Y. Crowell Company, 1958.

Lansing, Robert. *War Memoirs*. Indianapolis and New York: The Bobbs-Merrill Co., 1935.

Link, Arthur S. *Wilson*. Vol. V: *Campaigns for Progressivism and Peace, 1916-1917*. Princeton, N.J.: Princeton University Press, 1965.

_____. *Woodrow Wilson and the Progressive Era: 1910-1917*. New York: Harper & Brothers, 1954.

McConnell, Grant. *Private Power and American Democracy*. New York: Alfred A. Knopf, 1967.

Manners, William. *TR and Will: A Friendship That Split the Republican Party*. New York: Harcourt, Brace, & World, Inc., 1969.

Manuel, Frank E. *The Realities of American-Palestine Relations*. Washington, D.C.: Public Affairs Press, 1949.

Mowry, George. *The Era of Theodore Roosevelt and the Birth of Modern America: 1900-1912*. New York: Harper & Row, 1958.

Nagel, Charles. *Speeches and Writings: 1900-1928*. 2 vols. Edited by Otto Heller. New York: G. P. Putnam's Sons, 1931.

Neu, Charles E. *An Uncertain Friendship: Theodore Roosevelt and Japan, 1906-1919*. Cambridge, Mass.: Harvard University Press, 1967.

Odegard, Peter H. *Pressure Politics: The Story of the Anti-Saloon League*. New York: Columbia University Press, 1928.

O'Grady, Joseph P. *The Immigrants' Influence on Wilson's Peace Policies*. Lexington, Ky.: University of Kentucky Press, 1967.

Porter, Kirk H. *National Party Platforms*. New York: The Macmillan Co., 1924.

Pringle, Henry Fowles. *The Life and Times of William Howard Taft*. 2 vols. New York: Farrar & Rinehart, Inc., 1939.

_____. *Theodore Roosevelt: A Biography*. New York: Harcourt, Brace, 1956.

Reznikoff, Charles. *Louis Marshall: Champion of Liberty*. 2 vols. Philadelphia: The Jewish Publication Society of America, 1957.

Rischin, Moses. *The Promised City: New York's Jews, 1870-1914*. Cambridge, Mass.: Harvard University Press, 1962.

Rosenstock, Morton. "Louis Marshall and the Defense of Jewish Rights in the United States." Unpublished Ph.D. dissertation, Faculty of Political Science, Columbia University, 1963.

Saveth, Edward Norman. *American Historians and European Immigrants: 1875-1925*. New York: Columbia University Press, 1948.

Schattschneider, E. E. *Politics, Pressures and the Tariff: A Study of Free Private Enterprise in Pressure Politics, as Shown in the 1929-1930 Revision of the Tariff*. New York: Prentice-Hall, Inc., 1935.

Schiff, Jacob H. *Jacob H. Schiff: His Life and Letters*. 2 vols. Edited by Cyrus Adler. Garden City, N.Y.: Doubleday, Doran, and Co., 1929.

Schmeckebier, Laurence F., and Eastin, Roy B. *Government Publications and Their Uses*. Washington, D.C.: The Brookings Institution, 1969.

Seymour, Charles. *The Intimate Papers of Colonel House*. Vol. II, Boston: Houghton Mifflin Co., 1926.

Shapiro, Yonathan. "Leadership of the American Zionist Organization: 1897-1930." Unpublished Ph.D. dissertation, Faculty of Political Science, Columbia University, 1964.

Soloman, Barbara Miller. *Ancestors and Immigrants: A Changing New England Tradition*. Cambridge, Mass.: Harvard University Press, 1956.

Solvick, Stanley Donald. "William Howard Taft and the Progressive Movement: A Study in Conservative Thought and Politics." Unpublished Ph.D. dissertation, Department of History, University of Michigan, 1963.

Sulzberger, Cyrus L. *Is Immigration a Menace?* New York: American Jewish Committee, 1912.

Taft, Philip, and Ross, Philip. "American Labor Violence: Its Causes, Character and Outcome." *Violence in America: Historical and Comparative Perspectives*. Edited by Hugh Davis Graham and Ted Robert Gurr. New York: The New American Library, 1969.

Taft, William Howard. *The Presidency: Its Duties, Its Powers, Its Opportunities and Its Limitations*. New York: Charles Scribner's Sons, 1916.

Truman, David B. *The Governmental Process: Political Interests and Public Opinion*. New York: Alfred A. Knopf, 1951.

Wagenknecht, Edward Charles. *The Seven Worlds of Theodore Roosevelt*. New York: Longmans, Green, 1958.

Waldman, Morris D. *Nor By Power*. New York: International Universities Press, 1953.

Watson, James E. *As I Knew Them*. Indianapolis and New York: The Bobbs-Merrill Co., 1936.

Wiebe, Robert. *The Search for Order*. New York: Hill & Wang, 1967.

Wilson, Woodrow. *A History of the American People*. Vol. V. New York: William H. Wise Co., 1931.

Witte, Sergei. *The Memoirs of Count Witte*. Translated and edited by Abraham Yarmolinsky. Garden City, N.Y.: Doubleday, Page and Co., 1921.

Wolf, Lucien, ed. *The Legal Sufferings of the Jews in Russia*. London: T. Fisher Unwin, 1912.

Wolf, Simon. *The Presidents I Have Known from 1860 to 1918*. Washington, D.C.: The Press of Byron S. Adams, 1918.

Woodward, C. Vann. *The Strange Career of Jim Crow*. New York: Oxford University Press, 1966.

Articles and Periodicals

The American Hebrew. 1906-1917.

American Jewish Committee: Annual Report. New York, 1907-1917.

American Jewish Yearbook. Philadelphia: The Jewish Publication Society of America, 1905-1917.

Bemis, Edward W. "Restriction of Immigration." *The Andover Review*, IX (March, 1888), 251-63.

Berthoff, Roland. "The American Social Order: A Conservative Hypothesis." *The American Historical Review*, LXV (April, 1960), 495-514.

Bingham, Theodore A. "Foreign Criminals in New York." *North American Review*, CLXXXVII (September, 1908), 389-94.

Birdsall, Paul. "Neutrality and Economic Pressure, 1914-1917." *Science and Society*, III (Spring, 1939), 217-28.

Cohen, Naomi Wiener. "The Abrogation of the Russo-American Treaty of 1832." *Jewish Social Studies*, XXV (January, 1963), 3-41.

Dawidowicz, Lucy S. "Louis Marshall's Yiddish Newspaper, the *Jewish World*: A Study in Contrasts." *Jewish Social Studies*, XXV (April, 1963), 102-32.

Glazer, Nathan. "Social Characteristics of American Jews: 1654-1954." *American Jewish Yearbook*, LVI (1955), 3-41.

Goren, Arthur A. "A Portrait of Ethnic Politics: The Socialists and the 1908 and 1910 Congressional Elections on the East Side." *Publications of the American Jewish Historical Society*, L (March, 1961), 202-38.

Hall, Prescott F. "The Future of American Ideals." *North American Review*, CXCV (January, 1912), 94-102.

Hapgood, Norman. "Jews and the Immigration Bill." *Harper's Weekly*, LXII (April 15, 1916), 391.

Higham, John. "Social Discrimination Against Jews in America: 1830-1930." *Publications of the American Jewish Historical Society*, XLVII (September, 1957), 1-33.

Hoyt, Homer. "The Literacy Test and Immigration." *Journal of Political Economy*, XXIV (May, 1916), 445-73.

The Jewish Advocate. 1912-1913.

Kohler, Max J. "The Immigration Problem and the Right of Asylum for the Persecuted." *Jewish Comment* (Baltimore), October 24, 31, 1913.

Lee, Joseph. "Democracy and the Illiteracy Test." *Survey*, XXIX (January 18, 1913), 497-99.

Link, Arthur S. "A Portrait of Wilson." *Virginia Quarterly Review*, XXXII (Autumn, 1956), 524-40.

The Maccabaean. 1907-1915.

The New York Times. 1907-1917.

Panitz, Ester. "In Defense of American Jewish Immigrants: 1891-1924." *American Jewish Historical Quarterly*, LV (September, 1965), 57-97.

_____. "The Polarity of American Jewish Attitudes Towards Immigration (1870-1891)." *American Jewish Historical Quarterly*, LIII (December, 1963), 99-130.

Rappaport, Joseph. "The American Yiddish Press and the European Conflict in 1914." *Jewish Social Studies*, XIX (July-October, 1957), 113-28.

Roosevelt, Theodore. "A Proper Case for Arbitration." *The Outlook*, XCIX (October 14, 1911), 365-66.

Supple, Barry. "A Business Élite: German-Jewish Financiers in Nineteenth Century New York." *Business History Review*, XXXI (Summer, 1957), 143-78.

Szajkowski, Zosa. "The Alliance Israelite Universelle in the United States: 1860-1949." *Publications of the American Jewish Historical Society*, XXXIX (June, 1950), 389-443.

_____. "The European Aspects of the American Russian Passport Question." *Publications of the American Jewish Historical Society*, XLVI (September, 1950), 86-100.

_____. "Jewish Diplomacy." *Jewish Social Studies*, XXII (July, 1960), 131-51.

_____. "Paul Nathan, Lucien Wolf, and Jacob H. Schiff and the Jewish Revolutionary Movements in Eastern Europe (1903-1917)." *Jewish Social Studies*, XXIX (January, 1967), 3-26.

_____. "Private and Organized American Jewish Overseas Relief (1914-1938)." *American Jewish Historical Quarterly*, LVII (September, 1967), 52-138; (December, 1967), 191-253.

Ward, Robert DeCourcy. "Agricultural Distribution of Immigrants." *Popular Science Monthly*, LXVI (December, 1904), 166-75.

_____. "Immigration and the South." *Atlantic Monthly*, XCVI (November, 1905), 611-17.

_____. "National Eugenics in Relation to Immigration." *North American Review*, CXCII (July, 1910), 56-67.

Wolgemuth, Kathleen Long. "Woodrow Wilson's Appointment Policy and the Negro." *Journal of Southern History*, XXIV (November, 1958), 457-71.

For Product Safety Concerns and Information please contact our EU
representative GPSR@taylorandfrancis.com
Taylor & Francis Verlag GmbH, Kaufingerstraße 24, 80331 München, Germany

www.ingramcontent.com/pod-product-compliance
Lightning Source LLC
Chambersburg PA
CBHW071151300426
44113CB00009B/1159